The Personal Equation

KP,
Thanks for all your
help with everything.
I am glad we have
gotten to be friends.
Sincerely,

Shelton Palmer Sanford IV

The Personal Equation

A BIOGRAPHY OF

Steadman Vincent Sanford

Charles Stephen Gurr

The University of Georgia Press *Athens and London*

© 1999 by the University of Georgia Press

Athens, Georgia 30602

Designed by Kathi Dailey Morgan

Set in Minion by G & S Typesetters, Inc.

Printed and bound by Maple–Vail

The paper in this book meets the guidelines for
permanence and durability of the Committee on
Production Guidelines for Book Longevity of the
Council on Library Resources.

Printed in the United States of America

03   02   01   00   99   C   5   4   3   2   1

Library of Congress Cataloging in Publication Data

Gurr, Charles Stephen.

  The personal equation : a biography of
  Steadman Vincent Sanford / Charles Stephen Gurr.

      p.   cm.

   Includes bibliographical references (p.   ) and index.

   ISBN 0-8203-2108-7 (alk. paper)

   1. Sanford, Steadman Vincent, 1871–1945.   2. University of
Georgia—Presidents—Biography.   3. College administrators—
Georgia—Biography.   4. Educators—Georgia—Biography.
I. Title.

LD1982.7.S36G87   1999

370'.92—dc21

  [B]   98-30811

British Library Cataloging in Publication Data available

Frontispiece: A relaxed Chancellor Sanford, ca. 1944

To those educators whose labors sustain

Steadman Sanford's lifelong concern for

his "boys and girls of Georgia."

Contents

Preface

This book is the story of the life and career of Steadman Vincent Sanford, one of Georgia's most significant figures in the field of higher education. It should be made clear at the outset, however, that this work makes no claim as a contribution to Georgia's higher education history per se. The aim of the book is rather to reveal the role of the individual and personality in professional attainment and the fulfilling of professional ambition. The individual in this case is a white male southerner during a period of dramatic change in American life, 1871 to 1945. The subject might have been as interesting as a banker, a lawyer, or a minister. He was, however, a teacher, a school man, and it was as an educator that he became well known.

Our view of Sanford is highly internal. It is based in large part on letters, documents, and miscellaneous papers found in the Sanford Collection at the University of Georgia and on interviews with those who by and large remember Sanford favorably: colleagues, students, and family members. No attempt has been made to provide a broad critical assessment of his career based on external sources or interpretations. We see Sanford in Sanford's terms and from the viewpoint of the Sanford family. This is not to say Sanford is presented as a flawless character. Seeing a man in his own mirror can be touchingly revealing.

In February of 1997 at the close of more than two years of working on this book, I happened on a previously overlooked brief ap-
praisal of Steadman Sanford written by his protégé and colleague John
Drewry. Drewry, writing at the time of Sanford's death, spoke from
more than two decades of firsthand knowledge of his subject. With so
much of my writing on Sanford behind me I shuddered a bit for fear
of finding in Drewry's remarks some vitally important and undis-
covered fact or idea about my subject, something important enough
to require extensive reconsideration, rethinking, and rewriting. I was
pleased and a bit relieved that the article held no great surprises. I
found, in fact, a high degree of affirmation for my coverage of and
conclusions about Sanford. It was startling, however, to read at this
juncture in my project the following: "When the biography of the late
Chancellor is written. . . ." Following this were projections about that
future biography. Drewry said that the story of Sanford's life would be
"a volume of size and record achievements to compare favorably with
those of Charles W. Eliot of Harvard and Nicholas Murray Butler of
Columbia." Drewry pointed to the episodes of Sanford's life and career that, in his opinion, merited chapters: the stadium, football, the
Southern Conference, trips to Washington on behalf of the University
System, and so forth. "The man and the accomplishments are there,"
said Drewry. "A first rate writer will be required to do the job as it
should be done."

My initial despair lifted somewhat as I reflected on the contents of
my first draft, completed just before reading Drewry's comments. I
believe that Professor Drewry would have at least approved my choice
of subjects; his list of topics matched mine and those which he had
not mentioned I am certain he would have recognized as valuable to
the study. At least I had recognized "the man and the accomplishments." To what degree Drewry would have agreed with my interpretations and just how "first rate" the final product is, is another matter.

Acknowledgments

That an earlier biography of Steadman Sanford has not been written seems odd. The best explanation is that Shelton Sanford, Steadman's oldest child, long reserved that responsibility for himself. Some very fragmentary notes remain from that ambition, but when Shelton died in 1978 he had done little more than discourage others from attempting a biography. With Shelton's death his nephew Charles S. Sanford Jr., grandson of the chancellor, began the process of getting the impressive volume of his grandfather's papers and scrapbooks into the University of Georgia Libraries, where they could be available for use by those outside the family. Charles Sanford, himself a graduate of the university, maintains a keen interest in his alma mater and his grandfather's associated memory and legacy. His willingness to support the research and writing of this biography while keeping an editorial arm's length from this final product and its assessment of his grandfather led to the present volume. Charles Sanford helped in securing the logistical support from the office of the president of the university, specifically Tom Landrum and his staff, and from Karen Orchard and the staff at the University of Georgia Press.

Charles Sanford was also most persistent in helping locate individuals who had known his grandfather. My interviews with these sources provided valuable insights into my subject's personality and day-to-day habits. Of course the passage of time robbed me of the availability of Steadman Sanford's true contemporaries, but it was encouraging to discover that there was still an impressive array of keen-minded octogenarians who knew S. V. Sanford as kinsman or teacher or football fan or president or chancellor or colleague and friend. Among those university students of the period who provided informative interviews were Senator Herman Talmadge, Charles Gowen, Tom Paris, and Jasper Yeomans. Several sources were the children of Sanford's contemporaries who had themselves only slightly known the chancellor: Jack Spalding, James A. Dunlap, George Abney, George Marshall, Bill Hartman Sr., Dr. John Stegeman. I was pleased to have had a chance to interview Lamar Dodd shortly before his death. Dodd came to the faculty of the university after Sanford had become chancellor but fondly remembered Sanford as an Athens neighbor. Gwendolyn Caldwell, widow of Dr. Harmon Caldwell who followed Sanford as president of the university and as chancellor, was a helpful source.

I came to think of several of the new friends I made during this project as "talent scouts." They might not have known how important they were, but I want to thank them for leading me to additional interviews and sources: Elizabeth Powell, Susan Barrow Tate, and Billy Hudson, all of Athens, and with long-time university connections. Marvin R. and Sally Bruce McClatchey of Atlanta helped me in many ways, including the loan of family scrapbooks, letters, and photographs, as well as memories of my subject and his family.

Ralph Moor of Atlanta and Colonel Ben Moore of Butler, Georgia, provided some of my most insightful views of Chancellor Sanford in his daily work routine. Both these men worked with Sanford just before America's entry into World War II and retain crisply clear memories and thoughtful assessment, which they cheerfully shared. Charlotte Marshall of Athens was kind enough to share with me her family records on the Sanford line. Ann Cabaniss, on hearing of my project, presented for my reading almost three hundred previously unstudied letters between the Sanford family and son Shelton, who was in France during World War I. These letters have subsequently been added to the Sanford Collection at the university.

Beyond the University of Georgia proper several institutions are due credit for their help: Mercer University, the archives of the Georgia Department of Archives and History, the Board of Regents of the University System of Georgia, Gainesville College, and the Marietta Public Library. Roy Gatchell and Tim Pennell of the Archives of the Athletic Association of the University of Georgia were most important resources for my research into the important sport-related aspects of Sanford's career, especially in the building of Sanford Stadium. A most grateful thanks goes to the director of the Hargrett Rare Book and Manuscript Library of the University of Georgia Libraries, Mary Ellen Brooks, and her always helpful and cheerful staff. The Archives of the University were of great value to my work on the official records of the university. I became a weekly fixture among the workers at the library for the better part of two years. I thank them for putting up with me and helping me find my way.

Allie Reynolds, Robert B. Stephens, Nelly Rucker Lamar Walter, Stephen Lumpkin Upson, Harry Baxter, Beth Abney, Griffin Bell, Tyus Butler, Mike Cheatham, Charters Embry, Albert Esley, Judge Richard Kenyon, Hugh Mills, J. Aubry Smith, Henry King Stanford, Joanna Traylor, Klon and Patricia Waldrip, and Meg Gunn all came to my assistance in sharing leads, conversation, and memories. Thank you.

Thomas Dyer, who initially brought my name up in the discussions of a Sanford biography, has my thanks for his confidence in my ability and my apologies for my shortcomings in the resulting product. A few individuals deserve special mention for their patience at the most difficult points in this effort. Judson Ward of Emory University was gracious in giving my manuscript an initial reading and in providing helpful suggestions for improving it before submission to the University of Georgia Press. Janice Nylander transformed my manuscript into a decipherable document. Foster Watkins and Kenneth Coleman, my friends, colleagues, and mentors, were always encouraging. My wife, Rebecca, was a devoted and patient helper all through this project. I value her persistence in pushing me to give a more careful edit to the final product in spite of my unreasonable defensiveness at the time. Whatever is good here comes by the efforts of these people and institutions and those whom I may have overlooked. The flaws, oversights, and shortcomings are mine.

The Personal Equation

ONE

Beginnings

1871-1890

The story of American life, whatever the time period, is but a fusion of the small stories that were the lives of the men and women of the era under consideration. Steadman Sanford's life is important to a better understanding of the American society in the last decades of the nineteenth century and the first half of the twentieth. The mosaic that was America when Sanford died in 1945 had been shifting and changing since the day of his birth. The geographic elements grew to fill in much of this continent and leaped over great seas to plant important outposts and anchors of international responsibility in what had been far-flung corners of the world at Sanford's birth. Great new and diversely populated industrial, commercial cities arose from modest colonial seedbeds or sprang up overnight westward and around the Great Lakes. Technology and the economy played the major parts in effecting these changes. The accompanying social and moral challenges drew responses marked by a dramatic reform spirit. Progressivism grew from these roots, enlisting the social and cultural agencies as well as the political and economic mechanisms of the nation in the crusade against social injustice and for moral improvement.

This generalized view of one period of American history becomes a more familiar, event-specific interval when one considers the four wars that chronologically anchor and punctuate Steadman Sanford's lifetime, which spanned almost three-quarters of a century. He was born in the ashes of the American Civil War, was personally involved in the Spanish-American War excitement, had a son serve in Europe during the "War to make the world safe for Democracy," and died only a few months after the end of World War II.

To know and understand the life of Steadman Sanford is to put a specific amid the generalizations that are the stuff of history. What tiny glittering or dull fragment of the mosaic was the face of Sanford? What credence to the traditional story of America in his time does the life, experience, and the personality of Steadman Sanford give? What about it all does he depict? It may be that he provides us with a symbol of American life. Rather than represent a heroically proportioned "movement" such as Progressivism, a movement well described if variously interpreted via studies of the great progressive leaders, Sanford serves as a symbol of another element of the age. This other element may not dominate the history of the age, but it is certainly vital in appreciating the smaller stones and chips in our mosaic.

Steadman Sanford was not an "everyman" by any means. To attempt to depict him as worthy of examination only because he was one of the tiny cogs in a great wheel would be wrongheaded. He was, in the context of his locale, a large public figure. He was at the center of public higher education in Georgia for almost half a century. His labors were not nationally known or trendsetting or pioneering. The study of his career and personality, however, reveals the inner workings of leadership and influence on a state level within a distinct region of a nation, a region not in step with many of the changes that marked the years of Sanford's life. What seems remarkable about Sanford is his ability to achieve his goals despite the increasingly conflicted relationships between the traditional South and emerging twentieth-century America. He essentially addressed the coming century's challenges in the style of the past century. S. V. Sanford met the challenges of twentieth-century American change in the context of nineteenth-century southern institutions: family, education, personal contacts. His was an exercise in the personal equation, a dying American art form, of which he was without peer.

Steadman Vincent Sanford was born in Covington, Georgia, August 24, 1871, to Baptist parents, Charles Vincent Sanford of Greensboro, Georgia, and Elizabeth Mars Steadman Sanford of Murfreesboro, Tennessee, and Covington, Georgia. At age fifteen Steadman entered Mercer University at Macon and graduated with a degree in English in 1890. His first jobs were in Marietta, where on June 16, 1895, he married Grace McClatchey (1872–1952), a local schoolteacher and daughter of Methodist parents, Devereaux Fore McClatchey and Adelaide Grace Reynolds McClatchey. He taught at the Marietta Male Academy (1890–1892), was principal of Marietta High School (1892–1903), and served as superintendent of Marietta City Schools (1897–1903). When he joined the faculty of the University of Georgia as instructor in English literature in 1903, he began a career there which led him to the presidency of that institution and eventually to the chancellorship of the University System of Georgia.[1]

A detailed study of the Sanford lineage would provide a look at the Sanford forebears as far back as Robert Sanford I of England, who migrated to America and died in Westmoreland County, Virginia, in 1699. The present biography, however, looks back only as far as Steadman's grandfather and his generation. Shelton Palmer Sanford, Steadman's paternal grandfather, himself a well-known and highly respected Georgia educator, was born in Greensboro, Georgia, on January 25, 1817.[2]

By many accounts, especially the recollections of those who knew both Professor Shelton P. and Chancellor Steadman V. Sanford, there were any number of similarities between the two men. Both men were known for their kindness to the students in their care. They gave them sound advice, made them feel at home, and lent them money when they needed it to get through college. The younger Sanford was pleased to have those similarities recognized and acknowledged and it is obvious that Shelton Palmer Sanford was the model for Steadie's career in academics.[3]

In ways other than appearance S. P. and S. V. Sanford seem cut from the same cloth. S. P. Sanford was said to be "very fond of books, and availed himself most diligently of his opportunities . . . he pursued his studies with great diligence." He, like his grandson, was a product of rural nineteenth-century Georgia. He received his early education in Greensboro and graduated from the University of Georgia at Athens in 1838 with first-class honors. In 1840 he was named professor of mathematics (and later also astronomy) at Mercer, then located at Penfield. When the Civil War came Shelton Palmer Sanford served as captain of a militia district that included Penfield and the Mercer student body, but persisted in teaching throughout the war despite suggestions that Mercer be closed. When Mercer moved to Macon in 1879, Professor Sanford's reputation as a mathematician had been enhanced with the publication of his *Analytical Arithmetic* (1870). After forty years he was senior faculty member at Mercer as professor of mathematics and astronomy when his grandson entered in 1886.[4]

Throughout his career Steadman Sanford held his grandfather in highest esteem. There is no doubt that he was the role model and that his acclaim was a benchmark for the younger Sanford. It is significant that the style of both men reflects the "southern traditions" as they were interpreted within that culture in the latter part of the nineteenth century. The attributes of greatest value were diligence, loyalty, devotion to family and neighbors, kindness, and self-sacrifice. S. V. Sanford saw these characteristics on a large scale in his grandfather and devoted himself to emulating that model.

An extensive unpublished history of the University of Georgia included a very flattering biographical sketch of Shelton Palmer Sanford, in which his training is hailed as one of the university's greatest contributions "to the cause of education." The biographical sketch recalls the senior Sanford's sacrifice of fortune in order to "influence for good . . . the lives of thousands of young men."[5]

S. V. Sanford saw himself in concert with his grandfather's manner and frequently drew attention to stories that made favorable comparisons of the two men. The elder Sanford was noted for his "courtesy and politeness" to students: "to the lowliest freshman he was as gracious as if he had been conversing with some illustrious fellow scientist."[6] Such a manner was a common and favorite recollection of the grandson among those who knew him.

There are few written clues to S. V. Sanford's life before his Mercer days in the late 1880s. Significantly, the first "document" in the S. V. Sanford Collection is an 1890 note to S. V. Sanford ("Dear Steadie") from grandfather S. P. Sanford ("Grandpa"). The note admonishes: "continue to be prompt, punctual, courteous, available to all with whom you are brought in contact . . . the way to make a reputation that will be lasting."[7]

Steadman's maternal grandfather was Enoch Steadman (1819–1893), a Rhode Island native. He and his wife Mary moved to Covington in 1863, where Enoch bought land and established a twine mill. Enoch Steadman was a prosperous, well-respected businessman and community leader who served in the state senate in 1871–72 and 1873–74.[8]

The Charles Sanford family's move from Covington to Conyers in the mid-1870s removed the direct contact that would have obviously occurred had Steadman's family continued to live in the Covington house where he was born.

We know little of Steadman's father, Charles V. Sanford. He was a student at Mercer, where his father was on the faculty, when he entered the service of the Confederacy in 1862, serving in Cutt's Battalion until the end of the war in April 1865. He married Elizabeth Mars Steadman (1848–1904) on December 2, 1869. He worked for his wife's father in Covington, and he and his young family lived with her parents. When they moved to the Conyers community he "kept a warehouse." References to Charles V. Sanford speak of his "successful business enterprises," and his establishment of a "retail merchant business," but there are no indications of outstanding accomplishment. His obituary in the April 3, 1922, *Macon Telegraph* refers to his "prominent family," his father "Shelton P. Sanford, LLD., author of the famous Sanford's Analytical Arithmetic, and for sixty-three years professor at Mercer University," and his membership in the R. A. Smith Camp, Confederate Veterans of Macon. Additional information included the fact that his two sons were once members of the Mercer University baseball team. "Dr. Sanford (SVS), after leaving Mercer and becoming a member of the University of Georgia faculty, so fostered college athletics as to many times head the college conferences and is at present (1922) President of the Southern Intercollegiate Conference."[9] Apparently Charles V. Sanford was a rather dimmer light between the two shining scholars, his father and his son.

Charles V. Sanford and Elizabeth Mars Steadman Sanford had six children, five of whom lived beyond infancy: Steadman Vincent; Charles Dickerman, born in 1875 in Covington; Anna Maria, born in June 1876 in Conyers; Ethel, born in 1879 (d. 1880); Shelton Palmer, born in 1880; and Paul Hill, born in 1884.[10]

Family names and connections have always been significant elements in the process of defining personalities, but describing and explaining the life of S. V. Sanford requires an examination of matters beyond the family tree. Chronology and geography provide additional important means of understanding Sanford's beginnings. A straightforward genealogical entry of several lines in a multivolume biography of noted figures never left a southerner very informed, or understood.

Georgia in Sanford's infancy and early childhood was operating in the economic and social currents that were legacies of the "late war for southern independence" and what were, in the view of many white southerners, the tragedies of Reconstruction. Thus these themes were major influences over the family that guided the formation of Sanford's youthful values and notions of the world and people around him. Grandfather Shelton Sanford had been in his prime at age 45 when the Civil War started, and his father, Charles, reached adulthood as the war ended. The sons and daughters of the late-nineteenth-century South were heirs to experiences that would figure largely in their roles in the new century. They would rise to live in and lead a twentieth-century society, but they clung in some corners of their minds and hearts to antebellum sentiments and worldviews that fit awkwardly into the America that was about to undergo dramatic change.

It was the special burden of S. V. Sanford and his generation to sort out the wheat from the chaff among those views and values of old. What differentiated the leaders from the masses, S. V. Sanford from the greater crowd about him, was the keen ability to efficiently and appropriately evaluate the relationships between the facts of change and the relative applicability of the various modes and styles of a passing society in adjusting to and capitalizing on those changes. His success in this process accounts for the true power behind Sanford's "personal equation": the facility that set him apart.

Leadership in the post-Reconstruction South was most commonly visible in the distinctly political area. Georgia politics at the time of Sanford's birth was anchored deeply in the struggle by the majority white population, at least males with the right to vote, to somehow reconcile the postslavery society with the traditional dominance of white male, Democratic politics. Much of the political agenda during Sanford's youth and early manhood revolved around the suppression of the black population's political and economic significance. This process not only helped perpetuate racial tensions, it left a legacy of resistance to reform. Sanford ironically would have to battle that legacy throughout his career, a career that might just as well have been in politics but seemed predestined to be devoted to public education.

The Reconstruction Constitution of 1868 called for "a thorough system of general education to be forever free to all children of the State." However, it was not until control of the state's political machinery was back in the hands of Democrats in 1871, the year of Sanford's birth, that a real effort was made to act on that lofty notion. When a new constitution replaced the old Reconstruction-dominated 1868 document in 1877, it reaffirmed a "thorough system" of public education. This time a separation of races was spelled out, and the general notion of Georgia providing public education seemed generally accepted.[11]

By the time Steadman finished Mercer, Georgia was still far from achieving that elusive "thorough system." About 200,000 Georgia youngsters attended primary school for four months of the year, recently increased from three months and moving toward a six-month school year. The few secondary schools that existed were private and usually found in Georgia's larger towns and cities.[12]

In higher education the university in Athens in the 1870s was regaining its role as state leader in collegiate education following the interruptions of war and Reconstruction. It reopened in 1866 under the leadership of Chancellor Andrew Adgate Lipscomb, said to have possessed educational views that would "prove to be among the most modern and advanced in the United States."[13] Lipscomb sought to "modernize" the university by means of fundamental changes in the curriculum of the institution to place a greater emphasis on modern languages, moving from what he considered the negative effects of the classical models of higher education. He saw the need for practical education and attacked the "pretensions to culture" that, rather than usefulness to the student, became the object of classical education.[14]

Chancellor Lipscomb retired in 1874. Before his retirement he had strongly encouraged the trustees and the state to see the university as more than an institution or even several institutions, but as an agency for change and improvement in Georgia. He encouraged the university to reach beyond Athens or Dahlonega or Augusta to the "farmers, planters, manufacturers and mechanics" and the "industrial interests." He encouraged research and experiment for practical application beyond the classroom into the mines, fields, and industrial plants of Georgia. He saw the university as the General Assembly's agency for reaching and acting on Georgians.[15] Sanford came to echo many of Lipscomb's progressive sentiments.

In the remaining decades of the century, the university gradually returned to the traditional modes, undergirding the classical liberal arts model and reducing dramatically its commitment to agricultural education. Lipscomb successors Henry Holcombe Tucker (1874–78),

P. H. Mell (1878–88), and William Boggs (1888–98) carried the university to the edge of the new century in a tradition of the classical and counter to the models envisioned by the far-sighted Lipscomb. The creed represented in the phrase "New South"—industrial growth, economic diversification, and modern government—found no ally in the university.

When the General Assembly created the Georgia Institute of Technology in 1885, it was located not in Athens but in Atlanta and in time became a bitter rival to the university. In 1889, the establishment of the Georgia Normal and Industrial College at Milledgeville brought public education to the white women of Georgia as an outgrowth of the stimulation of teacher preparation. This further scattering of higher education around the state no doubt played a part in the establishment by the 1890s of a normal school in Athens to be supervised by the chancellor and forced the university to expand itself beyond its traditional roles, in self-defense if for no other reason. As the century came to a close, the state university had to defend itself not only against competing public branches and colleges but also against a serious threat from denominationalists, who attacked the legislature's relationship to the school in Athens, which they saw as making possible unfair competition for their institutions. An uneasy relationship with the agricultural interests of the state grew from what farmers and planters perceived as mismanagement of Morrill funds and negligence of agricultural education on the part of the university. The twentieth century dawned with much to be resolved in Athens and between the citizens and legislators of the state.[16]

The social-institutional tensions surrounding higher education in Georgia was only one manifestation of the conflict between change and tradition as S. V. Sanford began life in central Georgia in the 1870s. The villages he was born and grew up in and the larger towns where he attended college and would take his first job provide clues to the physical world that was the stage on which young Sanford witnessed the playing out of these tensions. It was here that the platitudes and wisdom of the ages come face to face with the challenges of change in the closing of one century and the dawning of another. In these surroundings Steadman Vincent Sanford began to take his measure of the situation, to make his judgments and evaluations, and to exercise his "personal equation."

The routines of Sanford's boyhood had not changed appreciably in rural areas for hundreds of years. Farming, the crops, the tools, the technology were not much improved or changed from biblical times. Diversity was not encouraged or welcomed, yet around the edges there were economically inspired changes in Georgia: increased urban migration, especially to Atlanta or mill cities like Columbus, Macon, and Augusta; rudimentary extractive industries such as granite in northeast Georgia; coal in northwest Georgia; and timber and naval stores in the southern end of the state. Still, by the turn of the century Georgia's economy was relatively less diversified than it had been in 1860.

The two decades of Sanford's youth were spent in small-town Georgia settings, Covington and Conyers, a few miles apart between Atlanta and Augusta on the Georgia rail line. During the 1870s and 1880s the two communities would have undergone closely similar experiences; had similar problems, entertainments, and diversions; been concerned with the same public issues; and shared similar economic service areas. Covington, Sanford's birthplace, was about forty miles east of Atlanta, less than fifty miles from Athens. Macon, post–Civil War home of Mercer University, where Sanford would attend college, was about sixty miles to the south.

The relative location of this "neighborhood" of Sanford's youth is significant, especially in that age before automobile transportation, when the rebuilt and expanded rail system of Georgia was the life's blood of outreach for the communities strung along the steel ribbons of their rails. In that age of wagons, carriages, and buggies, only by rail was there a practical means of movement for more than a few miles beyond a home place. The proximity of Covington and Conyers to Athens and Macon and the direct and close link to Atlanta and Augusta meant that the Sanford family world was under the significant influence of those Georgia centers of commerce, culture, law, and education but beyond the immediate influence of older, "finer," coastal, colonial Savannah and Chatham County. Sanford's community was up-country Georgia rather than tidewater; for generations before and later, that would make for significant distinctions that played an important role in his life and career.

The pages of the *Covington Enterprise* in those years reveal a place similar to many others in late-nineteenth-century Georgia: blacksmith shops, brick kilns, steam cotton gins, a "new photographic gallery over the Post Office, J. W. Crawford, artist." Local lawyers and dentists and drugstores were promoted on the front page; larger clothing and furniture retailers in Augusta and Atlanta carried advertising. The news was largely excerpted from other newspapers, regionally and nationally, and large segments of the front page were given over to excerpts from Shakespeare and other popular literary offerings.[17]

The rising tide of public education was evident in Covington when a school board election elicited the following editorial declaration in early 1871: "only religious freedom is more sacred in the estimate of enlightened freemen than the right to direct the education of the rising generation whose training is by the creator committed to the care of every parent." In making a choice for board member the editor advises, "Be careful and elect the right man."[18]

William Beebe's *Covington Enterprise,* like other weekly newspapers, lived by its advertising. This was an age of unregulated and exaggerated ballyhoo, especially in the patent medicine and related cure-all areas. Among the advertisements for sarsaparilla and seeds could be found painkillers and Indian bitters that we know now to have thinly disguised rampant narcotic and alcohol abuse. Ayer's Hair Invigorator was promoted alongside fancy cologne, ale, beer, syrup, molasses, buggies, and wagons. A regular feature of the front page was the Georgia Railroad, which ran between Augusta and Atlanta four times daily and four times each night. The week of Steadman Sanford's birth the editor complained of drought and dust.[19]

Conyers in the 1880s may be seen in the pages of its newspaper for that period, the *Conyers Examiner.* Steadman would have the opportunity to attend the local high school, which was opened in 1881, for a twenty-two week session at a monthly tuition of $1.00–$2.00 depending on class and ten cents per month for "incidental expenses." L. F. Daniel, B.E., served as principal. Steadman's father was among those listed as being drawn for grand jury duty in January 1881. That "a couple of Italian street musicians were in town this week" was no doubt of interest to a young boy like Sanford. Music was to be a life-long source of entertainment to him, and it seems likely that these street musicians would have held great fascination for any ten-year-old boy in Conyers in 1881. The more mature blades might have taken close note of Sarah Bernhardt's pending visit to Atlanta, where it was reported her "stockings will be displayed in store windows." Mad dogs, dying hogs, human suicides, and bad roads were of interest to publisher W. E. Hays according to the coverage given in his newspaper. Conyers, like Covington, revolved around a small axis where such matters stirred the mind and imagination in the 1870s and 1880s.[20] Tom Reed's "History of the University of Georgia" says Steadman had "all his precollege education at Guinn's academy in Conyers."[21] Beyond that, the records of Sanford's early schooling are blank. It is first in Macon at Mercer University that a documented track of young Steadman Sanford begins to form.

When Mercer made the move from Penfield to Macon in 1879, many of the state's institutions of higher education were in the process of adjusting to changing situations and demands in the last quarter of the century. Mercer's move to the leading city of central Georgia proved a good decision. Macon was to be a significant community in the life of Steadman Sanford as the home of his grandfather and grandmother, as the place where he received his undergraduate education, and as the last home of his father and mother, who moved there about the time Steadman completed his work at Mercer. It was Macon that the young S. V. Sanford family visited frequently.

Macon called itself and was "The Central City of Georgia," geographically as well as culturally, educationally, and economically. In an age in which every community boasted of its economic potential, beauty, and fortunate location, Macon was in fact just such a place. It had grown from an ancient site for Indian culture on the Ocmulgee River to a trade outpost to a point of transportation by rail and river and thus to a thriving commercial community of over thirty thousand inhabitants in the 1880s.

When Steadman went to Macon as a student the city enjoyed electric lights, gas, streetcars, handsome public buildings, and fine hotels. For all its fledgling urban features, however, Macon was like all Georgia towns, merely an interruption of farm and timber land. As an important rail hub, Macon was connected directly with Alabama, Florida, and South Carolina and the implied markets and sources beyond those border states. Other than agricultural products Macon's wholesale trade involved an impressive dry goods, grocery, hardware, and drug business. Many traveling salesmen called Macon home and beat regular trade paths throughout the South from the center of Georgia. Manufacturing had been economically important to Macon before the Civil War and the potential for that importance continued in the 1880s.

Macon enjoyed a system of free public schools, supported by the city and county. In 1889 there were also the following educational institutions: Wesleyan Female College, the oldest female college in the world and one of the largest and best; Mercer University; Pio Nono College; Mount de Sales Academy; the state-maintained Georgia Academy for the Blind, with a branch for colored pupils; Alexander Free School; a commercial school; and a number of private schools in which "stenography, telegraphing and type-writing are taught."[22]

Mercer, however, was most immediate to young Steadman Sanford as he carried on his studies and social life there in the late 1880s. There were 103 students at Mercer in 1889–90, Sanford's senior year. Steadman followed a fixed curriculum, the "classical" rather than the "scientific." In the *Mercerian* of 1889 the classical course is described: "[it] embraces a period of four years, during which time the following studies are pursued: Mental and Moral Philosophy, Mathematics, Physics, Chemistry, Geology, English, Modern Languages, Latin, and

Greek. The completion of this course entitles the student to the degree of A.B." Printed information indicates that in his senior year as a student of the classical curriculum, Steadman would have in his first term taken psychology in the philosophy area, astronomy in mathematics, heat and dynamical electricity in physical science, French in modern languages, and Shaw in English literature. During the second term of the senior year the prescribed courses were moral philosophy, chemistry and geology, French classics, and an elective in English classics.[23]

The liberal arts college (there were also a theological department, a subcollegiate department, and a law school) of Mercer had a faculty of nine: Other than Professor Shelton Sanford there were Joseph E. Willett, M.D., LL.D. in physics, chemistry, and geology; Rev. John J. Brantly, D.D. in English literature and mental and moral philosophy; Rev. Gustavus A. Nunnally, D.D. in history and science of government; William L. Dugan, A.M., professor of Greek; Thomas W. O'Kelley, A.B., professor of Latin; Robert L. Ryals, A.M., professor of pure mathematics; Emerson H. George, A.M., professor of modern languages; Kingman P. Moore, M.D., professor of physiology and hygiene. Professor Nunnally also served as president in 1889–90. As a Baptist institution, Mercer was governed by a Board of Trustees designated by the Executive Committee of the Georgia Baptist Convention, of which Professor Shelton P. Sanford, Steadman's grandfather, was secretary.

Of the ten members of Sanford's senior class only two were from the same county, Robert Lanier Anderson and Samuel Barfield from Bibb (Macon is the county seat). The others were either from central or north of central Georgia counties: Sanford from Rockdale, Bryan Well Collier from Spalding, Archelaus Maddox Duggan from Hancock, William Marvin Kelley from Washington, Andrew Washington Lane from Jasper, David Thomas Murdock from Chattooga, George Benjamin Stovall from Forsyth, and Baynard Willingham from Fulton County. The students in the lower classes reflected a similar pattern of home county origins.[24]

It is difficult to find a personality among the recorded and official records of Macon and Mercer in the 1880s, but there are occasional, important clues that help in seeing more of the young man who was Steadman Vincent Sanford. From the rolls of the social fraternities we see that Sanford was a member of Kappa Alpha fraternity. Sanford was also secretary-treasurer of the class of 1890. From these minor notes we may surmise something of his outgoing nature and willingness to work, traits which seemed to strengthen with each passing year. It is perhaps more revealing of persona and person to read the following observation about Sanford from a fellow student in one of the Mercer publications: "Since Steddie [*sic*] Sanford has become a junior, and a 'lady's man' it makes him mad to be thus addressed by his prospective father-in-law: 'why Steddie, how you are growing. You are almost as large as my daughter G———.'" [25] This bit of student humor at first blush might lead to the conclusion that young Steadman had met and was courting his bride-to-be, Grace McClatchey of Marietta. There is, however, no indication that was the case.

As the final decade of the century dawned Steadman Vincent Sanford completed his undergraduate education and started on his career. The next ten years mark the first stage of a long and illustrious professional career and family life. The world of S. V. Sanford the man begins; the tracks of his life, his courtship, his work, his social life, become visible. The scene of geography shifts now to Marietta, the cast enlarges to new friends, associates, colleagues, bride, children, all in what must have been one of the most exciting periods of change in American life, the 1890s.

That decade provided Sanford his first real-world opportunity to test his skills as a leader. He was on his own, devoid of local family associations, without his grandfather near at hand. It would be up to him to draw on those traditions and values which seemed most useful and thus most valuable to this new place, this new cast of characters, these changing conditions, this dawning new century.

TWO

Marietta

1890-1903

The 1890s were a period of considerable change in the life of S. V. Sanford. During those years he entered what was to be his life-long career, married, became a father, was a part-time soldier and public servant. In his twenties he cultivated new friendships and confronted the challenges of new surroundings in Marietta, Georgia, just north of Atlanta. Parallel to all these new experiences were important changes taking place in the community around him. Marietta was becoming a different place even for those who had been there all their lives. There was ample opportunity for Sanford to test his ability to deal with change and to make the most of it.

Marietta's electric lights were turned on in November 1889 and piped water came to the city in 1896. The telephone was in general use by 1898.[1] Technology had arrived with its many interlocking advances, one of which was illustrated in the bicycle craze. Sanford may have been among those who saw "the first female ever on the streets of Marietta on a bicycle," reported in November 1892 in the *Marietta Journal.*[2]

With all its technical progress, the Marietta to which Sanford moved in 1890 was not many years removed from the direct impact

of war. There were numerous reminders of the disruption and de-
struction of the closing months of the Civil War in that part of Georgia on the northern edge of Atlanta near Kennesaw Mountain. Steadman's oldest son, Shelton Palmer Sanford, recalled some remaining
evidence of the war that impressed him as a child near century's end.
Writing in the 1960s, Shelton said of the Marietta of his youth: "There
were many scars of the war to be noted as late as 1900." He recalled
that when rambling about the community and asking of this or that
burned shell of a building or declining earthwork, "the Negroes would
only say 'war times.' These two words explained a lot in Marietta."³

S. V. Sanford, however, harbored no long-lasting or burning re-
sentments of wartime events or glorified notions of southern deeds
and heroes. He had a fondness for the military and its trappings, but
that was expressed in the present tense as seen in his leadership of a
local unit called the Marietta Rifles and in his Spanish-American War
period involvement rather than in past glory or defects. S. V. Sanford
properly honored tradition but kept it clearly in perspective with the
events going on around him. Early on, Sanford was a man linked to
the past but ever ready for the future, a characteristic that would serve
him well for the remainder of his career.

Shelton Palmer Sanford reinforced this view of his father. In his
account of his youth he recalled that there were elements in the community of late-nineteenth-century Marietta that included a good
many northerners who had come since the late war. "Early in life
my father had let me know that all Northerners who came to Marietta were not carpetbaggers. Some had come with good intentions.
They were public spirited people with the good of the community at
heart."⁴

In explaining why his father moved to Marietta, Shelton said that
Professor Thomas Murray, principal of Marietta's Male Academy, was
in attendance at Sanford's graduation exercise at Mercer and asked
him to come to Marietta to teach with him. Shelton's account suggested that Professor Murray had been impressed by an address his
father had delivered on that occasion.⁵

Marietta was about to become a leader in public education among

Georgia communities when S. V. Sanford came to the Male Academy in 1890. Sanford would have been aware that he was committing himself to Marietta's determination for excellence during the infancy of an evolving public educational system. D. F. McClatchey, Steadman Sanford's future father-in-law, was among those who in the mid-1880s raised funds for schools for both boys and girls in the community.[6]

McClatchey was a locally important Marietta businessman who operated a grocery and general merchandise store in the town when Sanford arrived in 1890. McClatchey's colorful advertising copy in the *Marietta Journal* was always of interest to readers, and from the social notes and news of that paper it is obvious that both Mr. and Mrs. McClatchey were significant community figures. Grace and her siblings had their social comings and goings reported in "Marietta Matters" and "Local Leaflets" sections of the *Journal.* Grace's parents were involved in their church, the Marietta Methodist.[7] Young Sanford became a familiar figure in the McClatchey household when he began boarding there. Just when he first moved there is not known, but there is interesting correspondence concerning his departure.

In the summer months and during holidays when his school was not in session in Marietta, Sanford would return to his parents' home in Macon. Mrs. D. F. McClatchey wrote Sanford there in the summer of 1893: "I supposed when you left we would have you stay with us again this winter. Now Mr. McClatchey thinks we had best have no one as we have yet secured no servant, neither cook, [nor] house girl for wages."[8]

Mr. McClatchey, in the timeless fashion of husbands, has enlisted Mrs. McClatchey to break the news. Grace's mother continues: "We could have no one to give us as little trouble as yourself. . . . I must say with your deportment at my house I could find no fault yet with no servant to attend the room or half the time no cook. . . . Mr. McClatchey insists that for the present we should not try to keep a boarder, even you."[9]

It is telling of its time that Mrs. McClatchey expresses her concern about what Steadman's mother might conclude on hearing her son had lost his place: "I write so your mother can understand why you would go any where [and] assume it was not because you were troublesome."[10]

In closing Mrs. McClatchey suggested several possibilities including "the Elliot Cottage, next to the Seminary, or the Elmwood either."[11] In the fall of that year Steadman V. Sanford's flowery letters to "My Darling Grace" and signed "Your sincere lover, SVS" were written on letterhead stationery from the Elmwood. "My love is so deep and so strong that it almost makes me worship you. You are to me such a woman as was the wife of Pygmalian [sic]—true, sincere, kind, and loving. *No man will ever try as hard to increase your pleasure as I and none can make you as happy as I.*"[12]

We see, about a month later, in a letter from Grace to "My Dear Mr. Sanford" what may be considered uncertainty mixed with obvious devotion: "There are times when the dread and fear seize me, that I do wrong to love you, in spite of the desire of father, mother, sister, and brother and I ask myself—why do I love him? Just because he is he and I am I *that* is the only reason I can find. Lovingly, Grace."[13]

Grace wrote Steadman temporarily "breaking" their "engagement of a little more than a year ago" in a letter dated February 28, 1894. She had despaired of Sanford's "likes," among which she enumerated "card parties, dances, the punch bowl," and "other amusements."[14]

Grace's family, however, was on Steadman's side. He had made his place in the community by his well-publicized success in local schools, and from Grace's letters it is clear that her family heartily favored their future together.[15]

For several issues in August 1890 a Marietta newspaper, the weekly *Journal,* carried a small notice headed "Marietta Male Academy"; it read: "The Fall term of this institution will open September 1st. No change will be made in the established rates of tuition. The Principal will be assisted by Mr. Steadman Sanford, an honor graduate of Mercer University, and other competent teachers. A catalog giving particulars will be issued at an early day." It was signed: "Thom. A. Murray, Principal."[16]

In October the *Journal* reported rather flatly that at the Male Academy "Professor Murray is a teacher of ability and is doing his duty as principal." What signs of hope and promise there were in the coverage of the school seem reserved for young Steadie Sanford. "Professor S. V. Sanford, assistant teacher in the Male Academy is giving satisfaction to his patrons of the Academy."[17] Sanford's place as a community figure may be assumed to have soon been established given the note in the "Local Leaflets" column of the *Journal*, October 23, 1890: "Professor S. V. Sanford spent Sunday in Conyers."[18]

Following Christmas vacation and the beginning of the new year, S. V. Sanford's career stock began to rise precipitously. A lead item on page four of the February 26, 1891, *Marietta Journal* reported: "Professor Thomas A. Murray on last Monday tendered his resignation to the Board of Trustees as Principal of the Marietta Male Academy." The school was said to be on solid ground, and with "all the bad weather has had an attendance of over seventy pupils." Murray's act, the article assured, was "voluntary." He needed rest. Murray had been teaching twenty-five years and needed "the rest from the mental and physical worry incidental to the close and active duties of the school room." The resignation was to take place March 1. The trustees chose "Professor Sanford and Miss Baker to take charge of the school, both of them are fully competent to give satisfaction."[19] Just how much satisfaction Mr. Sanford was able to provide was abundantly clear by the time of school closing activities in June 1891.

Among other innovations, Professor Sanford instituted military drill to reinvigorate the student body and improve public perception of the Male Academy. The local newspaper made a most approving note of the innovation when it announced the coming "celebration" and exercises for the end of the school year.[20] In what was an obvious nod to his leadership of the academy by now, the editor noted: "Professor Sanford has arranged an interesting program for the occasion."[21]

The apparent success of the professor's first major public production in Marietta testifies to his possession of those talents that were his trademark for the next fifty-plus years in education and in the public eye. Even at the tender age of nineteen, Steadman Vincent Sanford was a showman with that deft touch of being able to convey his sincere warmth and personal concern for his students and his community.[22]

Young Sanford's debut was proclaimed a "Brilliant Closing Examination" for the Male Academy in a one-page full-blown, detailed article in the *Marietta Journal*: "An immense crowd was present. It was a representative of beauty, refinement, and culture. The music was delightful. There were several beautiful tableaux, and calcium lights were thrown upon the scenes." Professor Sanford announced the program, which included in part prayer, recitations, tableaux, poetry, stories, dialogue, parody, oration, a spelling contest, extracts from Henry Grady, and, of course, military drill. One no-doubt stirring item was a depiction of "Jefferson Davis in chains." Miss Grace McClatchey was cast as the fortune-teller in "The Gypsy Fortune Teller," one of the many short playlets also part of the festivities.[23]

S. V. Sanford's star was on the rise, rapidly and in an unusually high arc, or so it may be inferred from the tone and coverage of the article: "At the conclusion of the entertainment, a very unexpected event, not down in the program, was enacted. It was 'the caning' of Professor Sanford, the Principal of the Academy. Captain W. W. Wolfe of Atlanta hurried to the stage with a gold-headed cane in hand and presented it to Professor Sanford as a testimony of esteem from his pupils."[24]

The article was an homage to the community's new leading educator: "Professor Sanford is one of the youngest teachers in the State. . . . But we learn with pleasure of his thoroughness. As a competent teacher and disciplinarian . . . we have reason to believe him to be a courteous and upright gentleman. He is from one of the best families in the State, who have ranked high as educators, and he has a laudable ambition in his chosen profession and an energy that will win success."[25]

The first full term under Sanford's leadership proved a success. Following the closing exercises of June 1892 it was reported that "Professor Sanford and his able corps of teachers have given Marietta a good school and eminent satisfaction. Marietta is glad to have such faithful, pains-taking and competent teachers to instruct the youth. Professor Sanford is a young man, but he has shown aptitude, tact, and good judgement and deserves the esteem and confidence of our people." [26] Steadie Sanford had become Professor Sanford.

Steadman Sanford's second year at the Male Academy was to be his last. The impetus in the Marietta community to provide a public education for its youth was to bring an end to the Male Academy as well as its counterpart for females, Harwood. The closing of the academy, however, was another opportunity for Sanford's "laudable ambition."

O. B. Keeler, who was one of young Professor Sanford's first students in Marietta and remained a lifelong devotee, wrote about the young professor's successful methods in a 1935 piece in the *Atlanta Journal*. "It was on the threshold of the gay nineties—in September 1890, to be precise," begins Keeler, "that a slender youngster of 19 came to my home town, Marietta, a graduate, A.B. from Mercer University at that tender age, to be President of the Male Academy." [27] Sanford may have come to be president, but in fact he was hired and began the school year as assistant to the aging principal, Thomas A. Murray.

Keeler described the Marietta Male Academy as "at that time probably the toughest educational post in the civilized world." No headmaster in any English school was ever confronted with a job to compare with that one. "I don't say," claimed Keeler, "we Marietta Boys were harder cases than others, but we were thoroughly organized— the little boys (I was one) into Indians and cowboys; the bigger fellows in the Dirty Dozen and the Beauties." [28]

It is easy to read into the 1935 account Keeler's heroic memory of young Sanford. Recalling one of the frequent examples of mischief, usually perpetrated on the smaller boys by the larger boys, he describes in obviously worshipful and perhaps exaggerated terms Sanford's response to the bullying: "The young man from Mercer went into that combination [the Dirty Dozen] and hauled out the biggest boy, the ring leader, in this case, Charles Sanges and sent word for all the school to assemble in the Big Room, and then and there he thrashed the offender, half a head taller and twenty pounds heavier than himself, until he roared for mercy." Keeler proudly concludes, "and that, in a manner of speaking, was that."

Further recollections by the writer and former Sanford student attest to Sanford's "immense popularity with the boys." He played football, "the old rough Rugby game—where everybody kicked the ball," and he "made friends with the boys big and little." According to Keeler, "if there ever was a regular, he was one."[29] No higher praise was possible in that still simple time of the 1930s which, like the 1890s of the writer's memory, sought out and loudly proclaimed heroes near and far.

The paucity of existing correspondence for 1892 and 1893 leaves significant gaps in our knowledge of the specifics of Sanford's work and leisure during that period, but a letter from James D. Manget dated May 24, 1894, suggests that things were going very well for Sanford in his role as a teacher. "Dear Professor," began Manget, "Four long years you have been my teacher. Father says I have learned more since I have been going to school to you than I learned the whole time before." If the father was impressed with the student's progress under Sanford, the son was impressed by his teacher's kindness: "Not *one* cross word from you was ever spoken to me."[30] If young Sanford, as in the later recollections of his student O. B. Keeler, was a tough disciplinarian, willing and able to whip the biggest and toughest of the "Dirty Dozen," he was obviously also a dispenser of that same gentle kindness, understanding, and caring that his grandfather, Shelton Sanford, had cultivated with his Mercer boys in decades past.

The "First Annual Report of the Public Schools of the City of Marietta, Georgia; with Manual of Instruction and Rules and Regulations, Session 1892–93," provides some indication of the shifting responsibilities of Professor Sanford in this period. The report lists S. V. Sanford as "Principal and Teacher of High School." Grace McClatchey was at the academy building, Sanford's former headquarters, as B division, second grade teacher.[31]

The Marietta Schools reported in their first year a total of 742 students in attendance, 411 white and 331 colored, 72 percent of the persons of school age in the community according to their figures. This relatively high percentage was a source of local pride, and the report pointed out that Macon might claim only 54 percent and Athens 58 percent in public schools. There is no indication of private school attendance in these communities.[32]

The "Course of Study" for the Marietta schools established high ideals, claiming assuredly: "Our High School covers four years and can, if thoroughly taught, prepare a boy or girl for the junior class in our colleges, in fact, for the senior class in the Female colleges." A somewhat more "modern" point of view follows: "The Board should, however, arrange for a business course covering the full course in English and the Sciences but omitting Greek or French entirely, and Latin after the second year, and inserting in their stead, Book-keeping, Economics, and advanced Arithmetic." It appears that Sanford's previous commitments at the Male Academy when he took over leadership there (assuring attention to the "needs of the day") are reflected here.[33]

Sanford's first term at the Male Academy had ended with his promotion to principal, and thus by 1891, he was in a position to be seen and evaluated in the public eye. The 1891–92 school year gave Sanford the chance to demonstrate his educational philosophy and methods as head of the academy. When, however, in the fall of 1892, Sanford became principal of the newly created public high school, his public persona was considerably diminished. The identification with the public schools was no longer with principal Sanford, but with superintendent Joseph S. Stewart Jr., who held that position until Sanford gained it in 1897. Between 1893 and 1897 Sanford's public image was largely in the context of his pupils and his connections to the McClatchey family.

The creation of a local military unit in early 1894, however, provided a new opportunity for Sanford's abilities to be publicly tested and acknowledged. Sanford in that year addressed the need for an armory, community benefits arising from its support, and plans for generating support for the effort. Describing the evolution of the military group, Sanford said that it was initially organized with forty-four members but that many had left the community, leaving the present (1894) enlistment at thirty-seven "and for a company to succeed we must have sixty." He proceeded to explain that the present situation was not stable and was in need of important community support. Sanford outlined his plan for a new organization of support to be known as the "Marietta Rifle Association." The members of the association, for the payment of dues of seventy-five cents per month or $9.00 for the year, would "elect a President and form a Constitution, be exempted from Jury Duty, enlistment, drills, parades, and all military duty." The association would govern the Rifles as a division in keeping with "law of government and volunteer forces." A part of the rationale for this plan, according to these notes, was that "the town needs somewhere to entertain her distinguished guests. For example Speaker Crisp [Speaker of the U.S. House of Representatives, Charles Crisp of Americus, Georgia] had no good place to be entertained." [34]

In January 1894 the *Journal* reported that a military company was to be organized "backed by some of the pluckiest young men in town." A meeting was called at the fire engine house for January 29 to "commence enrollment." Speeches were to be made by several, but Sanford's name does not appear in this account. Later, when it reported on the meeting the *Journal* described the gathering as an "enthusiastic meeting looking to the organization of a military company—having enrolled thirty-seven men" and seeking to enroll as many as seventy-five. No individuals' names are given in this account. Early in February the *Journal* reported the election of S. V. Sanford as captain of the new company. [35]

For the remainder of the year there is seldom an issue of the newspaper that does not include some mention of, and usually high praise for, Sanford and his men. It was reported in late March that the Rifles had received their uniforms, dark blue coats with appropriate brass buttons and light blue pants with white stripes down the sides; Captain Sanford was described as "drilling the boys (about 45 in number) every week, and they are learning right along." In April the Rifles visited "by invitation" the Capitol City Guards Fair in Atlanta and Memorial Day ceremonies in Marietta. May activities included a ten-day encampment at Griffin, which was preceded and followed by community prayer services, sermons, and "liberal patronage and entertainments."[36]

The outstanding performance of the Rifles at their encampment was the subject of several items in the Marietta press during the summer of 1894. A mid-June issue of the *Journal* called them "the neatest company in the encampment," as they liberally quoted from the *Atlanta Constitution:* "They make a feature of going into dinner. The Marietta boys have with them two colored guitar artists, who always march in front of the company into the mess hall, making march music the while. In drilling the company is right up to the notch."[37]

Summer camps at Tybee and Cumberland Islands in 1895 provided Captain Sanford and his troops an opportunity to get to know members of similar companies around Georgia. These military based associations contributed to Sanford's active interest in related veterans' activities throughout his life.[38]

The defining event of Steadman Sanford's time in Marietta was not, however, the formation of the Rifles, his teaching, his professional advancements, or his civic responsibilities. His greatest Marietta accomplishment was his marriage on June 16, 1895, to Miss Grace McClatchey.

The ceremony was a quiet one, only a few friends being present. Newspaper accounts describe Grace as "one of the most popular teachers in the city schools." The groom received larger notice: "He is a graduate of Mercer, Captain of the Marietta Rifles and popular among his company. No young man in Marietta has more friends than Captain Sanford, socially or otherwise." Their wedding trip took them to Macon to visit the parents of the groom. From there they

visited Cumberland Island to attend the Teachers Association, returning to the city in a few weeks.[39]

Apparently Steadman's marriage coincided with a concerted effort
to advance his career somewhere beyond Marietta. In the Sanford
collection there are several 1896 letters of recommendation and mention of various positions in education around Georgia. The June 5,
1896, letter from R. N. Holland of Marietta, to the Honorable W. A.
Little Jr. of Columbus, is typical: "This letter of recommendation is
for my warm personal friend and fellow-townsman, Captain S. V. Sanford, of the Marietta Rifles. Captain Sanford is also one of our leading
educators and prominently connected with the public schools of the
city. He is one of our best and most popular citizens."[40]

After the death of his grandfather in July 1896, Steadman's father
continued to encourage him and talked to his friends about helping
his son search for a new position. Charles Sanford no doubt understood the sense of loss his son felt with the death of his grandfather.
In his August 5 letter he continued the encouragement but cautioned
his son to be ready for setbacks, "Dear Steadie, I hope you will get the
place you are trying for. You must, however, be ready for disappointments, as they come more often than success. It seems your friends
are doing all they can for you."[41]

The birth of Grace and Steadman's first child in 1896 provided a
new, more personal topic for the Sanfords. Sanford's father wrote in
February 1897 regarding his new grandson: "Grandma says that Shelton Palmer looks like a 'poor little God-forsaken child.' Shelton (uncle
to the child) says he looks a like little full-blooded Irishman. I think
he looks like a little London waif or news-boy."[42] Four Sanford children were born in Marietta: Shelton Palmer in 1896, Grace Devereaux
in 1897, Charles Steadman in 1901, and Homer Reynolds in 1903. The
growing family provided, in addition to much family joy and pleasure, more and more incentive for professional advancement.

A note to Captain S. V. Sanford dated February 1, 1897, from John F.
Howard of Barnesville, Georgia, contained what must have been
the disappointing news that "Professor Branson is not accepting

the Athens job, but is staying at Gordon Institute. I'll keep you informed." [43]

More encouraging news came the following day in a note Sanford received from R. E. Lawhorn, city clerk of Marietta: "Captain W. J. Hudson resigned the office of City Treasurer and you was [sic] elected to fill the vacancy." That action was confirmed in the February 4, 1897, *Marietta Journal*: "The City Council met Tuesday night and elected Professor S. V. Sanford Treasurer to succeed Captain W. J. Hudson, resigned." [44] Throughout the remainder of the year the treasury reports of the city published in the local paper were signed by "S. V. Sanford, Treasurer." Among these reports is Sanford's salary as treasurer of $12.50 per month. [45]

Never one to overlook the importance of the present in pursuit of the future while he looked for career possibilities elsewhere, Sanford cultivated his civic roles and responsibilities in Marietta. In July Sanford took part in the dedicatory services for the "newly furnished Sunday School rooms" in the new Marietta Baptist Church. Mr. R. H. Northcut tendered the room. "The response of Professor S. V. Sanford, in accepting the tender of the room in behalf of the Sunday School," said the *Journal*, "was a literary gem, beautiful in diction and tender in sentiment." [46]

Sanford's chance for advancement came in late July when Professor J. S. Stewart resigned his superintendency of the Marietta schools to become president of North Georgia Agricultural College at Dahlonega and Sanford was chosen as Stewart's successor at a salary of $1,350 per year. *Journal* readers were reminded of Sanford's family, "noted for their educational ability, prestige and influence," and the professor himself was credited for his "signal success" and "well-known moral and educational qualifications." He was said to be "fired with ambition to promote the best interests of the schools." The community need "have no fears," the students of the Marietta schools were in good hands and would graduate able to be successful in "first class colleges." [47]

With this change Steadman Sanford was in a position to regain public attention and exercise leadership on a broader base than that provided by the Rifles. One of the best indications of Sanford's return to educational prominence in the public eye and mind may be seen in the account of the June 1898 closing exercises of the Marietta public schools. In his role as superintendent, Sanford was once more allowed to demonstrate his special flair. The full account of the event from the *Journal* is reminiscent of the lavish pageantry of Steadie's first closing exercises at the Male Academy in the spring of 1891. More than three columns on the front page of the *Journal* on June 2, 1891, were devoted to the occasion. The account closes with a paragraph in tribute to the new superintendent: "The schools have been admirably managed and conducted by Superintendent S. V. Sanford. He has worked faithfully, earnestly, and intelligently and sought with tireless energy to make Marietta Public Schools the best in the state, and he has succeeded by the aid of his excellent corps of teachers. He comes of a prominent family of educators and sustains the enviable reputation that they made in his own work." [48]

Eighteen ninety-eight provided, in the Spanish-American War, a national excitement that came to overshadow even superintendent Sanford's local successes. The war also disrupted Sanford's Marietta routines. As was typical, however, even the disruptions provided Sanford with future assets.

Early in 1898 events in Cuba precipitated the entry of the United States into war with Spain, said to have been called by contemporaries America's "splendid little war." The conflict was brief and sometimes comically colorful. However, it not only provided the basis for America's entry into the twentieth century as a significant player in world diplomacy but gave the post–Civil War generation of service age Americans their first real chance for patriotic gore. Captain S. V. Sanford, like most of his fellow soldiers, did not make it as far as Cuba and the fighting. In fact Sanford did not get as far as Tampa where so many of the would-be combatants waited out the brief conflict.

The Marietta Rifles, as Company H, 5th Georgia Infantry, in 1894 entered the Spanish-American War as Company F, 3rd Georgia Volunteer Infantry, on August 24, 1898. The unit served in Cuba from January 18, 1899, to March 25, 1899, and was mustered out at Augusta, Georgia, on April 22, 1899.[49] S. V. Sanford would receive his honorable discharge at the end of September 1898, so he technically was a "participant" in the war for only a month. It appears that Sanford's experience was more typical of most soldiers serving during this time than were Col. Roosevelt's Rough Rider experiences in Cuba. Sanford spent his brief active duty with his men at Camp Northen near Griffin, Georgia.

There is an interesting letter concerning the war from Steadman's father Charles written in July 1898. Beginning on a light note he wrote, "Don't you let little Shelton Palmer enlist in your company, but leave him at home to take care of his mama and little Grace." It is perhaps revealing of the Sanford family's concern for its own in the face of the threat of war that Charles Sanford's letter to his son, the captain, evokes something less than a bellicose view of recent developments and prospects of things to come: "Dear Steadie, Your letter on yesterday did not read much like a warrior's letter but rather like a civilian, for you seemed to write more like a man whose time and mind was filled with school and educational matters than with things pertaining to war."[50]

Captain Sanford appears to have taken to heart his father's advice. There was little activity at Camp Northen and the situation at Griffin was getting to him. He requested leave from September 1 to 17 to go home to attend to private business. "Unless attended to at this time [it] would cause me serious loss."[51]

He wrote Grace on September 24, "there is not one word of news— everything is as dull and monotonous as can be." He mentioned the death of a friend from typhoid fever and he obviously yearned to get back to Marietta and his family.[52] He wrote again on September 26 that he had visited Macon where his mother was sick. He borrowed $75 and sent it home to Grace. He thanked his wife for "the last box you sent, it added much to our bill of fare." He had apparently been informed that his recent request for permission to resign would go through. "I hope they will not find out in Marietta that I have resigned until I come back to stay."[53]

Copies of official correspondence verify that on September 30, 1898, "Captain S. V. Samford [*sic*] 3rd Georgia Volunteers, having tendered his resignation is honorably discharged from the service of the U.S. to take effect this date."[54] In later years Chancellor Sanford remarked to a colleague that he had never envisioned the Marietta Rifles as a combat unit. He claimed to have recruited not soldiers but "fellows who looked good in a uniform."[55] Nonetheless, after 1898, for the remainder of his life the public Sanford wore proudly his status as a "Spanish-American War Veteran."

The summer after his active duty Sanford enrolled in summer school at the University of Chicago. In the main the few items of correspondence available to us from Sanford's Chicago stays address small and personal matters that were obviously of great interest and importance to both Grace and Steadman. "S. P. [Shelton Palmer] stood at the gate and asked Carrie [the maid] 'have you a letter from Dad?' He sat beside me for me to read it to him. 'Grace what does Dad say?'"[56] Little Shelton Palmer, almost three at the time, sounds unusually mature and pensive.

A late July 1899 letter from wife to husband contains an interesting combination of topics, practical business to wistful parenthood matters to professional politics. Grace asked Steadman which math book would be used in the Marietta schools in the coming year. She wanted to start working with the children in advance. Since Grace had served as a supply teacher, it is not certain that she was interested for the schoolchildren in general or for members of her own family.[57]

The University of Chicago would have been an exciting place in the 1890s. In that decade universities were the proving grounds of many of the "advance agents of Progressivism." The utility-minded in higher education were attempting to put an up-to-date definition of pragmatism among the creeds of the university. At Chicago John Dewey was about to make a name for himself as the leading figure in American Progressive education.[58]

While we have no evidence of Dewey's philosophies at work in Sanford's classroom, there is an interesting parallel in the style of Chicago's president, William Rainey Harper, and S. V. Sanford as he rose in higher administration. Laurence R. Veysey in his study of late-nineteenth- and early-twentieth-century higher education in America says of Harper: "He never learned that it might be poor form to appear too unreservedly enthusiastic or to exert oneself to the very limit in public. Instead he never got over the boyish desire . . . to show everyone continuously how hard he was working." [59] Harper engaged in practices that sound uncannily like those of Professor (and later administrator) Sanford: "Harper was capable of indulging in kindly sympathetic acts. He liked to call undergraduates to his office to have a chat." [60]

"It can be argued," says Veysey, "that the University of Chicago represented a blending of the small-town promotional spirit of the adolescent middle west with the big-city standards of sophistication." [61] He may not have consciously adopted that combination of influences during his two summers at Chicago, but S. V. Sanford certainly operated as if he had been injected with that combination.

At the turn of the century American higher education moved toward a model of utility and efficiency. The leading figure of American political Progressivism, Theodore Roosevelt, evidenced the kind of enthusiasm that might have pleased President Harper. Down in Marietta S. V. Sanford's enthusiasm found yet another outlet.

The Chautauqua movement created a whole new area for Sanford's energy during his final years in Marietta. Early in the winter of 1900 the newspaper reported that "A meeting was held last Tuesday evening having in view the organization of a Chautauqua assembly for Marietta. Professor S. V. Sanford is the promoter of the enterprise, and he has enlisted as supporters quite a number of wealthy and influential citizens of the town who will give the matter financial aid." [62]

The fiscal side of the enterprise called for the selling of twenty shares of stock at one hundred dollars a share, the election of Judge George F. Gober as president and Professor Sanford as secretary, and the plan to secure a "tent to seat 5,000." Sanford, in a role to which he would become accustomed and in which he would be highly successful, headed up the "soliciting committee." An initial Chautauqua session of one week was planned for the coming July, to be modeled on the programs in Gainesville, Barnesville, and Hawkinsville, Georgia. "It will," offered the *Journal,* "bring visitors who will spend money and help considerably in the dull season." The town would benefit from the advertising and "best of all, this movement contemplates the placing of the community upon a higher intellectual plane." The editor concluded: "Let everybody rally to Professor Sanford's support and make this the best assembly in Georgia." [63]

The Chautauqua, largely with the guidance of Professor Sanford, became a major topic of interest in Marietta in the winter of 1900. A long article explaining the evolving nature of the movement appeared in a later February issue of the *Journal.* Chautauqua was characterized as "dignified" and "high class" with music, including military brass bands and "aggregations of vocalists," playing a "prime place" in each meeting. Speakers, however, were the stars of the American Chautauqua movement and Marietta's version was going to include some of the brightest of them by offering handsome rewards.

By the end of June the Chautauqua program had been confirmed. General John B. Gordon was to be the featured speaker, addressing "the Last Days of the Confederacy" at 10:00 A.M. on July 4, and a tent had been erected on the "Hunt lot" on Cherokee Street. "It will seat 2,500 people." Post-Chautauqua accounts were filled with praise: it was "a great success, it did good, it was a moral uplift in culture and social prestige. The stockholders and managers did their work well. The public should feel grateful to them." [64]

In the spring of 1901 superintendent Sanford had the opportunity for a personal visit with Chancellor Walter B. Hill of the University of Georgia, who spoke at the Marietta school's closing exercises. Shelton Sanford, writing about his father's employment at the university in Athens, attributes Sanford's pursuit of a position at the university to Hill's influence. He was "so impressed with Chancellor Hill and the

University that he applied for an appointment and in due time he received it."[65]

Sanford's campaign for a position at the university was through Byron Bower, a Bainbridge, Georgia, attorney, who wrote: "your friend Judge Gober has already spoken to me very highly of your qualifications for the position to which you aspire. I shall take pleasure in favoring your appointment to the place in question."[66] Early the next month, W. E. Simmons of Lawrenceville wrote Sanford: "I have yours of the 23rd informing me that you will be an applicant for the position of Instructor in English in the State University and solicit my assistance. Believing you to be fully competent to discharge the duties incident to the position, I make an exception in your case, owing to personal considerations, to the rule heretofore observed by me under such circumstances, not to commit myself and assure you that it will afford me pleasure to render you any assistance within my power."[67]

U.S. senator from Georgia A. O. Bacon provided a late response to Sanford's request for a recommendation for the position in Athens. The senator apologized for the tardiness of the reply. "Should an opportunity offer, I will be glad to serve you if I can consistently do so," he offered. "I make this qualification as I do not know the circumstance connected with the filling of the proposed position in the University."[68]

In the spring of 1903, Sanford was still involved with the Chautauqua, serving on the program committee, according to an early May issue of the *Journal*. Sanford made the dedicatory speech for the new fountain in the Marietta square in late May. That is the last public account of his activities until the October 8, 1903, issue of the *Journal*, which reported, "Professor S. V. Sanford, of Athens University [*sic*], spent Sunday and Monday here with his family." In April the trustees of the university had elected Sanford to "Instructor of Rhetoric and English Literature" at a salary of $1,200 per annum, for one year. For a cut in pay of several hundred dollars, Steadman Vincent Sanford was headed to the place where his beloved grandfather had established a Sanford legacy.[69]

THREE

Athens
1903-1917

In his history of the University of Georgia, Professor Tom Dyer maintains that "more change occurred in the university during the first two decades of the twentieth century than in any preceding era."[1] The beginnings of many of these changes were in motion in the decade S. V. Sanford was establishing himself in the education profession in Marietta. When Sanford arrived in Athens in the fall of 1903, these changes were creating a new university.

It was, according to Dyer, the leadership of "two strong Chancellors, Walter B. Hill, and David C. Barrow," which "moved the university closer to the mainstream of American higher education." Between the beginning of the new century and America's entry into World War I, the University of Georgia emerged as an institution far more than a "gentleman's finishing school." It was becoming a "multi-faceted," coeducational, academically well-grounded, politically connected, if underfunded resource for the State of Georgia, newly sensitive to a broad constituency and to public service responsibilities.[2]

Professor Sanford's experiences during those early years of the twentieth century were as multifaceted as those of the changing university. Between his arrival in the fall of 1903 and his eldest son's enlistment in the American Expeditionary Forces in 1917, S. V. Sanford became a popular professor in the English Department; was the central, noncoaching faculty figure in the athletic program of the university; took a leave to study English and German literature abroad (1912–13); wrote literature and composition texts (1914); developed a widespread reputation as a public speaker; suffered the loss of his only daughter (1907); was instrumental in the establishment of a program in journalism at the university (1915); was awarded an honorary doctorate (1914); was promoted to professor of English (1913); established personal and family ties in the Athens community; and established the family home on Cloverhurst Avenue, which remained the center of family activities until his death.

The first mention of S. V. Sanford in an *Athens City Directory* is that of 1904, listing Sanford on West Dougherty, but no street number is given. The next available directory (1909) has the Sanford household at 125 South Milledge and by the 1916–17 directory the family is located at 359 Cloverhurst.[3] Those who knew Sanford still associate the house at 359 Cloverhurst with Dr. Sanford, Grace, and the boys: Shelton Palmer, Charles Steadman, and Homer Reynolds. Grace Devereaux, the daughter, did not live to enjoy Cloverhurst. Her death was one of the defining events in the household early in the Sanfords' Athens years.

Athens, the residence of Steadman Sanford for almost a half-century, was a bustling town when the new professor arrived in 1903. There were about twelve thousand residents, paved streets, electric lights, an electric railway, and four, soon to be five, rail lines. Shelton Sanford recalled the importance of those railroads during his youth when he thought of them as the only way of getting out of town.[4] It was, however, the educational field of which the community was most proud: "In the educational field of Georgia, Athens easily holds first place with the University of Georgia, the State Normal School of Georgia, and Lucy Cobb Institute, a high grade college for girls. Athens also has a magnificent system of city schools, unsurpassed in the United States."[5]

In its form in the summer before Professor Sanford became a faculty member, there was still a strongly traditional tone to education in Athens: male, white, with but a nod toward both women and African Americans. Educational opportunity for women and African Americans was available in Athens but not in mainstream forms or locations. A 1903 publication offered, "while the University of Georgia has no dormitories for women, they may obtain rooms near the Campus at reasonable prices, and take their meals at Denmark Dining Hall. A summer school for colored teachers is held in the buildings of Knox Institute in the western part of the city."[6] The Knox Institute was a product of Freedman Bureau effort and was the first school erected in Athens for African Americans. These arrangements were normal for the period and only gradually modified during Sanford's life. The repressive pattern of gender and race relations in Athens was in keeping with those of Conyers, Macon, or Marietta and familiar to the Sanfords as they came to Clarke County in 1903.

Athens took its lead from the University of Georgia, which bordered Broad Street's commercial district. The university not only provided architectural presence but was also a major force in the local economy and in local social, cultural, and intellectual leadership, despite having no more than three hundred students, including a class of subfreshmen and a faculty that numbered but twenty-five during the 1903–4 term. Generations of Georgians have come to think of Athens as one of their hometowns as a result of the time spent there as students. Probably no other community generates more adopted loyalties or attracts more formerly temporary residents to return and spend their lives there. That special university–Athens connection was a tradition when the Sanfords arrived, and their adoption of the community soon fit the familiar pattern.

It was no doubt difficult, at least initially, to overcome the close ties the Sanfords had to Marietta, Grace by family connections and life-time residence and Steadman by virtue of his many roles in the community over a period of almost thirteen years. The Sanford children were all young enough at the time of the move that the adjustment to a new community was probably less troublesome for them. In look-ing back, however, the oldest, Shelton, said that "the transition from Marietta to Athens was not without pain," recalling the comfort of having had along Powder Springs Street in Marietta "forty-four close relatives."[7]

"Steadie" would return to Marietta only for brief visits and family gatherings. He of course maintained his ties with friends and with the McClatchey and Reynolds families. He remained involved in matters such as the old Marietta Male Academy building. It was an important symbol of what had first taken him from Mercer to Marietta at the beginning of his career and eventually his marriage and family life. Steadman remained a trustee of the Male Academy as late as 1910 and his military associations provided another lasting Marietta connec-tion. When Sanford informed the Marietta Rifles of his move to the university and Athens, he was "presented with a very handsome silver saber by the company as evidence of the love which is borne him by the company and the high esteem in which he is held by its members." A newspaper account from 1903 described the departing captain as "a great favorite with the command and it is a source of deep regret that he will leave. . . . He has always had one of the best companies in the State, and there has never at any time been the least trouble with any of the men under his command."[8]

The past that preceded Marietta remained important, too. In Ma-con Sanford's parents provided the most significant connection. That connection was weakened by time and distance and by loss. During his first year on the faculty of the university, Sanford's mother died. In the spring before, his father had written him describing her illness, her high pulse and temperature, and the difficulties of running the household. "All the work," Charles Sanford complained, "falls on Annie [Steadman's sister who never married] and me."[9] In the sum-mer of 1904 Elizabeth Steadman Sanford died. Steadman's father lived on in Macon until his death in 1915, and Steadman's siblings remained in the community beyond that. These connections, as well as his loy-alty to Mercer and his grandfather's memory, made Macon a special place for S. V. Sanford.

Family illness was, unfortunately, a keynote of the Sanford household and extended family in these first years in Athens. In 1906,
Charles wrote his son in Athens regarding his concern for the health
of the Sanford children: "Dear Steadie, I got a letter from Shelton
saying you are 'much worried about the sickness of Charles Steadman.' I was hoping that the change from Athens to Marietta might
have done the little boy some good. [During the summer the family
had apparently returned to the McClatchey place.] I hope he has not
the fever and that you may soon see a change in him for the better." [10]

During the first decade of the century typhoid fever was a major
health problem, especially in the South. Sanford had lost comrades to
the scourge during the Spanish-American War period, and now his
children faced the same menace. Less than a year after Charles's threatening illness, daughter Grace Devereaux succumbed to the fever.

On July 24, 1907, Alex MacDowell of Savannah wrote Sanford of his
distress to "hear of Grace Devereaux's serious illness. It may relieve
your anxiety," he wrote, "to learn that during the recent typhoid epi-
demic in Savannah the treatment of the disease was almost universally
successful and with the high climate in Athens in her favor we shall
anxiously await for the news of her speedy recovery." [11] The child had
died the day the letter was written. Following a funeral at the Sanford
residence in Athens on Milledge Avenue, Grace was buried in the
Marietta City Cemetery, where her parents later were interred beside
her. Several of the notes and letters of sympathy at the time of Grace's
death were addressed to Mrs. Sanford in Marietta, where she stayed
for a time after the funeral. [12]

Among the many sympathy notes and letters was one from W. H.
Young, pastor of the Athens Baptist Church and Steadman Sanford's
pastor. Young apologized for not being with the family at Grace's
death. He had left town on a trip to Washington thinking that her
recovery was under way. [13] Another note in a childlike scrawl with the
salutation "Dear Shelton" simply says, "I'm sorry you got hurt." The
oldest child, Shelton, was thrown from a mule the day after the funeral and suffered an apparent concussion.

The tragic events of the summer of 1907 were still on the mind of grandfather Charles V. Sanford in Macon as he wrote his son in September advising him to keep Shelton home from school for a time. "He is not a strong child," his grandfather maintained, "and he has passed through a great deal this summer. With the hurt he received in his head which must of necessity hurt his brain, I think it extremely hazardous for you to allow him to study." Steadman's father was certain that his grandson's intellectual abilities and previous academic experience gave him the advantages that meant "he can easily afford to have the time from school without any loss to himself." [14]

The adjustments to Athens, a growing family, Grace Devereaux's death, and the passing of several other relatives made the first few years at the university stressful for the entire family, but both Grace and Professor Sanford as well as the boys withstood the traumas and plunged themselves into their new community, schools, friends, and challenges.

When the family moved to Athens, Grace maintained her membership in the Methodist Church while Steadman continued his Baptist affiliations. Some have attributed the divergence of denominations to the individualistic streaks of Grace and Steadman, as well as to their strong commitments to respective family traditions, Grace and Mc-Clatchey Methodism in Marietta and Steadman with his grandfather's strong affiliation with the Baptists, and especially the Mercer ties that survived in Macon. It may be that Steadman recognized the greater political connections among Georgia Baptists and the benefit of keeping a Methodist connection via Grace.

Social life, a large part of which in the South included church matters, also encompassed civic participation, political affiliations, and neighborhood and work-based friendships. Athens provided a busy network of such social connections and the Sanfords were eager and popular participants. They were members of the Athens Country Club, associated with patriotic organizations and veterans' groups, and were Democrats in political loyalty. From their arrival in Athens, however, the university would be, as for the community of Athens itself, the Sanfords' chief base of operations and friendships. Family connections with the university grew as each of their sons in turn became students.

In difficult times, such as the death of his daughter, Sanford drew strength from the university and his growing role there. In the year of his daughter's death, Sanford was promoted from instructor in English to the rank of adjunct professor and was made director of physical education. It was Sanford's interest in work with the athletic programs of the university that figured most prominently in his expanding role beyond the classroom and into the arena of intercollegiate sports.

Sanford had made friends and contacts in every phase of his life in Conyers, at Mercer, in Marietta, in the army, and of course these were all multiplied by his work at the University of Georgia. Many of these acquaintances called on Sanford in matters related to the welfare of youth, their own children, nephews and nieces, the children of friends, and the children of former employees. Sanford was known for his caring and personal treatment of students. Those who knew both Steadman and his grandfather, Professor Shelton Palmer Sanford, remarked on this trait that they shared. Obviously, the younger Sanford took great pride in carrying on this tradition of kindness and attention for which his grandfather was so well remembered. A letter dated October 28, 1905, from Blanton Winship on a letterhead from the Headquarters Department of the Judge Advocate's Office, Chicago, is revealing of this special facility: "My Dear Sanford, I have a young kinsman, Charles Willis—who is now attending the University of Georgia. I am greatly interested in his welfare and progress. I ask no favors you understand. But a little advice at the right time from one of my good friends would be appreciated and effective." [15]

Sanford became a well known and highly appreciated addition to the faculty. The 1905 edition of the *Pandora,* the university's yearbook, was dedicated to him even though he had been on the faculty only since 1903. "Professor Sanford is held in universal esteem by the student body. His uniform sympathy and helpful kindness has made every student his friend. His exalted Christian character and courteous bearing have endeared him to every one who has come within the circle of his acquaintance."[16]

While late in his life Sanford was known primarily in conjunction with his leadership of the University System as chancellor and the memories of him as builder of Sanford Stadium, he maintained a fond recollection of his teaching career in the university. Sports, however, early became an important adjunct to his teaching and occupied much of his attention. These efforts no doubt were more important for his professional future than was his teaching.

The connection between Sanford and the athletic program at Georgia is first documented in a penciled draft from him "in behalf of the Athletic Department of the University of Georgia," dated November 26, 1906. The document is a proposed agreement between the Athletic Association of the university and that of the Georgia School of Technology. This early Sanford involvement in sports at Georgia addresses several of the major recurring issues connected to collegiate sports during Sanford's entire career: school and town rivalry, civility, pride, fairness, schedules, and money. The agreement called for actions "to build athletic friendship and cooperation" between Georgia and Tech. The recommended actions included agreements regarding a traditional fall meeting of the two football teams in Atlanta, spring baseball schedules, tennis, and track competition. It called for a sharing of schedules and a division of profits or losses from gate proceeds.[17] The document, obviously not a final agreement, illustrates the challenges to Sanford's diplomatic skill that his involvement in sports provided.

Sanford served twenty-five years as faculty chairman of athletics at the university, the longest period for which he held a single title in his career. It was only when he was named president of the University of Georgia in 1932 that he gave up the position he had held since 1907. Sanford considered his quarter-century in that role one of his most demanding and rewarding experiences.

The first line of the minutes for the initial meeting of the association on April 10, 1907, captures the spirit of Sanford's central and critical role in that body: "At the call of Professor Sanford, the following gentlemen met in the Chancellor's office as members of the proposed Board of Directors of the Athletic Association." Those named were Billups Phinizy, M. G. Michael, E. H. Dorsey, J. W. Welch, D. C. Barrow, C. M. Snelling, John Moore, W. H. Bocock, S. V. Sanford, and W. D. Hooper.[18] For almost two decades this membership was constant, with the exception of replacements because of the death of some members. A survey of the minutes reveals Sanford as the moving force of the group. Except for the period when he and his family were in Europe (1912–13), Sanford is shown as the de facto chair of every meeting. Throughout minutes begin: "Professor Sanford stated the object of the meeting to be. . . ."[19]

The year 1897, the fifth year of football at Georgia, was a dark one for collegiate football, especially at the university and in the state of Georgia. On October 30, 1897, the university met the University of Virginia at Brisbane Park in Atlanta. Georgia lost 17 to 4, but the real tragedy was the death of Georgia fullback Richard Vonalbade Gammon from head injuries he sustained butting his helmetless head into the Virginia line. Mercer, Tech, and the university immediately suspended football, and the state legislature presented to Governor Atkinson for his signature a bill outlawing the game at public institutions. Rosalind Burns Gammon, the dead player's mother, intervened. She wrote: "grant me the right to request that my boy's death should not be used to defeat the most cherished object of his life."[20] The bill went unsigned by the governor and although the remainder of that year's Georgia schedule was canceled, football was resumed at Georgia in the fall of 1898.

The few years between Gammon's death and Sanford's move to Athens were relatively undistinguished in terms of Georgia's football program. Roughhouse and blurry distinctions between coaches and players, pros and amateurs, were the common elements in collegiate football at the turn of the century. According to John Stegeman's account, football during Chancellor Hill's administration "was largely shunned by the more strait-laced members of the faculty." Hill died in late 1905 and his successor, David C. Barrow, was by contrast a devoted fan of the game and publicly endorsed football, calling it "the best training of self-control that I know of." [21] It was inevitable that with the new administration there was more opportunity for Sanford to be a supportive faculty member.

The year Sanford was named faculty chairman of athletics (1907) represented the zenith of the nearly unregulated mayhem. The crowning issue of the 1907 season was the alleged use of "ringers" in the Georgia–Georgia Tech game of that year. In writing of the early days of football in the South, Fuzzy Woodruff postulated that "beyond a doubt the advent of the ringers was caused by the absolute domination that Vanderbilt had over the whole football situation in Dixie." [22]

In the days leading up to the Tech-Georgia contest in the first week of November 1907, newspapers in Atlanta charged the university with professionalism and demanded that Georgia provide a list of the starting lineup so that eligibility of the players could be established. In truth four professional athletes were hired by alumni in Athens in collusion with Coach Bull Whitney. When the teams came on the field there was still no player lineup available. "Just before the starting whistle sounded Professor S. V. Sanford of the University faculty furnished the referee, the Rev. Henry Phillips, with his battle front." Georgia lost anyway, Whitney left town, and Georgia was publicly reprimanded. Such was S. V. Sanford's inauspicious start of twenty-five years as faculty chairman of athletics at Georgia. He determined, however, that such a beginning would be the low point if it were within his powers to assure it. The Southern Intercollegiate Athletic Association suspended Georgia by mid-November and "before Thanksgiving Day Georgia had a thorough housecleaning. Whitney had resigned as coach and had been succeeded by Branch Bocock. The personnel of the team had been made Simon pure amateur." [23]

In that dark time surrounding the ringer incident, Professor Sanford was one of the few loyal followers of the Georgia team who made road trips with a handful of students to locations outside Athens. By 1910 Sanford had established his credentials as the most devoted and involved nonplayer or coach, so much so that he became sufficiently bold to take it upon himself to hire coaches on his own. In the spring of 1910 Sanford hired Alexander Cunningham, a Vanderbilt standout who was coaching at Gordon Institute in Barnesville. Cunningham coached until after World War I and, in bringing his star player Bob McWhorter from Barnesville, made one of his greatest contributions to Georgia's program. McWhorter, an Athenian, became the university's modest hero halfback scoring twelve touchdowns in his first two games as a freshman. He was All-Southern for four straight years and Georgia's first All-American during his senior year, as well as its first entry to be elected to the College Football Hall of Fame.[24]

John F. Stegeman's *The Ghosts of Herty Field* provides an excellent account of Georgia football in the period 1891–1916. He includes an in-depth look at the seriousness of the rivalry not only between Tech and Georgia but among all the southern teams during that period. Stegeman notes that strained relations between Tech and Georgia had reached the point in 1904 that "the two teams left each other off their schedules," much to the displeasure of fans on both sides who joined the *Atlanta Journal*'s campaign to get them to play each other again. With John Heisman as their new coach Tech fans were especially anxious, having gone eleven years without crossing the Georgia goal. Heisman had coached the Clemson team that had the year before routed Georgia.[25]

Just as Steadman Sanford arrived, football at the university was facing tough times. Heisman's improved Tech team was part of the problem, but additionally, the off-the-field behavior of some of the players was resulting in some difficulty for the program. S. V. Sanford emerged as the man Georgians and sports enthusiasts identified with the athletic program at the university and did so in nothing but the most positive of terms. In the ashes of 1907's scandal and the suffering of his family over the loss of his daughter that same year, S. V. Sanford began the groundwork for what would become a monument to his role as a builder, Sanford Stadium, the accomplishment for which he is best known. John Stegeman strongly identified Sanford with the resurrection of football at Georgia following the nadir of 1907: "The reverie of this kindly English teacher and the administrative energy of the same man years later were largely responsible for the transformation of a damp and shadowy valley on Tanyard Creek into the beautiful Sanford Stadium of today."[26]

When Sanford first began to dream along the lines of a great stadium, facilities for the athletic program at Georgia were meager. There was old Herty Field, a couple of offices in academic buildings, and a field house between Candler Hall and the infirmary that Stegeman said "consisted of a few lockers and a shower." Revival began under the leadership of an "all but bankrupt" Athletic Association, and in that association director Sanford's "personal efforts and endorsements" were "the only way to secure money."[27]

The man whom Stegeman described as "a pleasantly smiling man neatly dressed in a dark suit, bow tie, and derby" was more than a face at a conference table; he was also an ever-present fan. When Branch Bocock succeeded Whitney in 1908, he put together a successful team which, following two wins, headed to Knoxville to face bitter rival and favored Tennessee. Sanford was present for Georgia's 10–0 loss, but given the circumstances he described later, the loss was not all that unwelcome. It seems that Sanford, one of the few Georgia fans present for the game other than the players, was standing on the sidelines surrounded by hostile Tennesseeans near the goal. A Georgia back was tackled just short of the goal. A "grizzled mountaineer in a green frock coat and a four-gallon hat and full of sour mash, holding a .38 pistol pointed to the goal-line, 'the first man that crosses that line will get a bullet in his carcass.' Much to Sanford's relief, Georgia fumbled on the next play and Tennessee recovered."[28]

In 1909–10 the Athletic Association with Chancellor Barrow's encouragement and support began to solicit funds for a building program for sports on the campus. The chancellor notified the university alumni: "We are asking again for your aid for all who would add the advantages of physical strength to our students. We are going to build

Late in the summer of 1912 the Sanfords set their plans for travel to Europe, and in keeping with the social forms of the day they armed themselves with letters of introduction. The surviving examples make for an interesting view of the family's acquaintances and connections after almost ten years in Athens. Hughes Spalding, a former boarder in the Sanford household and now probably the Sanfords' most important Roman Catholic friend, wrote to Grace Sanford in July 1912: "You will find enclosed a letter from Bishop Keiley of Savannah to Bishop Kennedy in Rome. He will arrange for you and the professor and the children to see the Pope."[35] Clark Howell, editor of the *Atlanta Constitution,* provided letters of introduction to the Associated Press organization in Europe on behalf of the Sanfords; Governor Joseph M. Brown provided the following: "This will introduce you to Steadman V. Sanford a gentlemen of unquestionable high character, integrity and ability and worthy of every confidence and consideration due a gentleman. He belongs to one of the best families of the State of Georgia, U.S.A., and whatever courtesy may be extended to him will be greatly appreciated by me."[36]

R. C. Hazlehurst of the Taylor Cotton Company provided letters to a number of German commercial firms for Sanford. U.S. senator from Georgia A. O. Bacon likewise provided introductions and Melville Stone of the New York office of the Associated Press introduced Sanford as holder of "the chair of literature at the University of Georgia" and requested that S. B. Conger, the Berlin Associated Press representative, "make his stay pleasant and profitable."[37]

Thus armed and with tickets purchased through North's Tours on Peachtree Street, Atlanta, the Sanford family—the professor; Grace; Shelton Palmer, sixteen; Charles Steadman, thirteen; and Homer Reynolds, nine years old—sailed August 10 from Philadelphia to Hamburg on the Grafwaldersee.[38]

A clipping, presumably from the *Athens Banner,* reported that Sanford, "instructor of Rhetoric and English literature," had been granted a one-year "leave abroad to study and travel in Europe." Plans called for the professor to study at the University of Berlin October 1912 through May 1913, studying the novel, Shakespeare, and Gothic literature. "He will spend the month of June in France, and July and August next year (1913) in England, Scotland, and Ireland."[39]

There is little documentation detailing the Sanfords' year abroad. Impressions of these months come from Shelton's later recollections, scraps, and mementos; a single letter from Grace written on the trip over to "my dear ones at home"; telegrams from Athens; a letter from S. V. to his brother-in-law Marvin McClatchey in Marietta; and the like.

Hugh Hodgson Jr. and others kept "Coach Sanford" informed on football scores from across the pond. The oldest Sanford child, Shelton, was impressed, as was the rest of the family, with Berlin and Germany, how clean and beautiful they were, and the excellence of goods and meals, but also noted the persistence of Franco-German tensions. His younger brothers attended public school while Shelton studied at the Tilley Institute, a famous language school where diplomatic corps families attended. Shelton, almost fifty years later, would recall the German emphasis on efficiency, thrift, cleanliness, and scholarship, as well as the intense anti-British and anti-American tone at the Tilley. World War I would see headmaster Tilley interned by the Germans.[40]

The Sanfords relished their American connections, and the six-day delivery time for first-class mail from home kept the family in touch. The *London Daily Mail*'s continental edition provided newspaper reading for Sanford's comfort, and the American Community Church in Berlin provided another contact with home.[41]

S. V. Sanford's impressions of Germany are found in a letter from him to his brother-in-law Marvin McClatchey dated November 5, 1912. It comes as something of a surprise that Sanford seems more fascinated with the physical and organizational nature of things than with the people and the ways of the society. Much of his letter was given over to describing the businesses and services of Berlin and its suburbs: the postal system, the pattern of professional offices, and the like. He was especially impressed with the absence of skyscrapers and with the tendency to combine in city buildings residential and commercial functions. He described train transportation in and out of the city and commented on the fact that the Dresdner Bank with capital of "nearly 809 million dollars" had "fifty-two banks in the city." He closed on a familiar topic from back at the university: "I tried not to mention the Vandy-Georgia story—it was too bad . . . but Tech is still waiting to get beat so I won't kick." [42]

Professor Sanford had a project back in Athens that also occupied his attention during his European stay. A book that he had coauthored was in the editing stage while the family was abroad. There were a few notes from Peter Brown of the Department of English at the State Normal School in Athens regarding Brown and Sanford's grammar text. By April when the Sanfords were staying in Oxford, football news declined and baseball news picked up and Brown wrote more on details of their joint publication. [43] D. C. Heath and Company of Boston published their *Modern Course in English* in 1914. This high school level grammar was adopted by the state boards of education in Georgia, Alabama, Mississippi, Tennessee, and Oklahoma; a revised edition came out in 1923.

The Sanford family (incorrectly identified as the "Stanfords" on the passenger list) started back to Athens via the White Star Line from Liverpool to Boston on July 29, 1913. Among the souvenirs from their year abroad are hundreds of color postcards from their travels. Just before their departure the Sanfords bought silver teaspoons, watches, opera glasses, and cutlery in the West End of London. [44] Professor Sanford also returned with a "Certificate of German Study." In 1924 when he completed a self-report for Tom Reed, secretary of the Board of Trustees of the University of Georgia, Sanford was asked to list "the titles of graduate courses taken, and after such title give the name of the instructor, and the institution in which he taught." From the European period of study he listed: "Anglo Saxon, Dr. Brandl, University of Berlin, Germany; Middle English, Dr. Spies, University of Berlin,

Germany; Schiller, Dr. Schmidt, University of Berlin, Germany; Beowulf, Dr. Napier, University of Oxford, England; Shakespeare's Predecessors, Sir Walter Raleigh, Oxford, England."[45]

Among receipts from their stay in England are lecture tickets for
"Easter and Trinity" to the lectures of Professor Napier, Dr. Carlyle,
and Professor Raleigh as well as a receipt for five pounds two shillings
for "board and residence" for July 15, 1913, at Macauly House, Woburn
Place, Russell Square, W.C.[46]

On his return to Athens in the summer of 1913, Sanford learned
that he was approved for promotion to a full professorship in English.[47] The matter of rank, title, and degrees, so cherished by many
academics, was never of great import to Sanford. As president and as
chancellor, Sanford was addressed by the titles of the respective offices. In referring to Sanford, surviving contemporaries frequently
use the title "doctor." From his youth in Marietta, Sanford had been
known as "professor." A professional associate of Sanford's in the late
1930s, someone who worked daily with the chancellor and traveled the
state with him, reported that Sanford never referred to himself by any
of these degrees or titles, but rather simply as "Mr. Sanford."[48] In
conjunction with the university's recognition of his accomplishments,
and perhaps in part as a salve to those concerned about Sanford's
promotion without any graduate degree to append to his name, he
was awarded an honorary doctorate (Litt.D.) by the University of
Georgia in June 1914.[49] In 1932 Mercer would honor Sanford with a
doctorate of laws, but in his response to the question of "higher degrees" in the 1924 survey Sanford said "None."[50] So it was that one of
Georgia's leading educational figures of the century built his fame on
so simple a foundation as a B.A. from Mercer, a handful of graduate
courses, and the "personal equation."

With his recent European studies, the publication of his text, his
promotion, and the distinguished new title of "Doctor," Professor
Sanford faced the eve of the great war in Europe with a full complement of credentials befitting his ambitions. At the age of forty-three
his career path was at a fork in the road. In one direction was a con-

tinuation of his work with the athletic program and his teaching. That choice might have been the more comfortable and less challenging, and would probably have led to many enjoyable years in a graceful academic routine. Despite the fact that Sanford did not choose to make his long-term investment in the classroom, he was throughout his life and in the later memories of his former students fondly recalled as an inspiring teacher. At Georgia between 1910 and 1920, he taught English grammar, composition, and Shakespeare to women in summer classes. During the regular term he taught rhetoric and the English novel, usually to seniors. According to Tom Reed's account, "It was especially in the field of English Literature that [Sanford] excelled." Reed says that his English novel course "was of such excellence that it attracted the very best students in the University." [51]

Sanford's fine reputation as a teacher, however, could not be expected to keep him on the road of the familiar and routine. At the point in an academic career when many professors settle in, S. V. Sanford looked for new challenges. At the same time he continued those interests and connections he had cultivated over almost a quarter-century in education.

Sanford saw at the university before World War I the need for something new, a course and program in journalism. Professor Sanford found time to initiate just such a course and program shortly after his return from Europe. According to Tom Reed's account, for several years Sanford taught all the courses in journalism while working toward full recognition for the discipline as a distinct department of the university. "Dr. Sanford," says Reed's history, "was really the founder of the Henry W. Grady School of Journalism." [52]

The most definitive account of the beginnings of the journalism program at the University of Georgia is found in George M. Abney Jr., "Forty Years of Communications Education at the Oldest Chartered State University (1915–1955)," a 1959 M.A. thesis written at the university. When Abney, a Georgia journalism graduate of 1951, wrote his thesis, the university was offering forty-four courses in journalism, a considerable growth from that initial offering of a single course in 1915. During that great period of growth "the School has been guided . . . by two heads, Steadman V. Sanford and John E. Drewry." [53] Abney's account of the first two decades of journalism at Georgia testifies to Sanford's groundbreaking contributions to journalism at the university.

In 1913 the Board of Trustees of the university had acted on a resolution which read in part: "Inquire into the propriety and expediency of establishing at the University at an early date a school of Journalism in which shall be taught the branches required for editing and publishing newspapers and like periodicals." [54] On Sanford's return from Europe in 1913 he had undertaken to teach a class in journalism, which Chancellor Barrow in his 1913–14 annual report had cited as a "valuable course." [55]

The trustees' report for 1915 recommended the establishment of a school of journalism and joined the chancellor in praising the work of Professor Sanford's class. With this recommendation and the knowledge that "Professor Sanford would carry through for the next four years without additional costs," the university's Committee on Disciplines acted on the original 1913 resolution and recommended the school be established ancillary to the English Department. The committee was of the opinion that "the establishment of this school should not change Professor Sanford's relation to his classes, and should not relieve him of any duties in connection with his work [in English]." [56]

The title professor of journalism was authorized for Sanford. And for the 1915–16 year the English Department offered a course in journalism to be taught by Professor Sanford, who also had classes in English and the English language. The journalism course was entitled "newspaper writing" and was described as follows: "A course designed to give the student a knowledge of the making of the newspaper and to prepare him for work on the daily paper. The third term is devoted to the history, development, and strict analysis of the short story, with special stress on the magazine supplement of the newspaper." [57]

The Board of Trustees authorized a four-year degree for the fall of

1917 and the first degree in journalism at Georgia was awarded in 1921. Meanwhile course offerings expanded to seven in number: editing, reporting and correspondence, special articles, editorial writing, history and principles of journalism, psychology of business, and newspaper advertising.[58]

For Sanford the growth of offerings meant more work. He continued to offer English courses and his early agreement to teach journalism without additional compensation, originally a four-year offer, stretched into seventeen years. According to Abney, Sanford "always maintained a heavy load, sometimes teaching as much as twenty-four or twenty-seven hours a week and always eighteen hours, except for a few years when he was an administrative official. The average load then was fifteen hours. Even as President, Sanford taught a three hour course."[59]

Sanford in his annual report of 1921 recommended the naming of the journalism school for Henry W. Grady: "To name the Department of Journalism for Grady will honor one of our most illustrious graduates and one of the great journalists in America . . . and will give it prestige from the outset."[60] The recommendation, which was adopted, was pure Sanford in logic. Sanford's sensitivity to the value of visibility and beneficial connections is seen in his 1921 report: "It is my desire to make this work in the University of great importance . . . to associate the School with the daily and weekly press associations and conventions. With the cooperation of Board of Trustee members Clark Howell, Bowdre Phinizy, and Pleasant Stovall, three alumni editors of wide influence, we can make this department reach high water rank in a short while."[61]

John Drewry came to assist Sanford in 1921–22 and became director of the school in 1923. Still Sanford's 1922–23 teaching schedule showed six journalism courses together with two English courses. Despite what seems a heavy load of journalism, Sanford said in the same report he would like to offer a graduate course in "The Growth and Development of the Newspaper."[62] Although Sanford had single-handedly laid the foundation for the establishment as a school, he was proud of Drewry and pleased to have him head up journalism as his own focus was aimed toward other university matters. For the rest of his tenure, however, Sanford kept an active interest in the newspaper field and in its professional training, as will be seen in his involvement with the Georgia Press Association and the Georgia Press Institute from the 1920s until his death.

Together with his continued teaching and grammar text writing and his newfound interest and activity in journalism, Professor Sanford resumed with gusto his involvement in the sports programs at the university when he returned to the campus in the fall of 1913. The 1912 *Pandora*, which was published while Sanford was in Europe, hailed his earlier contributions to that aspect of life at the university in a full-page commentary headed "Sanford Field." This tribute to Sanford's determination to improve campus facilities for athletic teams credited him with overcoming what seemed the impossible task of securing a better playing field. Despite the nay-sayers, Sanford "went to work and picked out the present location, which at the time was a ravine with a small-sized river running through it. Today Georgia has the best athletic field in the South. Professor Sanford refused to allow the field to be named after him, but he reckoned without the appreciation of everyone who gave him credit, and as a small tribute to his great work named the park, Sanford Field."[63]

Coincidentally, the football season of Sanford's return marked the first stages of what John Stegeman called, in his *Ghosts of Herty Field*, the "end of an era." This was the last year for Bob McWhorter, Georgia's first All-American. The few seasons after McWhorter and before the outbreak of world war marked the end of the first quarter-century of intercollegiate football in the South. Professor Sanford would serve as one of the links between that first quarter-century and the football legacies of postwar southern football almost to mid-century.

FOUR

World War I

1917-1919

During the years between Sanford's arrival in Athens and the outbreak of World War I, administrative leadership in public higher education in Georgia was complicated by a kind of legal fiction regarding the relationship of the university in Athens to the other "branches" of the university at Dahlonega, Milledgeville, Savannah, Augusta, Atlanta, and the State College of Agriculture in Athens. Despite the technical branch status of these schools, the public considered each unit as independent of the others. Andrew M. Soule, president of the State College of Agriculture, with the advantage of federal land-grant funds, did his best to make perceptions a reality. Meanwhile in Atlanta, Georgia Tech, with its own Board of Trustees and strong community support, was reluctant to accept anything less than equality with the university.

At the university the individual charged with attempting to exercise administrative management of this unfortunate arrangement was the chancellor. Walter B. Hill was chancellor when Sanford joined the faculty. At his death in 1905 David Crenshaw Barrow was named chancellor, serving until 1926.

57

Barrow himself was a graduate of the university, and following a number of false career starts he was elected adjunct professor of mathematics in 1878. When Sanford came to the faculty, Barrow was dean of the Franklin College of Arts and Sciences, a position he had held since 1898. As chancellor, Barrow took for his program that of his predecessor Hill. The times, however, took Barrow, the faculty and the university into areas Hill had never foreseen, connected to the outbreak of and American entry into World War I and the coming of important federal support of higher education.[1] The Smith-Lever Act of 1914, in part the work of Georgia's Senator Hoke Smith, established the most significant relationship between the university and the federal government before World War I. The Act made possible cooperative agricultural extension service between the states and the U.S. Department of Agriculture, federal funds being distributed among the states on the basis of matching appropriations. During the 1920s this would come to mean the sum of over $350,000 at the university, an amount of considerable significance in terms of customary university resources. Andrew Soule as dean of the College of Agriculture took appropriate advantage of the importance of his area in light of this considerable windfall.[2]

Intramural administrative competition was a logical by-product of new funds, growth, and change. It was Chancellor Barrow's challenge to take these internal struggles along with university competition with the state's private institutions and make a modern statewide accepted university from a collection of factions. Barrow's administration was remarkably successful given these challenges. The university grew in enrollment, in faculty, in schools, and in fiscal and physical ways.

The United States' entry into the war in April 1917 marked the beginning of America's seventeen-month direct participation and the brief period in which the university felt its impact. In the fall of 1918 shortly before the armistice was declared, a contract was established between the university and the federal government to set up Student Army Training Corps programs. In spite of the brevity of these programs they provided S. V. Sanford with a new outlet for his energy and valuable insight into a growing connection between higher education and the federal government.

Steadman Sanford enjoyed making scrapbooks of newspaper clippings throughout his career. The scrapbooks from the period of World War I include clippings from a wide variety of sources: the *Atlanta Constitution,* the British *Daily Mirror,* the *New York Times Review of Books,* the *Michigan (University) Daily,* the *Athens Banner-Herald,* the *Savannah Morning News,* the *Athens Daily Times,* and the *Academic Review.* The subject matter of clippings ranged from the expected educational and sports topics to national and state political commentary and military affairs. The latter, military affairs, occupied much of the Sanford household's interests as it did the nation's and the world's between 1914 and 1919. The war not only brought out the professor's old interests from his Rifles of Spanish-American War and militia days, it took on very special meaning for the Sanfords as their oldest son, Shelton, sailed to France in late 1917, staying there until after the armistice as a second lieutenant.[3]

As the summer and fall of 1916 passed, with America and President Wilson delaying entry into the war, Steadman and Grace Sanford and their three boys followed the world news while their major focus remained on family matters: college for Shelton and the worry with career plans, the coming to an end of high school days for Charles, the beginning of that period for the youngest, Homer Reynolds (Cutie), and household finances. Sending his regrets to an invitation, Sanford wrote, "The high cost of living is a deterrent force.... I may add that my wife at this very moment is in Atlanta visiting Rich and Brothers, Chamberlin-Johnson-DuBois, and other similar enemies of man making preparations for Easter and thereby rendering my bank account in red lines." The professor continued, providing a positive assessment of Georgia's upcoming baseball season.[4]

Professor Sanford meanwhile was busy revising his textbooks, teaching, and managing the athletic program for the university as faculty chairman of athletics.

Early in the new year of 1917, the war was yet to overtake sports as a chief item in Sanford's correspondence. He corresponded with coaches and a variety of sports-related contacts.

In June 1917 Professor Sanford learned of the opportunity for the university to provide a quartermaster training course for the enlisted grades. Various training programs were being considered, and it comes as no surprise that "Captain" Sanford saw a role for himself on behalf of the war effort and in the name of his beloved University of Georgia.

The proposed training program was to prepare men to "maintain lines of communications between internal and marine shipping ports to the front, accumulate war supplies and distribute supplies to troops in action." The trainees would be relieved from other military duty and would be part of the business staff of the army.[5]

Captain Ralph H. Hess of the U.S. Army Quarter Master Corps wrote Sanford describing the general organization of students into an infantry company, the expectation of a minimum of drilling, and the simple style of uniform. "It is assumed," wrote Hess, "that the military organization of the group will be placed in the hands of an instructor or student who has had some experience." S. V. Sanford was just the man for the job. In a June 30 telegraph, Hess reported to Sanford that the University of Georgia's plan for a quartermaster course had been approved.[6]

Sanford was invited by the Bureau of Patriotism Through Education to be a part of their speakers' training conference: "We cannot win the war unless there is universal public sentiment in favor of its vigorous prosecution and a thorough understanding of the vital issues involved."[7] There is no indication that Sanford attended the training session, but during the remainder of the war the professor was a popular speaker for the various Liberty Loan campaigns. He was touted not only for his great speaking ability and academic standing but also for his own military experience during the Spanish-American War and the fact that his son "was over there with Pershing."

Shelton Sanford had left Athens in the summer of 1917 for basic training in the Atlanta area. He applied for a provisional second lieutenant's commission in the regular army. Shelton's extensive wartime family correspondence is filled with his anxiety about getting a promotion and his subsequent career path following his military service. Throughout, the young soldier solicited his father's advice.[8]

At the end of August, Shelton and his father were together in Washington before the younger man's assignment overseas. Shelton wrote to his mother that his father had taken him to see Georgia Senator William J. Harris, who was "very cordial." Shelton was impressed with the senator's knowledge of his family and its connection. "He knew me. I don't know how. He called up his brother Col. Harris . . . and explained to him that Professor Sanford (you remember him?— married Grace McClatchey) and son would come over to see him. We went then to the War Department and Col. Harris introduced us to Major Jones who is the gentleman I have to report to."[9]

Shelton was initially assigned to duty in Washington. From there he reported to his mother in September that he was in a "Branch Office" at the Intelligence Department. He and others had been denied their request for transfer, and Shelton anticipated being "doomed to stay here for the rest of the war and I am afraid our chances for promotion are slight." Thus began a continuing theme of Shelton's wartime correspondence, his concern about being promoted. As usual, however, the caring son ended his letter to his mother on a positive note: "I feel my lot is much better than those left in Macon and Atlanta," but with a touching proviso, "except that they are nearer home."[10]

Shelton had not left the United States before he wrote his father regarding communications with his superiors: "I don't know what to say about the work up here. Shall I appear satisfied with it or not? The truth is that I should not, for any body could do what I am doing. Let me know what to write him." He continued his solicitation for advice: "Do you know what I can do to stay in the army after the war? It seems to me that this would be desirable for I would hardly be fit for anything else then. Let me know what you think about it and if there is anything I can do."[11]

In the old and well-respected tradition of the South, connections were considered important keys to success. S. V. Sanford had long known this and used that knowledge well. Son Shelton, in a letter to his mother, confirmed the tradition: "above all I am going to try to be with the best people I can for that can not fail to help me."[12] In letter after letter Shelton recalls having seen or talked with or heard from some Georgia connection: Phinizy, Hodgson, Harris, Atlanta and Athens family names that represented the proper connections.[13]

When word came down that Shelton's unit was being sent to New York for probable assignment in France, his mother and father made plans to meet him in New York before his departure. The exact sequence of events is not clear, but apparently Professor Sanford had to return to Athens before Shelton sailed early in October; Grace, however, stayed in New York. Three letters written at this juncture provide a most revealing snapshot of S. V. Sanford as father, husband, and politician/educator.

Grace was still in New York; Steadman had returned to Athens by way of Washington. He wrote Grace:

> I left Washington Sunday morning and arrived in Athens at 7:00 about two hours late. In talking with Professor Cunningham he said of Shelton: "During my intimate association with him during the summer, I found a great liking for him and am greatly interested in his future." I appreciate those words about Shelton very much. I am enclosing a copy of a letter that I have this day written our friend [Senator W. J.] Harris about Shelton. Please destroy it upon reading for you might drop it and it will serve no purpose to retain it, but will do harm if it should fall into the hands of others. I can't see how the letter will hurt; of course it may not amount to anything for sometime to come. I wanted you and Shelton to see that I was still doing all I can in his behalf.[14]

The letter to Harris opened with a page devoted to Georgia politics including Sanford's observation that "Senator Hardwick's days are numbered." The professor went on to describe a conversation in the smoking room on the train from Washington to Athens in which a "blow hard" made claims as to his qualifications to run against and defeat Senator Harris. In a display of his wit Sanford noted: "After hearing his conversation I was greatly encouraged to announce for the Presidency. I know it would give Mr. Wilson great uneasiness to have me in the race."[15]

Sanford then turned to the real topic: "I do not want any political pressure, but if you can request your brother to bring about his promotion to first Lt. you will never have cause to regret it. I will repay you with everlasting gratitude. I know that Major Jones does not know his peculiar educational qualifications for there is no way to tell except through some good friends like your brother. If you can do this in a diplomatic way, all of us will remember it for life."[16]

Steadman Sanford was forthright in his desire to have his son promoted, and he obviously wanted both his wife and son to see that he was. The third revealing item is the letter on the same date to Shelton from his father: a combination of caring, fear, hope, admonishment, and down-home health care suggestions. Most fathers have felt as much for, if not written or said as much to, their own sons:

> While it is awful hard to see you leave us it is the only course to follow. Do your duty and you will not fail. [He goes on to describe a local draft dodger incident.] I could not bear a stigma like that.
>
> Enjoy yourself, be careful, do not get discouraged even if you never get a promotion. Keep your bowels open and then you will not be despondent, nor will you have a cloudy brain. Remember in your position you must be accurate and cheerful and nothing will help you more than a little medicine now and then.
>
> My own desire is to see you grow into a man, well qualified to meet all responsibilities. Don't forget your religious obligations—they will help you whenever other things fail. Keep us posted at all times. Remember you will never be out of our minds as long as you are absent—so don't forget us.
>
> If you should ever need money don't hesitate to write or wire and it will come at once. Affectionately your Daddy.[17]

In the summer the university had been approved to train one hundred students in the quartermaster course. By the end of the year three groups enrolled in separate five-week courses had involved almost two hundred men. Other than Professor Sanford, "Director in Charge of the University Training Course in Army Supply Service," other training personnel included W. A. Shelton, who taught transportation and economics; E. L. Griggs, field services and military administration; Hershel Carithers, vouchers; T. W. Reed, vouchers; John E. Talmadge Jr., buying, selling, and keeping; and W. A. Hooper Jr., military drill. In addition to having overall administrative responsibility, Professor Sanford taught the quartermaster manual and U.S. Army regulations.[18]

As students completed their course work they were called to various depots, chiefly Charleston and Jacksonville, with a few sent to Camp Gordon. It comes as no surprise that Sanford maintained a close connection with "his boys" after they left Athens. Sanford carried on an extended correspondence with Captain Hess on their behalf. He persisted in his assertion that he was sure these men should be classified as sergeants. Sanford was keen to notice that despite their completion of his course, once the boys arrived at Charleston they were not so identified. "Nothing will be done and they will be lost in the large number assembled there [Charleston]," he complained. "Not to make them sergeants at once will put the University in a false light and will put a damper on the second course to be given here in September. The situation as it now stands is very embarrassing to the University and particularly to me."[19]

Sanford's protests resulted in at least a partial concession. The Department of the Quarter Master Corps notified the university program that at least a portion would be promoted to sergeant and the remainder to corporal. Sanford made several trips to Washington at the close of the summer to make his case for the boys and to promote the extension of training at the university. Among the issues which he continued to pursue other than the promotion matter was his preference to have his boys assigned to Camp Gordon (in Georgia and smaller in size than Charleston or Jacksonville) and the urgency of placing men soon after their completion of the course in order to prevent their risking being drafted without regard to their training.[20] Sanford's invitation to Captain Hess to visit the program at Georgia and be the Sanfords' guest in their home was in keeping with the personal touch of hospitality that was a Sanford trademark.[21]

Before the quartermaster training program at the university came to an end Shelton was in France. In responding to his son's first letter from overseas Professor Sanford blended his pride in his "boys" with that in his own son: "I made four copies of your first letter and sent one each to Grandpa Homer, D. F., and Marvin. The Quarter Master Course has some fine men. I just wish they would make them all sergeants."[22] He must have been thinking about his own three sons as well as his students when he closed: "We have just read tonight's paper of the first losses of American troops. I am afraid that is the beginning of a long death list."[23]

Shortly after Shelton's arrival in France the quartermaster courses at Georgia came to an end. Sanford wrote his friend Lt. C. W. Wall at Camp Gordon in Atlanta that he expected that type of training to be discontinued in the colleges and carried out at regular bases, probably Jacksonville.[24] In December the work was completed. Richard Schwab of Atlanta wrote Sanford: "Thank you for your many kindnesses to me personally. I want to express my admiration for your splendid work and interest in the Third Quarter Master Class. The spirit of helpfulness, which you so unselfishly manifested, has been a source of inspiration to me, and I am sure, to the other men who have come into contact with you during the past few weeks."[25]

Knowing what we do about Sanford's lifelong attachment to his students we might imagine that Schwab's thank-you was more important to the professor than Captain Hess's December 17 communiqué: "The University of Georgia has rendered very worthy service in the work it has accomplished and your personal services in connection therewith are highly appreciated."[26]

Through the end of 1917, all the year 1918, and well into late 1919,

Shelton wrote his observations and impressions of the people and places with whom he came into contact. He alternately bragged or complained about the mess, weather, news from the papers, letters from home, shortages, prices, the course of the war, and his own hopes and fears. His letters to his father are a bit more formal than those to his mother, or of course his brothers. The letters to his brothers are both teasing and serious. Among those written during the first months in France was one to Homer Reynolds. "How are your girl friends? Or have you dropped them all since you got in High School?" To the other brother Charles who was just beginning his college work at the university: "Study all you can of German at school. It may come in very handy to you some day, and it will never do you any harm. You have as good a start as the others in your class and a very great advantage in having been to the country yourself." [27]

To his mother during the same week, Shelton wrote asking for "some more of the chocolate like we got in New York." To his father: "I have had occasion to see General Pershing once. He is the greatest man in France today and the most impressive looking. I have never seen a better looking soldier. The French people are full of praise for him." [28]

One of the ongoing themes of wartime letter writing was the matter of lost or delayed letters and packages. For a lonesome young Shelton Sanford, the matter must have exacerbated his homesickness. It did not take long for his father to react to his son's concerns and complaints. Apparently Steadman Sanford wrote the Statistical Department of the Army to which Shelton was assigned with details of his son's plight. The professor received a long reply dated November 19, 1917, assuring him that "all packages are forwarded to your son as soon as they are received." The letter goes on to describe to Sanford the general activities of Shelton's outfit and continues: "I shall be glad to greet you at any time you are in Washington. I am always glad to say howdy-do to the mother or father of any of our boys, and I am always ready to do anything I possibly can to look after the welfare of the boys. It is against army regulations for an officer to accept a present of any kind from anyone, but I am going to take the liberty of accepting the box of cigars you are sending and distributing it to the boys over here who are not allowed to go over there, with the good wishes of the Dad of one of the boys who has gone over there."[29]

The closeness of the Sanford family is evident in letters from Shelton to all its members. Shelton wrote his father, "above all let me know how each member of the family is." When family news came he was quick to comment: "I also got your letter today telling me about the Chi Phi dance. I am so glad that Charles and Cutie are being rushed by the Frats. Charles does not say anything about dancing. Make him learn to dance if he has not already done so. There is nothing worse at college than a boy that don't [*sic*] dance."[30]

In the new year Shelton reported to his father that he had signed up for a $100 per month allotment. "This one hundred dollars shall be forwarded to you from Washington the first of every month."[31] As the good son, Shelton was careful to report that he had written to "Grandpa" recently. "I am glad to have suggestions about who to write. I want to write to everyone I should, but of course I don't care to do any unnecessary writing as my time is limited now."[32]

Shelton could not have known how many letters and how much time in Europe lay ahead of him, but as early as his third month in France he wrote his mother and father asking, "What is your opinion about what I should do after the war? I would like to take the examination for the regulars. Be sure to answer immediately about this. When the national army disbands they will all be out of jobs and competition will be pretty severe."[33]

Many months later Shelton complained that he had not gotten much direction from home about what to do. It appears that his father and mother wisely let him discover more of himself as time passed and were reluctant to provide glib answers at this stage of his first experience away from home. If his father failed to guide his destiny, at least with a visible hand, he did hold his oldest son as close to the Sanford household as written communication would permit. On January 11, 1918, Steadman Sanford wrote:

Dear Shelton,

It is now eleven o'clock and we are still up sitting around the fire doing many and diverse things. Your mother is knitting you a sweater, Homer Reynolds is playing the Victrola, Charles is absent being down at Costa's to a little dance being given by Henry Marshall Fullilove, and I have been writing on my grammar. This will give you a little word picture of the household. While we sit by the good fire, keeping warm and comfortable, our hearts naturally turn to France, and we wonder where you are tonight and whether or not you are comfortable and well cared for in all the necessities of life.

Sanford continued with a description of the recent bad winter weather in Georgia, the coal shortage, and the disruption of the train schedules due to war demands, as well as the problems associated with managing to make scheduled basketball games. The anticipated arrival of a traveling (by train) minstrel show was doubtful:

All the girls around the town are the same as ever. There is very little doing for them this year. Drop Mrs. McWhorter a little card, for she would appreciate it. She asks about you everyday and seems so interested in your every movement. She is a real friend of yours—genuine. Charles has just returned—midnight—from his dance at Costa's and is radiant with happiness. Had a fine time. Took Elizabeth Arnold. He is all excitement for he says that the bridge across the river—The Oconee Street Bridge—has washed away, and that people can almost walk across the river on ice.

Well, here is hoping that you are as comfortable as we are. We are anxious about you, but trust that you will take care of yourself. We miss you all the time, more than you can tell, but particularly when we read of the terrible weather abroad. Sickness is worse than bullets in every war. Keep yourself in fine condition at all time. Let us hear details as to your equipment, and promise me that if you haven't every thing you need that you will get it or cable us for it.[34]

Professor Sanford's "family" had been enlarged beyond those mentioned in the letter to Shelton. By virtue of having had them under his care during their quartermaster training, there were now early in 1918 scores of other young men he referred to as his "boys," and Sanford's concern for his son's well-being extended to all of them. During January of that year there were many letters between Sanford and his quartermaster boys. From Camp Johnson at Jacksonville, Julius M. Elrod wrote thanking Sanford for "the help you gave me in getting my grade of sergeant in the army. "I am," he wrote, "endeavoring to be a credit to your instruction."[35] To Sergeant L. M. Gardner he wrote a two-page, typed, single-spaced letter assuring him that he would get his commission. Sanford reported his own son had been sent to France and told Gardner that he was writing Gardner's mother in Montezuma, Georgia.[36]

On January 13, 1918, Sanford wrote from Jacksonville where he had gone to check on "his boys": "Many of my Quarter Masters came to see me tonight. They seemed as pleased as if their own father had come. I came down to see just what is taking place and to see if I could do anything for the boys. They don't seem to know that they have taken the course at the University and so far have not recognized that they are non-coms. The boys do not blame me but seem to think I can help them."[37]

Despite his difficulties in such matters, Sanford willingly continued his connections with the war effort as best his situation would allow, serving as an instructor in war aims courses in the summer of 1918 at the university and making Liberty Loan speeches around the state. The chairman of the Elbert County Liberty Loan Commission was informed that Sanford would be speaking at a local rally. "You will find him," reported the writer, "most entertaining. Wherever he goes they always wanted him back. He has a son with Pershing, he has spent time in Germany and is Professor at the University. He saw action in the Spanish-American war."[38]

As 1918 came to a close Shelton remained in France but away from the fighting and, much to his dismay, away from a promotion, about which he wrote incessantly. Letters to his father turned more and more to the details of the military campaigns and Shelton's assessments of the situation. He continued his interest in his brothers, writing both of them often. Shelton's letters to them indicate the style of caring for which the family was famous. In a letter to Charles he wrote; "I sure am glad you insisted (and Cutie) on my bringing along that flash light. If I did not have a light I would never find my billet. Tell mother not to do too much Red Cross work but to rest some time." [39] He reported to his mother that he was "glad to learn Charles and Cutie are dancing. I am not worried about Cutie. He will always be able to care for himself in that respect. But Charles is more like me. I never would have learned to dance if you had not made me." [40]

Connections with the university were an important part of the Sanford family, and Shelton frequently reported to his father of having written Professor Lustrat or Dr. Campbell, Dr. Stephens, or Dr. Pond. The cultural connections which had been so much a part of the household are reflected in Shelton's apparent excitement when the great-grandson of Victor Hugo was assigned as a liaison officer in his unit. He wrote several times of talks with him.[41] Shelton grew philosophical about his fellow troops and their anxieties about the war: "Those not on the front are afraid the war will end before they get there. The ones that have been there are not as anxious to get back. That curious kind has to be warned not to look over the top (of the trenches) to see if the war is still going on. There is no use looking over to see. She is still going on. This war does not take the old kind of bravery anyway. The men that are killed and wounded in personal combat are few. It is more like being killed by lightning or an earthquake." [42]

Shelton closed this letter on a note that revealed his growing maturity: "Are you giving your Novel course this year? I wish I had taken that in college. I believe it must be the best course in college. The little I know about it from hearing you talk about it at home has helped me a lot over here. When I get a chance I want to read all those novels. I find people that talk about them all the time and I feel so ignorant."[43]

Family instructions to write specific people, family, friends, university people, or otherwise occasionally got the best of Shelton. In March 1918 he wrote to his mother: "I wrote Mrs. Mell, Scudder, and Sterling. As yet I have not sent the cards to the people Daddy suggested. I can not get suitable cards. You do not seem to realize I have not got the stores of Paris here for selection Roland Ellis has. I am supposed to be at the front and business has been slightly upset in these parts. As soon as I get a leave I will send all these cards."[44]

In a lighter vein Shelton wrote his father that his old teacher from their Berlin days of 1912–13, Herr Tilley of the Tilley Institute, had been interned by the Germans. "It struck me as funny—he being so openly pro-German."[45]

Talk of the weather, prices, sports back home, and food dominated family letters. Shelton wrote his mother in November of 1918: "It is time you were teaching Daddy and the boys to eat Cauliflower, Cabbage, Brussel sprouts, stewed onions, and lettuce. I don't feel right unless I have some of them for both dinner and supper so the war has done some good anyway, even if it is about to end."[46] Indeed the war was about to end but Shelton remained in Europe well beyond Armistice Day.

Shortly after the armistice, Shelton wrote to his mother: "During this year (and some over) that I have been in France, I have worked hard and conscientiously. I have seen many promoted over my head some who deserved them and some who did not, but I recognized those mistakes were unavoidable and have held my head up and tried to look cheerful though some of them were bitter pills. But it is all over now and I remain a second lieutenant. If I could only have gotten into it here things would have been OK. But I am delighted it is all over. We should never need another such army."[47] Shelton proved to be wrong on two counts. He would get a promotion before he returned to the States, and we would need another such army.

The year 1918 ended with Shelton still in France and still very much concerned about his fate on his return. He wrote his father about the possibility of staying in the military and the hope of getting into the regular army, but he also held out the possibility of trying his hand at something else: "I would not mind teaching a while anyway until something could develop. I think that I have had sufficient training to teach math, French, or German and though a teacher does not stand much chance of ever being wealthy, still he always holds a position of respect and comparative comfort. And as you say he can start out fairly well." [48]

His mother's McClatchey family had made overtures about going into business or working with them in Atlanta, but Shelton apparently did not feel comfortable with the prospects of the business world. Shelton had the example of his father before him and had seen the very real advantages to the profession of teaching, but he no doubt anticipated the fiscal limitations of that line of work.

At the beginning of 1919 Shelton wrote his father a note of thanks for having helped urge along a recommendation for the long-discussed and anticipated promotion to first lieutenant. "I certainly appreciate you going to all that trouble," he wrote his father in regard to a letter his father had "sent to Homer and Senator Harris. I know how distasteful it is to do such things, but I think you will agree with me that it is necessary. For in our army as in all other armies pull, or personal touch is the main counter. I have seen enough of it even in the French army. But I do not want you to feel that I have not done my part." [49]

Early in March Shelton wrote his father. "I know you were as glad as I was to know my promotion came through OK. My rank and pay date from February 26. It means about twenty-five dollars extra a month. I don't think I would say anything about it at all. Just let me come back like I had been a first lieutenant from the beginning." [50]

As peace negotiations dragged on, Shelton remained in Europe. As he moved from France to Luxembourg and into Germany, each letter anticipated an early return. Finally, in July he wrote: "All's fixed. I sail on the La Tumaine from Harve Tuesday. Don't write any more. I am sure to be on my way within a week." [51] The crossing took fifteen days. He sent his mother a cable from Newport News, Virginia, as soon as

he landed on July 28. His wartime correspondence ends: "I am trying to get the 30 day leave as daddy suggested and should be home
within a week. I am very anxious to know if you are all well. Much
love. SPS." [52]

The concern for his life after the war which Shelton had been so
preoccupied with during his absence was given prompt if initially unsuccessful attention by his father during the summer of his return.
Shelton was discharged at Camp Gordon in Atlanta on August 23,
and at his father's urging, made application for a Rhodes Scholarship
within a month: "I gladly gave up my plans of studying medicine at
Johns Hopkins University in order to serve my country. Now that
the war is over I am very anxious to begin the study of medicine. I
would be delighted to study medicine as a Rhodes Scholar at Oxford
University." [53]

Shelton, whose earlier devotion to the study of medicine had not
been obvious, did not get to Oxford, but at a great sacrifice to his
family he completed his M.D. at Harvard Medical School.

As treaty talk dragged on in Europe, most Americans began to
return to their prewar interests and lives. For returning soldiers like
Shelton, the beginning of the decade of the twenties might have
loomed as the start of a troubled period, lost generations, disillusionment, and insecurity. For those who had remained at home, life
returned to more or less normal. The overwhelming American inclination toward returning to normal helped propel a mediocre Republican into the White House and kept that party in power until the
depression created conditions that led to the Roosevelt victory of 1932.
S. V. Sanford, good southern Democrat that he had been and would
remain, withstood the Republican ascendancy, focusing little on national matters but rather making a new reputation in the organization
of southeastern intercollegiate sports, especially football, and his ex-
haustive efforts to build a major athletic facility at the university in
Athens.

FIVE

The Decade of Sports

1920s

During the 1920s Sanford's chief diversion beyond family and the classroom was the sports programs of the university, especially the football program. In that same decade he took the lead in founding the Southern Conference, the intercollegiate sports organization he presided over as president throughout the twenties. The capstone of the decade, however, was Sanford's conception of, planning for, and building of Sanford Stadium, considered by many his most noteworthy achievement.

With the coming of World War I, Georgia's 1917 and 1918 football schedules were suspended. Fifteen members of the 1916 team and two of their coaches joined the army; Coach Cunningham became a general.[1] The war's interruption of sports gave Sanford time to make his own contributions to the national effort. Full-time sports did not return to Athens until the same year Shelton Sanford returned from France. The professor had done his part: taught his quartermaster boys, made Victory Loan speeches, and sent his own son "over there." With the return of peace, it was time to resume the battles of the gridiron.

Coach Cunningham rejoined the army as a career officer following the 1919 season, and the new decade was ushered in with the coaching leadership of one of his assistants, H. J. Stegeman. Stegeman had played football for Alonzo Stagg at Chicago in 1913 and 1914. He came to Athens in 1919 to initiate an ROTC program at the university but instead became Cunningham's assistant and after one year was named head coach of all major sports at Georgia. Shortly he dropped baseball, and in 1923 he was named athletic director. Stegeman was the first of three great coaches of Georgia football during the 1920s: Stegeman, 1920–23; Kid Woodruff, 1923–28; and Harry Mehre, 1928–38.[2]

As faculty chairman of athletics, Sanford was most aware of and involved in the dozens of details related to the entire sports program on a day-to-day basis. The accounts of the association through the 1920s are filled with an array of fiscal relationships and obligations for which Sanford felt responsible. Each year there was the matter of schedule contracts, part of which involved negotiating agreements with the opponent schools over division of the gate receipts. Tens of thousands of dollars each year came from this source and were paid out on such expenses as field upkeep, travel, officials, coaches' salaries, equipment, training table expenses, laundry, physicians, rain insurance, and guarantees to other teams. Each year the figures increased, but for most of Sanford's years, the association stayed in the black.[3] Sanford's fellow board members recognized his extraordinary efforts and occasionally made tangible expressions of that recognition. On May 20, 1920, the board of the Athletic Association sent Sanford a check for $300 "as a slight token of our affectionate regard."[4]

Georgia football in the twenties was jam-packed with important, or at least interesting, benchmarks. For Georgia fans who considered the "real" game of the year the meeting with the Engineers from North Avenue, the first half of the decade must have been quite a disappointing interval. For six years (1919–25), there was no contest between the traditional in-state rivals. The 1916 meeting between the two had resulted in a 21–zip victory for Tech. With the resumption of play in 1919 there was a postwar possibility for revenge, but Georgia fans insulted Tech before a baseball game by casting aspersions on their players' patriotism, maintaining that during the great war Georgia boys were "over there" and Tech boys were in Atlanta. Furious Tech fans and their Atlanta supporters united in refusing to play the Georgia boys in any sport until 1925.[5] Traditional Auburn and Virginia rivalries had to serve the fans in the interim.

Just as one tradition was interrupted, another was formalized. In 1921 the Georgia team was officially designated as the "Bulldogs." Legend has it that Stegeman's first team was composed of the original bulldogs, so named by Atlanta sportswriter Cliff Wheatley after an especially tenacious defensive series against a powerful Virginia team. The season was Georgia's first undefeated one since Pop Warner's 1896 glory. Stegeman's subsequent teams were less successful; his final season (1922) ended in a 5–4–1 record as the reins were turned over to Kid Woodruff.[6]

Before Woodruff took over from Stegeman, Professor Sanford arranged for the beginning of a spectacular series of inter-sectional games that became standouts of the Georgia football seasons during the twenties. The series began when Sanford set up the 1921 meeting between Georgia and Harvard at Cambridge before a crowd of 25,000. Harvard won 10–7 but the closeness of the contest was a shock to sportswriters and a delight to Georgia fans, especially Professor Sanford.[7]

In his capacity as faculty athletic chairman, Sanford was not only the employer of coaches and master of schedules but also chief publicist and troubleshooter for the program at Georgia during the twenties. The stadium project, which was completed toward the end of the decade, seemed to be the crowning glory of these efforts, but between the postwar resumption of football and the glory of victory over Yale in 1929, S. V. Sanford had a plateful of details that paid little in the way of honor and glory. Professor Sanford's correspondence files for this period are littered with the tracks of the sometimes rewarding and often frustrating business of sports.

One single issue, the suspended rivalry between Tech and Georgia, persisted as a matter in need of attention to such a degree that it alone would have occupied the full time of lesser men. Professor Sanford, however, merely juggled that ongoing controversy along with a host of other major and minor crises and victories for almost half the decade before the matter was resolved.

Following the unfortunate 1919 incident between Georgia students and Tech supporters, the Atlanta newspapers took a special interest in the rival.y. Clark Howell, editor of the *Atlanta Constitution,* carried on an intense correspondence with Sanford related to the resumption of the contests between the two schools. In late 1920 Howell pushed Sanford to respond to accusations that Georgia was not working to reestablish relations between the schools.[8] Howell, as a member of the Board of Trustees of the university (1896–1927), had reasons beyond his newspaper for promoting the resumption of good will, and Sanford, in view of both the power of the press and Howell's position on the board, was sensitive to the editor's concerns.

Others decried the continuation of strife between Tech and Georgia. One 1921 letter to Sanford was from one who claimed to "have been closely identified with Georgia-Tech rows since the first fight," but felt the public was fed up: "The general feeling throughout the State is that the two State Universities, supported (however grossly inadequately) by State funds, ought not to be rearing two sets of boys who hate each other."[9]

As matters finally were resolved in 1925, in a speech made at the dedication of Woodruff Hall, the gymnasium on the Athens campus, Sanford spoke of Tech and Georgia basketball and other rivalries. In that speech he referred to the tradition of "bitterness, discord and strife" and called on all parties to "work against that." In calling for an end to that kind of competition Sanford outlined his view of sports and "competitive games" as "immensely important in making for an efficient man." In that same speech Sanford acknowledged the apparently disproportionate ballyhoo surrounding football and justified that situation on the basis that the gate revenues from the gridiron provided the wherewithal for all college students to participate in physical education.[10]

While it is easy to present Sanford in such a way as to make all his actions seem altruistic and selfless and to depict his work with sports at Georgia as a thankless labor, it is obvious that a very human Steadman Sanford enjoyed the benefits of the relationship as well. Prominent Atlanta attorney Harold Hirsch was an important supporter of the university and its athletic program and someone whose friendship Sanford enjoyed. An interesting relic of their correspondence is a typed letter on Candler, Thomson, and Hirsch letterhead to Sanford dated October 10, 1921, containing a handwritten postscript. The body of the letter, typed no doubt by a secretary, reads: "I am having sent to you today, with my compliments, via parcel post, an overcoat. I trust you will accept it in the spirit in which it is given and that it will prove to be of use to you." The handwritten postscript read: "Seven tickets for Harvard. HH." [11]

Sanford's largesse with football tickets sometimes proved more of a liability than an asset. E. R. King, a Fort Gaines, Georgia, attorney scolded the professor: "I received your card asking me to attend the football game at Athens. As a friend of the University, I would advise you to quit broadcasting the state with such invitations. Your institution is having a hard time now getting appropriations from the legislature. You are placing emphasis on physical programs instead of mental training. You are dividing the University from the masses. Keep your invitations if you want to help the state." [12]

For every killjoy, however, there were many more devoted fans, some of whom were eager to advise Sanford on schedules, coaches, and players for the Bulldogs, whatever the sport. A letter from Washington, Georgia, to "My Dear Cousin Steadman," dated August 8, 1923, puts in a good word for "another Babe Ruth," a good boy of eighteen, weighing in at 190 pounds, with lots of baseball potential, and the son of a "poor widow." The signature of the "cousin" is illegible as is the name of the prospect. If he made it, he is lost to the records. [13]

From 1923 until 1928 George C. (Kid) Woodruff was Georgia's head football coach. He had come to the university as a student from a prominent Columbus business family in 1908, was an outstanding athlete, and was captain of the 1911 football team at Georgia. Woodruff and Sanford had a long and mutually supportive friendship, which started with Woodruff's student player days and extended through the coaching years and beyond. In an unusual arrangement, Woodruff agreed to take on the coaching job for the nominal sum of one dollar per year. Keeping his profitable business interests afloat in Columbus in the off season, Woodruff would return to Athens each fall to prepare his staff and players.

Coach Woodruff and Professor Sanford early on established a partnershiplike arrangement whereby Sanford acted in loco parentis in the coach's periods of absence. The Woodruff-Sanford correspondence during the mid-twenties is largely about encouraging the boys, helping them pass their exams, and making sure they had sufficient funds to keep them in school and well fed. After leaving the coaching position, Woodruff repaid Sanford in part by his generous support for the building of Sanford's stadium.[14]

Among the many letters between Harold Hirsch and athletic chairman Sanford are strong indications that Woodruff's appointment owed some special thanks to the professor's behind-the-scenes efforts. Following Woodruff's first season as head coach, Sanford wrote Hirsch regarding the movement of Stegeman to athletic director and line coach and Kid Woodruff's appointment: "It has taken me forty days to bring matters at this end to a successful conclusion. It has been apparently slow, but very fast for *faculty* men." [15]

In the midst of what must have been for Sanford an act of juggling the "do-it-now!" demands of influential Georgia alumni and business leaders and the glacial pace of tradition-bound professors, the years-old issue of the suspension of play between Tech and Georgia was resolved, S. V. Sanford again playing a most important part. The rivalry was resumed during Coach Woodruff's third season. Woodruff's last encounter with the Engineers had been when he was captain of the 1911 team that beat Tech 5–0. The 1925 return match was a disappointing reversal; this time it was Tech the winner 3–0. The following year the Engineers left the field as victors over the Bulldogs, 14–13. In

Woodruff's last year as coach, the "Dream and Wonder" season of 1927, Georgia was beaten by Tech 12−0.[16] Despite the less than auspicious beginnings of the renewal of the old rivalries, fans from both schools were delighted with the resurrection of this great tradition. Many credited Sanford with working to end the suspension of games; one supporter labeled the renewal "the best news in seven or eight years."[17] Clark Howell wrote Sanford congratulating him on the re-establishment of the series and offered to have his newspaper fund a special trophy for the winner of two of the next three games between the schools.[18]

It was, however, not enough to get the two great in-state rivals lined up against each other on the gridiron again; the renewal led to new and difficult challenges for schedule-builder Sanford. L. W. "Chip" Robert, an important Atlanta architect and Georgia Tech supporter in his capacity as a member of the executive committee of the Georgia Tech Alumni Association, wrote Harold Hirsch late in 1926 to complain about what he considered an unfair Georgia-sparing schedule leading up to the big game between the rivals. According to Robert, Tech had specific understandings regarding positions in the schedule: "The dropping of Vanderbilt by the University, and the switching of Auburn back one week, and then taking on Clemson, one of the weakest teams in the South for the Saturday before our game is absolutely in violence to our understanding."[19]

Robert proceeded to lay the blame on Professor Sanford, referring to the scheme of meetings as "his schedule." Regarding the schedule as it stood Robert asserted: "under no circumstances can (we) consent to this. I feel quite sure that you understand this situation and will have same corrected." In a second letter to Hirsch, also dated November 30, 1926, Robert asked that "you take it up right away with Professor Sanford."[20]

A telegram from Harold Hirsch to S. V. Sanford dated December 3, 1926, read: "Considering our contractual relations with Tech and as a Georgia alumnus, I seriously object to anything that would tend to be a breach of contract or breach of faith, and I believe changing schedule as you contemplate doing would be a violation of the contract and violation of faith." [21]

Among the "new traditions" established by Sanford during Kid Woodruff's reign was a scheduling coup that probably made all the Tech complaints seem worth the trouble. On the heels of the Bulldogs' journey to Cambridge to face Harvard, Sanford began efforts to bring together an inter-sectional "Battle of the Bulldogs," pitting Georgia against Old Eli, Yale, often considered institutional forebear to the university in Athens and in the twenties a perennial powerhouse in the east. The series that lasted for almost a decade (1923–1934, excluding 1932) started with Woodruff's inaugural year (1923) and a 40–0 walloping of the southerners by their Yankee brethren. The second match resulted in a more balanced 7–6 Yale victory, but in 1925 Yale handed Georgia a 35–7 loss. In the next to last Georgia-Yale game, Yale won 19–0. [22]

The week before the 1927 Yale game Coach Woodruff announced his pending retirement. That year's Bulldogs, known as the "Dream and Wonder Team," featuring two All-American ends, Tom Nash and Chick Shiver, shocked the Yalies 14–10, giving Woodruff an almost perfect end to his career. Unfortunately, the otherwise stellar season concluded in a bitter mud battle with Tech, which resulted in Georgia's single loss that season, 12–0. A trip to the Rose Bowl and a national title slipped from the Kid's grasp. [23]

For non-Georgians S. V. Sanford's name became familiar in the arena of southern football by way of his role in the creation of a new intercollegiate conference. The Southern Conference and Sanford's role in its origins go back to the Southern Intercollegiate Athletic Association (SIAA), the organization from which the original members of the Southern Conference seceded in 1920–21. When Sanford became involved in the SIAA in 1908 he saw, as did the representatives of other larger schools, that due to the great variety of types and sizes of institutions, the organization no longer served them to the fullest. According to an early article on the founding of the Southern Conference, "the larger institutions felt that it would be impossible for them to enact more stringent and more progressive regulations than then existed in the old organization." [24] At the 1920 Gainesville, Florida, meeting of the SIAA, Sanford led the withdrawal of fourteen member institutions: Alabama, Auburn, Clemson, Georgia Tech, Georgia, Kentucky, Maryland, Mississippi A.& M., North Carolina State, North Carolina, Tennessee, Virginia, V.P.I., and Washington and Lee. The new Southern Conference was formally organized in Atlanta in February 1921.[25]

Sanford was chosen as the new organization's first president in 1921 and was reelected annually, in suspension of the constitution of the conference regarding limited terms, until 1931. At that time Sanford's multiple responsibilities forced the organization to cease drawing on his leadership talents.

In a 1925 speech before the Southern Association of Colleges and Secondary Schools, Sanford commented on the beginnings of the new athletic conference and its broader responsibilities: "The time, however, has arrived when organizations of the type of the Southern Conference and other similar athletic bodies must work more closely in connection with the academic side of college life. The college has broadened, and now we recognize that we must care for the intellectual, the moral, and the physical." [26]

From Sanford's initial membership in the old SIAA and through his leadership of the walkout and years as president of the new conference, he maintained the high ideal of establishing what he considered the appropriate relationship between athletics and academics. Throughout his years of association with sports at Georgia, Sanford championed a high road for intercollegiate sports. He asked the question which he thought central to a measure of the value of college sports: "Do you believe that intercollegiate football, as now conducted, contributes anything of real value to the cause of education to which your institution is dedicated?" [27]

Sanford obviously believed there was real value. He proceeded to outline in five points his defense of intercollegiate sports. He maintained that athletic contests improve the physical condition of the students, improve the morale and manner of the students and the public, increase the loyalty of the students to the colleges, create and foster an institutional solidarity afforded in like degree by no other agency, and that "they afford a laboratory training for the development of character such as is not afforded elsewhere in the life of the undergraduate."[28]

Sanford then compared the Association of Colleges and Secondary Schools and the Southern Conference. Both, he maintained, were in the business of "untangling the knotty problems with the college" and eliminating "evils and abuses." In his next litany of abuses which he said the Southern Conference had been instrumental in eliminating, Sanford revealed the heart of his philosophy of making intercollegiate athletics not only compatible with, but complementary to, the academic aims of postsecondary education. The abuses he cited as special targets of the conference were the "tramp athlete," the migrant players who "gave the colleges a black eye"; "short-term" or "re-appearing athletes," who showed up in the fall only to disappear after the season, reappearing in the fall; "special students" who do not meet entrance requirements; and the practice of letting freshmen play on college teams. Southern Conference students, Sanford pointed out, were limited to five years of competition from the date of first matriculation, and no student was allowed to engage in athletics unless he met the scholastic requirements of the institution involved.[29]

In the 1920s collegiate sports, especially football, faced many of the same criticisms they face today. Sanford considered it part of his role as head of the conference to answer charges that to him threatened the game and thus threatened the boy. His 1925 address contained the central core of his defense of the game. To the charge of overcommercialism he responded that the evil was not in the income derived from big-time football. The revenue from football gate receipts financed the nonpaying sports of baseball, basketball, track, cross-country, tennis, and golf. "Is it," he asked, "the desire of any institution to maintain a program of intercollegiate athletics for a handful of men who are already physically fit? No. The aim of every college may be stated in three words, Athletics For All."

Using his own institution as an example, Sanford explained that "not one dollar has ever been given for the physical training of the young men in the University of Georgia by the trustees or by the legislature," but rather had come "from gate receipts of that much abused game of intercollegiate football." [30]

While he deflected criticism of inappropriate recruiting tactics, Sanford readily admitted that zealous, but misdirected, alumni and friends are inclined to attempt to persuade able young athletes to come from their high schools to their alma mater. It was, however, his contention that "proselyting has grown less and less each year in our larger institutions." He added that institutions could eliminate this evil in others by refusing to schedule games with teams "the ideals of which are admitted to be low [and] an outrage to sportsmanship." [31]

Sanford also addressed the issue of the high salary of coaches relative to faculty members. "If this is true," said Sanford, "it is an easy problem to solve." He went on to explain that colleges must simply create departments of physical education, which would be administered on the same basis as other academic departments where the "professor of physical education would be elected in the same manner as the other professors of the institution, would receive the same salary, and would have the same tenure of office." This would, he said, remove coaches from positions that "depend too much upon the whims of a fickle body of alumni." He expressed the hope that the day would come when every coach would be a distinguished member of the faculty, and that salary levels for coaches and professors would be the same. With a slight touch of humor he added that the equity should be accomplished by "lifting professors' salaries to that of coaches, rather than lowering coaches' salaries to those of professors." [32] "It is our duty," Sanford concluded, "to save the boy and then save the game; in the past we have tried to save the game at the expense of the boy. Let us now adopt a new policy—save the game and save the boy." [33]

Sanford's leadership in the new conference was motivated by his desire to have sports programs in his region achieve an equal footing on the national level with the older northern and eastern conferences. The new conference may not have lived up to all the ideals Sanford mouthed, but his efforts probably did curtail or at least interrupt some of the more unsavory excesses of college sports in the South. Sanford had seen and been a part of those early and unfortunate episodes of hired ringers; the new organization that he headed represented a considerable move toward respectability for southern football and for student players and fans.

During the mid and late 1920s, Sanford's reputation as an advocate for and defender of collegiate athletics increased to national levels. In his affiliations with the National Intercollegiate Athletic Association, Sanford served on the American committee for the 1924 Olympics. When in 1925 the NCAA voted to cooperate with Yale alumni to erect a memorial to Walter Camp "in recognition of his distinguished contributions to American college sports and sportsmanship," Sanford, by then a member of the association's Executive Board, took on responsibility for soliciting contributions from colleges in the South, a region defined for NCAA as the "Third District." [34] For the next two years the usual demands of Sanford's routine were increased by the volume of correspondence related to this effort. Eventually a total of forty-three schools in the region for which Sanford was responsible took part, providing more than twenty-five thousand dollars to the effort. The level of institutional participation ranged from $1,500 to $50. Interestingly, Georgia Tech made a $1,500 contribution while the University of Georgia provided $1,000. When Sanford filed his October 1927 report, Mississippi A.& M., Clemson, and L.S.U. were the only Southern Conference schools not taking part. [35]

When the final reports for the fund drive were being compiled in late 1927 in preparation for a 1928 dedication of the memorial, Sanford took special notice of the results of his efforts with the Southern Conference schools. In October 1927, he reported to E. K. Hall, chairman of the Walter Camp Memorial, "Nineteen of twenty-two Conference institutions have taken part. I am sorry that I could not make it 100 percent. I have never worked harder on anything than I have this Memorial drive." [36] Considering the number of successful efforts in which he had taken part, this was saying a great deal.

While it was true that Sanford demanded a great deal of himself on behalf of such undertakings, it was apparently also true that he could be firm with and demanding of those with whom he worked, especially in his role as conference leader. Sports writer Ed Danforth revealed that tougher side of Sanford during the Southern Conference days: "Dr. W. D. Funkhouser of the University of Kentucky, a Southern and Southeastern Conference veteran said of him, 'Dr. Sanford was president of the old organization year in and year out, and he ran the show. I mean he ran it. He was a dictator beyond challenge. Beside him, Hitler and Mussolini are weak-kneed invertebrates.'"[37]

Sanford no doubt enjoyed the importance of being involved in such extensive regional and national efforts, but what he found most rewarding was the recognition he received for his role on his own beloved campus. The 1927 edition of the *Pandora* carried one such important acknowledgment of his efforts at the University of Georgia. The athletic section of that edition was dedicated to Sanford, "Faculty Director of Athletics and Founder of the Southern Conference for his true and lasting love and friendship to those who make Georgia's teams."[38]

Sanford's appreciation for the importance of sports reached beyond those students who made the teams. Not all his time caring for sports at Georgia was devoted to football, the conference, scheduling, and stadium building. There were less visible items in the sports program at Georgia that involved Sanford's time and attention. For example, prominent Atlanta physician and friend to the university Frank K. Boland corresponded with Sanford on behalf of tennis, promoting the building of some good courts and planting the idea for the eventual hiring of a tennis coach for the University.[39] Often Sanford's daily mail included complaints about sports overtaking academics at the university; sometimes a frustrated parent or student wrote to complain of a perceived mistreatment which they felt Sanford could correct. Despite his high visibility in sports at the university, he was known to be fair-minded, even by the critics of athletic activities.

As the man most identified as Georgia's consistent link to sports over a long period, Sanford occasionally suffered the emotional strains as well as the accolades generated by the university's team followers. Coaches and players were transient figures; Professor Sanford was the constant of the matter. In the fall of 1928 Sanford received a letter marked "personal" from "Wm. B. Kent Sr." of Alamo, Georgia. Kent had been captain of the Georgia team when Von Gammon was killed in the Virginia game of 1897. Kent wrote thirty-one years after that tragic event ostensibly requesting that his fifteen-year-old son Billie Kent Jr. be sent a complimentary ticket to an upcoming football game to be played in Savannah. The senior Kent described his son as a "good baseball player, [who] plays fine basketball, and plays any game well." He was "155 pounds and is nearly six feet tall," and "is wild over football." Kent asked Sanford if he could "take him in charge and help him to achieve the victory he desires?" Had it ended there the letter might have been similar to hundreds of others in which ambitious fathers, uncles, brothers, cousins, and mothers promoted the athletes of their family and those of family friends. What makes this letter significant is the remaining portion, which is devoted to replaying the Von Gammon death and Kent's perceived slight in conjunction with the dedication of the Von Gammon memorial:

> I can never forget that when Von Gammon was killed executing a command that I gave, I did the same thing I told him to do—that I jumped down over him and asked him where he was hurt and he held his hands to his head and then I said, "Von, you are not going to give up, you have too much Ga. grit to give up, get up and get in the game, we will beat them." He said to me, and these were his last words in life, "No, Cap, I'll never give up." He never regained consciousness and died a real hero. I can't understand why the University does not memorialize the above as it is just as it happened. The University overlooking me in this respect has kept me away from the games and from the campus as I thought that I deserved more than I ever got, altho this may be very weak in me to do so. After Von was dying and the boys on my team, I was Captain you know, did not want to play any more and the command was given to "play ball," and the boys said they just did not have the heart to play

with Von dying and the command was given a second time to "play ball" and I told the quarterback to give me the ball and I ran thru the center of Virginia's line for 60 yards and would have made a touch down the next run, but the game was called and the playing of Billie Kent went into history and that was my last year.[40]

He closed, "we love Georgia and will always stick to her. My boy wants to go there and beat my record. Will you let him do it? I am, Yours most loyally for 'Georgia.'"[41]

Although Sanford had not been at the university when Von Gammon died, he was prominent in the dedication of the memorial on November 5, 1921, accepting on behalf of the university the circular bronze plaque presented by the University of Virginia on that occasion. For Kent, Sanford represented Georgia football throughout its history, even in the years before he had come to Athens. Such was the case in the minds of legions of fans over the years.

After the twenties new generations of Georgia supporters came to extend that associational relationship even more, thanks to the building of Sanford Stadium. Those who write about Georgia football never neglect to acknowledge the importance of the man who conceived the idea of the stadium and worked so diligently to bring the idea into reality. In *Touchdown* John Stegeman and Robert Willingham maintain, "Dr Sanford had a recurring dream of building a great stadium in the tangled valley of Tanyard Creek that separates the north and south campuses." Sanford felt it unfair for college teams with large followings to have to play their game in large cities where facilities were available to accommodate the fans. He insisted, "every athletic contest should be played on the college campus. Athletics belong to the students."[42]

Writing on the same theme Jesse Outlar wrote: "Dr. S. V. Sanford . . . was the mastermind behind the building of the stadium," and he "had not only carried the athletic banner for Georgia, but he was a trailblazer in athletics for the entire South. He was also one of the first to visualize the impact of football, the coming of paved highways, and the magnetism of intercollegiate football in the Southland. It was the natural thing for the stadium to be named for him. No other name was ever mentioned or considered." [43]

Today there are few around who remember that there was a playing field named for Professor Sanford before the building of Sanford Stadium. From 1886 until 1911 baseball games at Georgia had been played on Herty Field, sharing that space with the football team. When Sanford became involved with the Athletic Association, he soon promoted the notion of securing a better baseball field. He picked the site, solicited support locally and around the state, and saw the completion of a new field for the 1911 season. An article in the 1912 *Pandora* devoted a full page to a tribute to "Sanford Field" and the man responsible for its creation. The field was described as the best athletic field in the South, "a park surrounded by a ten foot high fence, large grand-stand, which will hold about a thousand people," with concrete bleachers, which "will easily accommodate a thousand more." Professor Sanford, said the *Pandora*, "refused to allow the field to be named after him, but he reckoned without the appreciation of everyone who gave him credit and, as a small tribute to his great work, named the park Sanford Field." [44] The field was in use until 1943 when Stegeman Hall was constructed on that site.

The first specific reference to Dr. Sanford's interest in building a new football facility appears about a dozen years after the building of Sanford Field in a letter from Harold Hirsch to Sanford dated December 12, 1924: "I am terribly interested in that stadium proposal we talked about the other night. . . . I have talked to Chip Robert, his concern is building about 12 of these . . . over different parts of the country. He will do a free estimate. But of course I would not let him do this. I will pay for the survey and undertake to raise through alumni funds of $60,000–$70,000 if the City of Athens does preliminary work. Keep this confidential." [45]

In this same letter, Hirsch discussed the use of City of Athens labor to prepare the site and the possibility of a plan for a 25,000-seat stadium, 12,000 seats initially with the remainder added later. Hirsch proposed concrete rather than wood construction and estimated the project could be completed at $5–$7 per seat.[46]

It is apparent from comments made by Dr. Sanford in his 1925 address to the Southern Association of Colleges and Secondary Schools that if the University of Georgia was to conform to his public philosophy of the role and importance of revenue-producing sports in support of the total athletic program, a new facility was essential.[47] The files of the Athletic Association contain copies of letters in late 1924 among Hirsch, Sanford, and Robert. It seems clear that by the beginning of 1925 the idea of building a stadium had been accepted by important supporters, but caution was being exercised regarding the particulars of location, capacity, projected cost, and means of financing the project. Some unsigned notes in the Athletic Association archives report: "It was not until 1927 that the actual plan for the construction was formulated in the mind of Dr. S. V. Sanford."[48]

At a 1927 meeting of the Board of Directors of the Athletic Association at the Athens Country Club, Sanford explained his plan for the financing of the project following numerous behind-the-scenes discussions and decisions by a handful of leading interested parties. At the Athens meeting Sanford spoke chiefly to the point of financing the project. He asked for "moral support and financial credit" in seeking signatories to a note for the Athletic Association. In an effort to involve a large number of people, endorsements limited to $500 or $1,000 were solicited. The response was gratifying. So much so that one source claimed "many would-be guarantors were not given a chance to endorse."

With the word out of Georgia's plan, Sanford began to hear not only from supporters but also firms that were anxious to be considered for the project. Ultimately, there were ten bidders representing firms in Atlanta, Macon, Memphis, Jacksonville, Chattanooga, and Charlotte. The bids as read before the Athletic Association on May 1, 1928, ranged from a low $129,500 from J. S. McCauley Company of Atlanta, to the high bid of $206,778 from T. S. Manley and Company of Chattanooga. A committee, which included Snelling and Sanford, was to submit these to the Trust Company in Atlanta.[49]

At the February 1928 meeting of the Board of the University Athletic Association, Sanford reported that the Trust Company of Georgia
would lend the Athletic Association $150,000 to build the new sta-
dium. Subsequently in March 1929, the Trust Company agreed to
lend an additional $30,000 at 7 percent requiring $50,000 in signature
guarantees, "similar to that secured for the first loan." In a note to
Sanford, Daniel MacDougald apologized, "I am sorry I could not get
the rate back to six per cent, but that was all I could do. They are
putting it over as a matter of accommodation and really did not care
to make the loan."[50]

A typed list with handwritten notations and headed "Original
Guarantors of the Sanford Stadium" is among the items in the Stadium Folder at the archives of the Athletic Association. There is a
second list in the *Georgia Alumni Record* of October 1929 headed
"Friends and Alumni of Georgia Who Made the Stadium Possible."
The two lists are identical, but neither indicates whether the list includes new guarantors of the second, smaller loan or whether this is
only those who signed to guarantee the initial loan of $150,000. There
was a total of 277 names on the lists. Ninety-eight were identified as
from Atlanta, seventy-five from Athens, forty from Columbus, and
the remaining sixty-four scattered among fifteen other Georgia communities.[51]

There was an abundance of nagging details and time-consuming
problems in the months between the original solicitation for guarantors and completion of the stadium. Construction had started in the
summer of 1928, by which time Sanford had become dean of Franklin College and Snelling had replaced Barrow as chancellor. Most of
the troublesome items such as the difficulty with the Clarke County
work forces ended up on Sanford's desk. The initial discussions about
building a stadium had involved the Clarke County work forces, who
were generally deployed in the maintenance and improvement of
county roads. In agreeing to help clear the site for the stadium, the
county had apparently bitten off more than the public was ready for
it to chew. Tate Wright, clerk and county attorney, wrote Chancellor
Snelling in July 1928: "Since beginning work on the stadium the

county forces have scarcely done any other work in the county. Citizens are complaining. We have to quit the stadium work for now."[52]

Snelling immediately forwarded the complaint to Sanford, chief troubleshooter for the project. Building the stadium involved Sanford far beyond producing the idea, working to raise the funds, and assuring a dramatic opening schedule for the new facility. Nineteen twenty-eight saw him deep in his new role as dean, newly appointed to the executive committee of the National Collegiate Athletic Association, with the building of the stadium bringing more and more demands on his time. The pressure had mounted early in the year as the financial intricacies of the Athletic Association's borrowing for the project became more complex. Marion Smith of Little, Powell, Smith, and Goldstein, Atlanta, wrote Sanford of the urgency of incorporating the association, an essential step in getting approval for the loans. The business of the Athletic Association suddenly took on more formal dimensions, and S. V. Sanford was the vital player on behalf of the organization. The minutes for a February 1928 meeting of the association are revealing of Sanford's critical role. In those minutes, all four action paragraphs begin with Sanford initiating the discussion or introducing the issue.[53] It all took its toll. For several months early in the year Sanford was at home ill. The scores of well-wishers repeatedly attributed his situation to overwork.[54]

Sanford's dreams, however, kept him going despite it all. In September he wrote to invite Yale to play the dedication game for the new facility. In the following weeks Sanford left no stone unturned, contacting anyone with Yale connections to urge the acceptance of the invitation. It paid off. George Nettleton, chairman of Yale's Athletic Association, wrote October 26: "Our board gratefully accepted your friendly proposal that the Georgia-Yale football game on October 12, 1929, be played at the new Georgia Stadium as the occasion for its dedication."[55]

The November 1928 *Georgia Alumni Record* lavished praise on Sanford for his accomplishment, getting "the great Blue team of Yale [to] leave its New England home for the first time in history in order to travel southward and dedicate Georgia's new stadium." The *Record* called this "the crowning point in Georgia's rise to national recognition in athletics." Paying tribute to Sanford, the article declared that he "for a quarter of a century has been the moving force in Southern athletics and who during the same time has carried Georgia teams from obscurity to nation-wide fame."

The article closed, "what shall we name the new stadium? There is but one name that can be given it. No other could ever be suitable. Let us use an old, familiar name again—*Sanford Field*." [56]

The great day toward which Sanford had worked so diligently came on October 12, 1929, in the words of sportswriter Jesse Outlar, "the most memorable day in Georgia's proud football history." [57] As if to second the accolades, Harry Mehre, in just his second season as head coach, directed his "Flaming Sophomores" to a stunning 15–0 upset of old Eli. The team included several sophomores from what were then called "whistlestops": Marion Dickens from Ocilla, Herb Maffett from Toccoa, Red Maddox from Douglas, Red Leathers from Athens, Bobby Rose from Valdosta, Spud Chandler from Carnesville, Weddington Kelly from Newnan, Jack Roberts from RFD, Alabama, and Tommy Paris from Gainesville. It was, however, sophomore Vernon "Catfish" Smith of the big city of Macon who was to be the hero of the day. [58]

The story of the events surrounding the game are as legendary as the well-known tale of the game itself. The details of the game are for other accounts. The preliminary planning and anticipation were the important elements for Professor Sanford. Among his many scrapbooks in the collection at the University Library is one hand-labeled on its inside cover as "Book 1, Yale." The outer identification says simply "1929." From this scrapbook, covers bulging with yellowed clippings from newspapers far and wide, it is possible to sense Dr. Sanford's excitement in the days surrounding the big event of October that year. Along with newspaper accounts are found black and white photographs of the progress of construction of the stadium and a copy of the proclamation making October 12, 1929, an official state holiday, Abraham Baldwin Day. Sanford had composed the document which credited Baldwin, a Yale man, with the founding of Georgia, the nation's oldest chartered state university. The links between Yale and the University of Georgia had long been noted, but in his schedule-building campaigns Sanford had always emphasized that connection in developing support for a series of games between the two schools.[59]

In the days preceding the game Athens newspapers were filled with little save items related to the coming contest. Headlines on October 10 announced: "Athens Ready to Receive Thousands for Yale Game; Dedication Program Ready." The subhead declared that "Simplicity Will Mark Dedication of Stadium Here." The lead paragraph quoted none other than Dean S. V. Sanford who announced that the dedication would be "carried out with dignity and simplicity."[60]

There was a long list of "distinguished guests expected to attend the game." Outstanding among them were the governors of Connecticut, Georgia, North Carolina, Alabama, and Florida, as well as senators and congressmen from Connecticut, Georgia, and North Carolina. The General Assembly of Georgia was to be well represented by the secretary of the Senate, the secretary of state, the Speaker (Richard B. Russell Jr.), and clerk of the House. Richard B. Russell, chief justice of the Supreme Court of Georgia, and Mrs. Russell were also expected. Among those present were to be presidents of ten colleges and universities, railroad presidents and officials, Southern Conference representatives, prominent business and professional men, more political figures, military officers, and newspapermen from around the country.[61]

Thirty-five thousand overflowed the new facility, which was touted as containing 32,000 seats. Those who had to pay did so at $3.00 per ticket. A great many, however, were invited, nonpaying guests. The *Banner-Herald* made a front-page story of the variety of transportation which would bring the crowds to Athens: "Thousands Will be Brought here via Trains, Auto, Plane." Twenty-seven special trains and sixty airplanes were expected. The local police department was to be "augmented" and "local ambulance concerns [were] planning to be ready for any emergencies that might arise." Elsewhere there was discussion of an anticipated 7,000 automobiles parked on the campus for the game.[62]

The big day arrived, thousands gathered, speeches were made, and, indeed, the game was played. Chancellor Snelling in his remarks generously acknowledged Professor Sanford's part in it all: "This beautiful and wonderful stadium, the dream come true of the Honored Dean of the University and Faculty Chairman of Athletics stands as a monument to his vision, and his indomitable courage. Here his name is written large in the annals of the University."[63]

On Sunday the *Athens Banner-Herald* reported on the events of the preceding day: "Sanford's Dream Realized as Yale Dedicates Beautiful New Stadium. Dr. Sanford was called to the center of the field, and there, in the presence of governors galore, men high in the educational world and thousands of loyal alumni, he was presented with a silver loving cup and $1,500 in gold coins as a gesture of their esteem and appreciation of the great labor he had done in making possible the new stadium plant. His greatest moment was Georgia's victory. It was a fitting climax to the honors which had been bestowed upon this quiet, ever-smiling, friend of all Georgia boys."[64]

Georgia won, beating Yale 15–0, Vernon "Catfish" Smith making all Georgia's points. The Georgia upset of Yale seemed almost tailor-made to honor Sanford. The sophisticated *New Yorker* magazine, in its weekly issue following the game, explained old Eli's loss. It seems the Georgia players were wise enough to "plug their ears with cotton during the half an hour of bugle calls and speeches, that preceded the game. This gave them an enormous advantage on the Yale men, who had been taking in the speeches and were timing their plays to suit the rhythm of 1880s oratory. They were hot, bewildered, blinded by perspiration, and groggy with words."[65]

Winning was important, no matter the respective team strategy, but for S. V. Sanford that victory on October 12, 1929, while sweet, was but a small piece of a much larger whole. A football victory, even a football team, for Sanford was only a device, enjoyable though it may be, for working toward higher aims, the aims which ultimately Sanford seemed always to be advancing. In writing "An Appreciation" in the *Pandora,* Sanford revealed the goals beyond the yard stripes: "One purpose of the stadium is to bring to the University its alumni that they may renew their acquaintance with members of the faculty, may see the student body, may learn more intimately the needs of the institution, and may be drawn more closely to Alma Mater. Not only is the purpose to bring back the alumni, but to bring the people of the state on the campus of this institution that they may learn to love, to support, and to protect it as it so justly deserves to be for the vital part it has played in the history, the life and the development of Georgia." [66]

SIX

Beyond Sports

1920s

In spite of the apparent domination of sports in his life, S. V. Sanford was involved in a variety of other matters during the twenties. Approaching his second decade at the university, Sanford could have been at the peak of his career, but it was only a busy preliminary to the most challenging and important part of his career as an educational leader.

During the twenties the Sanford children reached adulthood. Shelton, the oldest, completed his medical education at Harvard; Charles and Homer Reynolds were graduated from the university. While Grace Sanford expanded her own role outside the home, serving increasingly higher positions in the State Federation of Garden Clubs, she continued to focus on her chief role of wife and mother.

Family letters in the Sanford collection reveal the tender regard they held for each other. Family tradition holds that as the oldest child, Shelton was given a special consideration and that the whole family made sacrifices in order for him to go to Harvard. Grace Sanford's attachment to Shelton has sometimes been given as the reason he never developed a brilliant medical career. Rather than take an internship in a prestigious New England hospital, Shelton was encouraged by his mother to come back near home, taking a residency in Atlanta.[1] Someone who married into the family attributed Shelton's lackluster career, spent chiefly in the military medical service, to his bland personality rather than the site of his residency.[2]

Grandson Charles Sanford, in recalling his visits to the Sanford home in Athens in the late 1930s and early 1940s, remembered that Shelton's room, by far the most elaborate upstairs in the house on Cloverhurst, was considered sacrosanct. When the sons visited in later life each occupied his boyhood room, Shelton always in the large room, the younger brothers in their smaller quarters.[3]

Shelton's primogeniture is reflected in one of the rare remaining letters written by his father to the "household" while he and Grace Sanford were out of town. The senior Sanford wrote from Austin, Texas, where he and Grace had gone to promote the adoption of one of his grammar texts. All three boys were at home on Cloverhurst: "I hope you, Charles, and Homer Reynolds are getting along alright. There is no reason why all of you can not have a good time. I want them [the younger boys] to have a good time but I do not want them to throw away money for that purpose during these days of H.C.L. (high costs of living)."[4]

The Sanfords enjoyed a comfortable life, but not without exercising some care for money matters. The family, however, valued its reputation more than financial status. The middle child, Charles Steadman Sanford, turned twenty-one in 1922. In December that year he wrote his mother from Atlanta: "Sometimes I get kinder [*sic*] blue and ashamed to admit that I am your son because everybody has such a good opinion of you and I know that I am unworthy of all that you have given me. I will amount to something and my intention is to some day be as honest, upright and true as my *mother* and *father*. I may not ever have any money and I may not even be a big man, but I shall always strive to be honest like you and dad and Cutie and Shelton, but if I should be a big man, honest or have a little money I shall always, with pride, look to you all and say you made me what I am today."[5]

Seeing their successful father and well-respected mother in such highly public roles probably outweighed the fiscal limitations of the family, although money was always a focal point of ambitions. Steadman and Grace Sanford's friends included the financially well-fixed as well as the socially well-placed of Athens and Atlanta and Marietta, so the models of wealth were always near at hand.

Sanford's salary before he became dean in 1926 was typically modest for professors of that time. Additional income came in spurts from the sales of his grammar texts. The amounts from this source were not insignificant, and the prospect of more adoptions and thus sales kept Sanford focused on revisions, new editions, or totally new books. In the early 1920s, Sanford was pushing his publisher to consider a new book, but he did not get much encouragement.[6]

There were occasional windfalls related to Sanford's efforts on behalf of the athletic program, but nothing on which the family could count. Small loans, usually in amounts of several hundred dollars from Athens banks, tided the family over in pinches. The Sanfords joined many other American families in the mid-twenties who borrowed money to buy an automobile. In August 1925 they purchased a new Buick for $1,525, $525 down and four quarterly payments of $250.00.[7] When Sanford's father, Charles V. Sanford, died in April 1922 at age 77, S. V. Sanford received $630.00 from the settlement of his estate.[8]

The Sanford household enjoyed a level of comfort enviable to many but certainly not lavish. The center of family life, the home on Cloverhurst, was a stylish and comfortably large two-story frame and shake rendition in the English cottage style. On the ground floor there were a broad front porch and a deep side porch. The living room was entered from the front and the library from the side porch. Through an archway behind the living room was a large dining room with bay windows to the west, and farther back a large kitchen and pantry. An inviting back hallway divided the kitchen from the east side of the house, where just off the side porch was the bright, sunlit library; behind that was a bath adjoining the parents' bedroom, the only one on the first floor. Up the stairs a wide hall led to Shelton's large bedroom in the front of the house; on either side of the hall were smaller bed-rooms, a bath, and a storage room.

The house sat on a large corner lot which eventually included a small frame garage and a vegetable garden in season. A flower garden was a source of family pride, and the location of social gatherings during Sanford's presidency and chancellorship. The Sanfords enjoyed entertaining small groups of friends, usually extended family or Athens faculty friends and occasional out-of-town visitors in for a football weekend. Gatherings as a rule numbered about ten; the dining room table would seat twelve comfortably.[9]

Our best clues to entertaining at the Sanford home come from an autograph/guest book which contains sporadic entries from 1913 until 1945. A photograph of the Sanford home pasted to the inside cover indicates the importance of that house in the social life of the Sanfords. The initial entries in the book are from the Sanfords' time in Europe. The Cloverhurst entries date from early 1914. As with so many good intentions, it seems obvious that the family did not rigorously adhere to any resolve to make sure their guests signed the book on all occasions; there are great gaps. What is found there, however, is revealing. On those occasions when the Sanfords made use of their guest book the signatures were names familiar to important university and Athens social circles: Barrow, Bryan, Bocock, Cobb, Carithers, Gordon, Hill, among others. The Hodgson name appears again and again as do such out-of-town luminaries as Clark Howell Jr., Governor Joseph M. Brown, George F. Gober of Marietta, and George C. Woodruff of Columbus and the playing fields of Athens. Football weekends seem to have been the most common excuse for the Sanfords to have a gathering of friends for dinner. On these occasions the guests were likely to include visitors from Valdosta, Griffin, Cedartown, Fitzgerald, Eatonton, Macon, or Blakely. Well before his presidency or the chancellorship, in those years before the term was used, S. V. Sanford was networking.[10]

On evenings at home, when he was not occupied with entertaining guests or working on one of his many scrapbooks, Sanford exercised his creative genius with word games and puzzles, and apparently, according to one scrap from his correspondence, songwriting. In October 1924 the Columbia Gramophone Company wrote Sanford to inquire about the rights to the waltz, "Dream of Heaven." According to this letter, it "was written by [Sanford] and introduced by the Garber-Davis Orchestra on one of our records several years ago." The story of Sanford's waltz ends there, but Sanford's enjoyment of word contests is well documented through the twenties. Sanford entered a "P-word Contest" sponsored by the Blackburn Distribution Company of Atlanta in May 1922 aiming for the grand prize of a "$1900 Oakland Sedan." That year a "B-word Contest" netted him a tenth-place prize of $20 from Lisle Daniels and Company of St. Paul. The big take for that year, however, was a $1,000 second-place award in an "S-word contest" sponsored by the Atlanta Newspapers.[11]

Sanford's fame as a word contest expert spread far and wide, and this talent added to his list of kindred spirits: football fans; Baptists; Spanish-American War veterans; quartermaster men; Marietta, Macon, and Conyers friends; Chautauqua contacts; and now word contest fad followers. From his fame as a grammar text author, Sanford had come to expect random questions regarding English usage, grammar, and punctuation. In the twenties eager word-contest entrants sought his wisdom. From such odd sources sometimes come extraordinarily meaningful messages. In April 1924 one such contact must have been especially cherished by Sanford. John G. Harrison, professor of philosophy at Mercer, wrote Sanford at the university thanking him for his "kindness to my boy in helping him with one of the recent word contests." He continued: "I am now meeting my Ethics class in the recitation room in which your grandfather taught. This is the first time that I have ever used it. I scarcely ever go through a period without some happy memory that attaches to his great character and noble service. How proud he would be of your success and distinctions."[12]

The decade of the twenties marked Sanford's transition from professor to college administrator. The decade opened with S. V. Sanford teaching English, journalism, and Anglo-Saxon.[13] Outside of these classes he helped sponsor the campus newspaper, the *Red and Black,* and was, as he had always been, an unofficial advisor to needful students and parents whether or not they were officially connected to his classrooms or areas of immediate concern. His classroom responsibilities must have seemed like respites in light of the conflicts and complaints his nonclassroom efforts generated. Parents of students at the university, many of them friends or acquaintances of Sanford, had always felt free to enlist Sanford's support when problems arose for their offspring. Dealing with angry, disappointed, or hurt parents was probably more to Sanford's taste than fending off the sometimes small-minded, campus politics–inspired complaints of other faculty and administrators.

Early in the month Judge R. N. Hardeman of Louisville, Georgia, wrote: "My dear Sanford: This letter is written to you personally and more or less confidentially, though you may discuss its contents in a general way if you see fit." The content and tone of the letter made it obvious that Judge Hardeman wanted desperately for "something to be done," and clearly, his expectation was that Sanford would be the agent of action.

The judge had sent his son to the university "because I have a deep interest in my state and in her institutions." The son, Jim, he described as high-standing, honorable, and tenderhearted. He went to Athens "to work and not to play and he went at it." He returned home "practically a nervous wreck." Hardeman said he understood the antics associated with youthful pranks, wearing a redcap, and so forth. He drew the line personally, however, at the head-shaving his son took. He also objected to what he considered the coarse language directed at the "damned fresh" he heard on the streets during a recent visit to Athens. It was, however, the physical abuse of a beating inflicted on his son that had driven him to complain. The son had undergone fraternity hazing which left him "so sick and exhausted that he fainted, had to have a physician and came home. . . . It was my avowed purpose to go to Athens and swear out warrants for the young men whose names I knew and prosecute them with all my vigor through the courts of my state. It was my first impulse to publish public articles in every daily paper in the state, calling attention to the situation as I found it."

He chose instead to write Sanford "as an old friend to let you know that I am not the only one that feels that our faculty at Georgia should at least make an investigation, and if necessary, command that such horse-play and rough stuff be cut out." He concluded: "I will leave to your own good judgement and ask you to make no reference to this letter that can in any way add to the discomfort of my son." [14]

There is no written record of how Sanford responded, but usually in such matters he would have the student come by for a visit. As was the case in so many of the concerns of students and parents, there was not much that Sanford or any individual could do to radically alter what was by then an established campus culture, for good or evil. What was possible, and apparently what Sanford did so well, was to acknowledge the imperfections of the situation, show a genuine interest in the welfare of the student, and at the same time work to bring to bear the subtle pressure of his own influence to change things for the better. It was Sanford's special talent to be approachable and a listener, and then to be a mediator between indignation and reality.

In dealing with his peers, his colleagues, and those on the faculty who held superior positions by virtue of their titles, Sanford occasionally had to be more concrete with his responses to complaints. Such was certainly the case when a few days after the Hardeman letter he received a thinly disguised complaint from Andrew Soule, "King Andy," president of the College of Agricultural and Mechanical Arts: "The *Red and Black* comes to my table occasionally, and I notice that there is seldom any mention made of various matters affecting the welfare of the Georgia State College of Agriculture which I think would be of interest to the community as a whole. I am wondering if it would be possible for you to designate someone from this side of the campus to represent the College in this connection. The fact that about one-third of the students enrolled in the University are in agriculture would appear to make this a fair and reasonable proposition."

Soule closed by saying he was not a critic, but was acting in a "get-together movement that will enable us to work together for better advantage." [15] As always Sanford was accommodating. At the close of that decade it was Soule who presented President Sanford with some of his most troublesome resistance when Sanford undertook university reorganization under the new University System.

One of Sanford's most rewarding academic roles was related to the teaching of journalism and the promotion of the discipline on the campus and across the state. There were a number of collateral benefits to his involvement with the newspaper field. Weekly small-town newspapers were the most important grassroots means of communication in Georgia between the turn of the century and World War II. In the larger towns and cities the daily newspapers transcended the small-town folksy role and served as important political and economic agents. Whether small weeklies or big town dailies, S. V. Sanford, through his avenue of journalism education, became perhaps the best-known Georgia educator among Georgia newspaper editors. The advantages of such visibility were not lost on Sanford.

Because of his association with journalism at Georgia over several years, Sanford had former students in newspaper offices around the state, and he continued to seek to enlarge the connections between the newspaper folks and the university. In 1921 Sanford spent a good deal of his time corresponding with editors around Georgia about the possibility of offering some means of linking them together via a University of Georgia School of Journalism connection. Apparently he had in mind a weekly newsletter, possible news service, and other unspecified "special services." This idea did not get very far, but when the Georgia Press Association and the Georgia Press Institute were formed, Sanford's interests and previous efforts did not go unrewarded. His careful cultivation of that important center of influence during the 1920s paid off handsomely during his presidency and chancellorship.

Sometimes seemingly frivolous matters interrupted the professor's already crowded schedule. B. P. O'Neal of Macon wrote in June 1921 to complain about not having been awarded a letter for tennis as a

Steadman Vincent Sanford, "Steadie," as student at Mercer University, Macon, 1889–90. Box 23B, Sanford Collection.

Grace McClatchey, ca. 1890. Box 67, Sanford Collection.

The Sanford family, ca. 1895. Standing left to right: Charles Dickerman Sanford, Steadman Vincent Sanford, Anna Maria Sanford. Seated left to right: Shelton Palmer Sanford, Elizabeth Steadman Sanford, Charles Vincent Sanford, Paul Hill Sanford. Box 23B, Sanford Collection.

Left: Captain S. V. Sanford, of the Marietta Rifles, Company H, 5th Georgia Infantry, 1895. Box 23B, Sanford Collection.

Below: Captain Sanford, center, Camp Northen, Griffin, Georgia, ca. 1895. Box 23B, Sanford Collection.

Grace Devereaux Sanford, born Marietta 1897, died Athens 1907. Box 67, Sanford Collection.

Four generations of Sanfords, 1896. Standing left to right: Steadman Vincent Sanford, Charles Vincent Sanford, Shelton Palmer Sanford holding great-grandson, Shelton Palmer Sanford. Box 23B, Sanford Collection.

Left: Professor S. V. Sanford at the University of Georgia as he appeared on the faculty page of the 1904 *Pandora.* Photo in possession of Mr. and Mrs. Marvin McClatchey, Atlanta.

Below: Professor Sanford's first graduating class, Marietta High School 1898. Seated: Miss Marion Atkinson. Standing left to right: James D. Manget, Guy A. Moore, Professor Sanford, James J. Daniell, Oscar Bane Keeler. Box 23B, Sanford Collection.

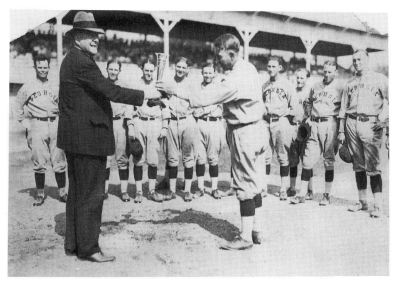

Sanford with University of Georgia baseball players, ca. 1920.
Box 5, Sanford Collection.

President Sanford at
right at the university
arch, ca. 1933. Box 67,
S. V. Sanford Collection,
Hargrett Rare Book and
Manuscript Library,
University of Georgia
Libraries.

Sanford Stadium under construction, 1928. S. V. Sanford in dark suit at the center. Box 35, Sanford Collection.

Sanford inspects his stadium in progress, 1929. Sanford in dark suit with shovel. Box 35, Sanford Collection.

Sanford Stadium filled to capacity, 1929. Archives of the University of Georgia Athletic Association.

Georgia Press Institute dinner, ca. 1932. From left: John Paschal, *Atlanta Journal*; Dean Drewry, University of Georgia College of Journalism; unidentified; Milton Fleetwood, president of the Georgia Press Institute; Mrs. Sanford; Dr. Sanford; Miss Emily Woodward, founder of the Georgia Press Institute. Box 23B, Sanford Collection.

The S. V. Sanford residence on Cloverhurst, Athens, ca. 1930. Box 67, Sanford Collection.

Contract signing for University System building projects, ca. 1938. Standing left to right: Harmon Caldwell, George Woodruff, and unidentified regents. Seated: Chancellor Sanford and regent Miller Bell. Box 23B, Sanford Collection.

Chancellor Sanford at his desk, Board of Regents office, Atlanta, ca. 1941. Photo courtesy of Ralph Moor.

August 11, 1938, Dr. Sanford presenting President Franklin D. Roosevelt with honorary degree from the university at Sanford Stadium. Photo by Henry Gates from photographic archives of the Lamar Dodd School of Art. Courtesy of the Office of the President, University of Georgia.

The chancellor holding forth, spring 1941. University of Georgia Athletic Association Archives.

Last public photograph of Sanford, receiving 4-H Club's highest award, honorary membership, from Virginia Knight, president of the Georgia 4-H Council, Milledgeville, August 1945. Photograph by Georgia Agricultural Extension Service. Box 67, Sanford Collection.

W461311
PRESIDENT RECEIVES DEGREE AT UNIVERSITY OF GEORGIA
ATHENS, GA.--Dr. S. V. Sanford, Chancellor of The
University of Georgia, Governor E. D. Rivers of
Georgia and President Roosevelt (Left to Right)
pictured in a gay mood at The University, August
11th, where the President received an honorary
degree of Doctor of Laws.
CREDIT LINE(ACME)   8/11/38   Burs DC

A note from James A. Farley, FDR's postmaster general, to Sanford.
Photos and editorial comments about the president's busy day in
Georgia, August 1938. Box 23B, Sanford Collection.

JAMES A. FARLEY
NEW YORK

November 5, 1938

octor Sanford:

In going through some pictures I

cross the attached and I thought you

like to have them.

With every good wish, I am

Sincerely yours,

[signature]

. V. Sanford
rsity of Georgia
s, Georgia

The chancellor's sons. Left to right: Homer Reynolds, Shelton, and
Charles Sanford, ca. 1941. Box 67, Sanford Collection.

S. V. and Grace Sanford and first grandchild Charles, son of their son
Charles and Anne Sanford of Savannah. Golden wedding anniversary, 1945.
Box 67, Sanford Collection.

Dedication of Sanford memorial at Sanford Stadium, October 20, 1945.
Left to right: Harmon Caldwell, Governor Ellis Arnall, Charles S. Sanford Jr.,
Robert Troutman, unidentified. Box 23B, Sanford collection.

student at the university. What might have been a brief note of complaint became a tightly reasoned, multipage single-spaced typewritten missive.[16] In September that same year Sanford's publisher, D. C. Heath, forwarded a letter of inquiry from Frank Watson of Hiawassee, Georgia, for his response. Frank wondered, "where should a child write his name on an essay after the paper is folded?"[17]

In the spring of 1924 Sanford wrote to Thomas W. Reed, secretary of the Board of Trustees of the University of Georgia, in response to a series of questions about the preparations, publications, activities, research, and workloads of the faculty. Sanford reported that his only earned college degree was the bachelor of arts from Mercer and that he had no higher degree other than honorary. He listed the graduate courses he had taken in Berlin, at Oxford, and at the University of Chicago: Anglo-Saxon, Middle English, Schiller, Gothic literature, Beowulf, Shakespeare's predecessors, English literature, and advanced rhetoric. He provided the titles of his three textbooks published by Heath and Company of New York (*Literature and Composition,* 1914; *Composition and Grammar,* 1914 and 1923; and *English Grammar,* 1914), noting that these books had been adopted for use in the schools of Georgia, Alabama, Mississippi, Tennessee, and Oklahoma.[18]

Regarding research in which he was then engaged, Sanford reported that he was working on three manuscripts: "The Spirit of America as Exemplified in Poetry and Prose, The Negro as Art Material, and a Freshman Rhetoric." There followed a question as to whether or not his workload permitted research. Sanford replied that the load was too heavy to write books or articles, saying what he had managed to do had been "under extreme difficulty."[19]

Asked about his interest in teaching graduate level work, Sanford reported that it was essential and expressed his interest in teaching historical English syntax, the growth and development of the newspaper, and Georgia's contribution to literature at that level. When asked what "additional equipment" he might need to enable him to offer these courses, he replied, "two student assistants to help me in grading my English papers."[20]

The questionnaire concluded with an inquiry as to what work he should be relieved of, if any. Sanford's response cuts in two different directions. He mentions not one course he teaches nor one extracurricular activity for which he is responsible that needs relief. He obviously doesn't want to drop anything; rather he suggests, "I really need an assistant to aid me in this outside work that means so much to the University of Georgia."[21]

The "outside work" that year included lectures and speeches all around the state as part of the ongoing routine of making friends and allies for the university. Nineteen twenty-four found Sanford speaking at Buford, Georgia, at Augusta's Richmond Academy, and at the dedication of a new gym in Tate, Georgia; making eligibility judgments for the Southern Conference in regard to tennis, track, baseball, and basketball; responding to more individual grammar questions prompted by his publisher; promoting a system of district summer schools; and dealing with complaints like that of the *Athens Banner-Herald* that May: "I know you have nothing to do with the editorial and news matters of the *Red and Black,* official organ of the Athletic Association, but I know you would not approve the enclosed clipping": The clipping from the *Red and Black* complained that the *Banner-Herald* had not covered a recent track meet on the campus.[22]

While these visible university-related matters occupied Sanford's time, behind the scenes partisans were taking sides and forming camps around the question of the future leadership of the university. Old friend Judge George Gober, Sanford's Marietta associate, member of the University Board of Trustees, occasional faculty in the law school, and frequent guest in the Sanfords' home, had taken it upon himself to form the center of one of these collections of contending forces. As one whose future role at the university would be affected by the outcomes of the struggles among these groups, S. V. Sanford no doubt took to heart an April 1924 missive from the judge: "Having been charged with putting the women into the University, I am deeply interested in having a proper Dean to look after them."[23]

Gober was promoting Anne Brumby as dean of women and his

letter directed Sanford to write several influential parties on behalf of Gober's goal. "We can," wrote Gober, "call a meeting if necessary, the regulars can go to hell." He allowed that, given the right preparation of his handpicked allies, "there is no reason why this crowd cannot control the matter." Gober suggested Sanford might write trustees Fleming and Callaway "but I fear they are illiterates."[24] That is, they would not be supportive of Gober's plans.

It seems legitimate at this point to inquire into the Sanfords' position vis-à-vis the coming of coeducation to the University of Georgia. Among the Sanford letters Gober's contain the only direct reference to women becoming part of the university. Sanford's early career in Marietta had involved teaching and working with young ladies and women, and Grace Sanford was active in the women's organization that had worked for years for coeducation at Georgia. Sanford's early ally Gober was always considered an advocate of the admission of women to the university. The movement for coeducation had first taken shape more than twenty years before Sanford came to Athens, and Chancellor Walter B. Hill, who was said to have inspired Sanford's ambitions to become part of the university, was favorable to the admission of women. Women had been students in the summer school since the year before Sanford's arrival, and his roll books from his early teaching at the university indicate that he taught many women students during those sessions. Some became long-term Sanford devotees.

There is nothing to indicate that the inevitable full admission of women presented Sanford with any undue concern. A study of the coming of coeducation to the university found "no comprehensive written description of the roles played by certain individuals which gave impetus to the development of co-education as a distinct phase of the University's growth."[25] Coeducation at the university was accomplished and a nonissue by the time Sanford became a university administrator.

Gober remained a friend and ally throughout the 1920s, but the fact that his methods stirred some of the more progressive university faithful must have complicated Sanford's diplomacy with groups and individuals of conflicting interests and motives. By the end of the decade, after Sanford had become dean and while Snelling was university chancellor, Gober was briefly dean of the law school, but his methods and tactics had offended to the point that within the year he was maneuvered out of that position to make way for "a more professional leadership" in the law school, Harmon Caldwell.[26]

Contributing to the complexity of the situation in the mid-twenties was the anticipation of Chancellor Barrow's retirement and speculation about his replacement. In 1925 Barrow's resignation was accepted by the Board of Trustees. Before the June meeting of the board to consider Barrow's successor, Sanford had become one of a large field of "nominees" for the position. The field included Governor Charles H. Brough of Arkansas; Dr. E. A. Alderman, president of the University of Virginia; Dean Snelling; President Soule; and Colonel L. R. Gignilliat.[27]

Thomas Dyer's account of the selection process reports that "with the retirement of Chancellor Barrow in 1925, Snelling became acting chancellor, and a year later shed his acting status to become the university's chief executive."[28] Robert Preston Brooks implies that the Board of Trustees of the university was most interested in President Alderman, among those being promoted, but that when Alderman removed himself from consideration the board, with no strong candidate among those remaining, appointed Snelling acting chancellor.[29]

Sanford may have initially been optimistic about his own chances to become chancellor. Judge Gober wrote Sanford early in 1925 that Soule would not be a serious candidate for the chancellorship given his record of heavy-handed dealings with a number of important people. "He has provoked so much antagonism through the state," wrote Gober, "that his election would be unfortunate for the interests of the University."[30]

In addition to Gober, an impressive array of Sanford boosters made their support known. Alex Cunningham of Gainesville, identifying himself as "Captain, Infantry, USA," wrote Sanford in March that when he heard of Barrow's resignation he "naturally thought of [his] old friend," and that he was "deeply interested in doing all [he could] for [Sanford]." Cunningham credited Sanford's work as "doing more for the upbuilding of the Georgia spirit than any other." [31] Writing from Georgia Military College at Milledgeville, E. T. Holmes, president of that institution, said he was "gratified to see that your name is prominently mentioned, and if you want the place, I earnestly hope that it will come to you." [32] H. D. Russell, a Macon lawyer, supported Sanford for the position, agreeing with a recent *Macon Telegraph* editorial which had held that the successful candidate "should be named from among those who have served so long and so faithfully the cause of the University." [33] President Holmes of Georgia Military College wrote again in May: "the impression of those with whom I have talked seems to be that, at the present, you are the strongest man whose name is before the Board." [34] While the credibility of Holmes's support might have been undermined by another letter from him, written the same day, seeking Sanford's support for a position at Mercer, Sanford no doubt chose to overlook or dismiss any connection between the two matters. [35]

The trustees met in June but postponed action until September 11. In that interval Sanford continued to receive encouragement. In late August Luther Elrod forwarded to Sanford a copy of a letter he had written Judge Samuel H. Sibley, a member of the Board of Trustees: "I am writing to suggest a man who is a Georgian and whose people for generations have been leading educators of the State. But he has insisted that I not do so. I think the time has come that I should do so over his protests. The man to whom I refer is Professor S. V. Sanford." Elrod pointed to Sanford's role as "a teacher, authority in the English Language, author of books on English, scholarship, and popularity with both branches of the University." [36]

As the September 11 meeting of the trustees neared, the volume of correspondence about the position grew. By the mid-twenties one of Sanford's largest and most widespread advocacy groups was made up of public school leaders around Georgia. Recommendation after recommendation, many directed to Judge Sibley, spoke of Sanford in the same terms, not mentioning his role in sports at all but rather emphasizing his scholarship, his publications, his character, his speaking abilities, and his capacity for work. H. B. Carreker, superintendent of the Dublin, Georgia, Public Schools; J. H. Purks, superintendent of the Madison Public Schools; G. W. Glausier, vice president of the Georgia Education Association; and M. C. Allen, superintendent of the Calhoun Schools, all wrote similar letters in September.[37]

When the board met in Atlanta on September 11 there was a flurry of nominations, including Sanford, Soule, and Snelling, as well as General Walter A. Harris, Judge Sibley, and Leo W. Branch. Sibley declined to be considered. From those remaining for consideration none had received a majority of votes through five ballots. Harris's father, a member of the board and former governor of Georgia, withdrew his son's name after consulting with him. The board then elected Snelling acting chancellor by a vote of twenty-six to one.[38]

Apparently there was a core of faculty concerns regarding Barrow's successor. One of the Young Turks of the university's English faculty wrote to some important opinion makers in the state asking that they help prevent the selection (for the chancellorship) of "a politician, preacher, or anyone who considered the University a 'sort of glorified business college' or a 'peg upon which to hang athletic trophies.'"[39]

If the proceedings of June 1926, the election of a new chancellor and a new dean, may be considered a contest, then S. V. Sanford, critics or detractors notwithstanding, took second prize, presidency of Franklin College and deanship of the university. This new position was given to Sanford by a vote of 21–5 by the trustees, acting dean Robert Preston Brooks taking the short end of the balloting.[40]

W. C. Kellogg of Augusta, Georgia, wrote Sanford one of the more flowery letters of congratulations on June 20: "The office is no easy one to fill; yet, if you will pardon the bluntness of the implied compliment, I feel sure that you will meet every requirement and shed dignity and lustre upon it. The Lord knows that education in Georgia is in a bad way, from Grammar School to University. Lack of funds, public indifference, selfishness and politics, bigotry and ignorance, false theology, and mean liquor are just a few of the reasons de etre [*sic*], the life of an educator is bound to be for years to come one of self-sacrifice, a via dolorosa [*sic*] that may end in failure, save for the inward consciousness of work well done, duty accomplished and a sure and certain treasure laid up in heaven where moths, rust and politics cannot disturb."[41]

Back on earth Thomas W. Atkins wrote to Sanford from Louisiana State University: "I am pleased to know that you have been made Dean of the University of Georgia, I regret, however, that you may be forced to drop your athletic activities because we need men of your type to aid in keeping athletics clean and on a high plane."[42]

The deanship did lead to a shift in athletic responsibilities. Many of the tasks of faculty chairman of athletics were transferred to the newly defined office of dean of men. According to a communication from S. G. Backman to Chancellor Snelling which outlined the job description of the dean of men, "It is very necessary that the Dean of Men be placed in charge of athletics and all its branches. In this capacity he is to act as assistant to Dr. S. V. Sanford, who is to maintain, as far as his work will allow, his connection with athletics. The Dean of Men is to relieve Dr. Sanford of all duties in connection with athletics, that he may designate."[43]

It was important for Sanford to maintain his links to the programs of athletics at Georgia, especially in light of his plan to build a great football facility on the campus. The plan was not widely shared before 1927, but rumors of such an enterprise had begun to create a stir among students, alumni, and important supporters of the university as early as the first year of Sanford's deanship.

Harry Hodgson pushed Sanford in the fall of 1926 to be sure to inform George Foster Peabody "fully about the stadium." Peabody, for the first quarter of the century, was one of the university's leading benefactors, and to inform him of plans for large buildings and great expenditures was thought by Hodgson to be politic.[44]

In his treatment of the twenties at the university, Thomas Dyer points out that there were "serious concerns" about the prominence given to intercollegiate athletics, the high salaries of coaches, and when plans of the stadium became widely known, "how the institution might fund the construction of a new stadium."[45] The same shadows of questions came from the more critical corners of the student body early in 1927. A student publication, the *Iconoclast,* attacked "hired athletes" and "the borrowing of $200,000 to build an athletic stadium while dormitories were falling apart."[46]

Sanford had already found himself on the defensive about the stadium in the early months of his deanship. President Soule of the agricultural college needed reassuring that the stadium plan was "no plot" in response to the outcry from that quarter surrounding the site selection, which seemed to threaten "King Andy's domain."[47]

Chancellor Barrow's report of June 1919 for the year 1918–19 contained subreports from both Charles Snelling, who was then dean of the university, and Andrew Soule, president of the State Agricultural and Mechanical College.[48] This report for the academic year 1921–22 is noteworthy for its inclusion of favorable comments about Sanford from Chancellor Barrow. He called attention to the "growth in the spirit of fair play in athletic contests" and his gratification at the advances made in this matter. "Professor Sanford," he said in crediting him for this progress, "is a capable and tireless worker." Barrow's brief review of athletics was largely a report on Sanford.

Barrow commented on the great improvement in the athletic field: "The untiring and intelligent efforts of Dr. S. V. Sanford have been very largely responsible for this result. This has been recognized by the University community and the general public by calling the park Sanford Field. In a way the name has been a spontaneous outcome. It has, however, never had the official approval of your Honorable Body. Now that the work is so far advanced as to be nearing completion I venture to suggest that your official sanction be given."[49]

Chancellor Barrow's endorsement of Sanford's activities was no doubt an important element for Sanford's continued success as a significant player in the politics of the university. That support was criti-

cal at every step of the early stages of planning for and building Sanford Stadium. In his last annual report, Chancellor Barrow's opening
comments on athletics reaffirmed his steadfast approval of Sanford's
leadership in that area: "The report of the Faculty Chairman shows
that as regards inter-collegiate athletics, the session was successful,
both from a financial point of view and as to the records of the teams.
More gratifying than either of these, however, is the record of the
players themselves, both on the playing field and in their social and
personal relationships. Wherever our teams have gone, they appear
to have made pleasant and lasting impressions as men as well as
athletes." [50]

When Acting Chancellor Snelling made his report a year later his
comments on athletics were simply excerpted quotations from Professor Sanford's "fine summary of the most important year that the athletic activities have ever had." In selectively quoting from Sanford,
Snelling clearly indicated the importance he placed on broad student
participation in the athletic program rather than focusing on the success of the major sports teams. Figures Snelling provided via quotations from Sanford show seventeen intercollegiate teams, with "five
hundred and sixteen men taking part in these contests," and a nota-
tion that "more than eighty percent of the student body took part in
Freshman and inter-collegiate athletics." [51]

The 1927 annual report is the first in which Sanford has the opportunity to speak directly and completely for himself as president of
Franklin College and dean of the university. His opening comments
clearly revealed an important element of the philosophy Sanford was
to pursue as a major administrator in public higher education in
Georgia, a role he was to play, under different titles, for the remaining
eighteen years of his life.

The latter period of Chancellor Barrow's administration had witnessed growing behind-the-scenes maneuvering and scheming in several quarters for control of the destiny of the sometimes warring elements within the state's institutions of higher education. In the late
teens and throughout the 1920s Georgia's higher education suffered

from irregular legislative support. In an atmosphere of infighting and jealous pursuit of funding, every effort to seek appropriations ran a risk of inciting some investigation by legislators who feared to see "godlessness or elitism" at work in the university. Without certainty of funding, planning and progress were haphazard at best. When state funds did come there seemed to be an inclination to give special consideration to the College of Agriculture, which found favor among the largely rural membership of the state legislature.[52] The term *sacred cows* somehow seems apropos.

By the time of Snelling's chancellorship and Sanford's deanship, it was apparent that the existing organization of Georgia's public higher education, the University of Georgia together with its branches, was not viable. Reorganization, however, was years away.

Premature state-level efforts to bring organizational reform failed in the early 1920s and the problems among the branches persisted, but reform was taken off the table as a publicly debatable issue. The exacerbation of problems came with a flurry of public college building in Georgia. By 1930 four state-supported junior colleges brought the total to "twenty-six colleges, schools, and experiment stations."[53]

S. V. Sanford made his opening shot in the initial paragraph of his 1927 report. Sanford's comments mark a distinct turn from the more passive approach of Chancellor Barrow's administration and toward the more aggressive position favored by Chancellor Snelling: "A clear statement of the duties and responsibilities of the several administrative officers of the University is greatly needed. Methods of procedure must be devised which will promote the unity of the University and the efficiency of its operation. . . . While the duties and responsibilities of every administrative officer should be defined, care should be taken to give him room for the exercise of initiative, originality, and constructive imagination in mapping out plans for the development of the institution. If such persons were encouraged to exercise more authority, more power, more initiative, the institution would make more progress."[54]

In many respects this first report from Sanford as dean represents a manifesto which was his guiding principle from that point forward. He almost seems to be outlining his view of a sound University System for the State of Georgia and in the process drawing up his own job description as chancellor of a true university system. Recalling his "more than twenty years" of working with the administrators of the University of Georgia, Sanford allowed that had "a man from outside been elected to the deanship," he "would be in a serious predicament as to his duties." Sanford believed he had the unique qualifications for leadership that were part of the association with the present, as he considered it, less-than-perfect system of higher education in Athens and across Georgia.[55]

Sanford pulled no punches in describing the pitfalls of an organization with ill-defined responsibilities and powers. "Perhaps," he speculated, "it is not the fault of anyone that such conditions exist—it is perhaps, one of our many traditions that have been preserved. Sentiment is fine—but efficiency is a better business quality."[56] Coming from anyone other than a veteran university figure, Sanford's boldness in proceeding to outline the "problems that confront the University and its branches" might seem inappropriate. His experience in and devotion to the university were such that his boldness was not unexpected or challenged, at least not openly.

His citations of the views of several prominent leaders in higher education around the country indicate that Sanford had given long thought and devoted considerable study to movements and trends which might help Georgia solve some of what he considered to be higher education difficulties. Junior college proliferation was considered a threat in several parts of the country, and Sanford agreed that the ambitions of these two-year institutions to grow into four-year, degree-granting institutions drained the resources and fragmented the progress of higher education in Georgia, as elsewhere. He made no bones about the prevention of these trends: "Some one should be responsible and see to it that needless duplications of effort is [sic] eliminated, and should protect each institution in the lines assigned to it."[57]

Sanford was familiar with the thus far abortive efforts to create a true university system in the state. The economic difficulties of the depression, which came sooner to the South, made it clear that the arguments for efficiency instead of local political favor-granting would sooner rather than later lead to a successful reform in higher education in Georgia. It was as if Sanford's first report anticipated the series of organizational changes and personal moves that would lead, by 1935, to his becoming chancellor, not of the University of Georgia, but of the University System of Georgia: "Georgia needs leadership in many lines but in none so much as in higher education. Permit me to say, as the Chancellor himself might hesitate to say, that no one is better qualified to present the cause of higher education to the people than the Chancellor of the University of Georgia. . . . He can bring to pass a unification of our system and a workable plan for the support of a University and its branches. My plea is that as the State needs an able and wise leader in higher education, and the time has come for the Chancellor, not in name but in fact, to be the head of the University system, rather than the head of a single part here in Athens." [58]

The journey from deanship of the University of Georgia and the presidency of Franklin College to the chancellorship of a reorganized system was not to be a short one. Almost ten years would pass between Sanford's first report as dean and his chancellorship. On the organizational chart, the move seemed simple. Dean Snelling became the university chancellor; Sanford became the dean. The university chancellor became the system chancellor; and Sanford became president of the University of Georgia. Finally, Sanford followed Snelling into the chancellorship. For the intervening six years, 1926–1932, before Sanford became university president, he staked his claim while tending relationships that had led him to this place in his career.

As dean, Sanford continued many of the practices that had endeared him to students and parents over the years. Students wrote to thank him for supporting their attendance at special conferences, parents wrote to thank him for his kindness to their sons, and Sanford wrote any number of letters to anxious parents reporting on the progress, or lack thereof, on the part of their children. While the far greater part of these communications were laudatory of Sanford's efforts, occasionally disappointed students or parents thoroughly took it out on the dean. A particularly disappointed writer who signed his April 1927 letter to Dr. Sanford "a boy that was once a student but am not now" took the entire university to task for playing favorites in allowing athletes to return to school under circumstances which kept the nonathletically inclined out of college. He called the university a "money-making machine" for misleading his father about his ability to succeed there. "Why in name of God didn't you tell him that [I] was not ready for college and not let him spend his money for nothing, or something else. I think you owe me an apology for what you said and owe my father one also. Well I could write you many more things but am tired. Understand I don't want to hurt your reputation nor your feeling I am telling you what I think. Hope you Good luck."[59]

The heavy volume of Sanford's correspondence included some with people who would be among the state's best known and most powerful figures: Ellis G. Arnall, a student at the University of the South, later became governor during Sanford's chancellorship; and Eugene Talmadge, at the time Georgia's commissioner of agriculture, became governor during part of Sanford's presidency and chancellorship. Both were in correspondence with Dean Sanford in the spring of 1927. Arnall wrote about visiting Sanford and the possibility of attending Georgia the following year, and Talmadge heard from Sanford on behalf of James W. Setze. Setze was identified as an agriculture department employee whom Sanford and his brother-in-law D. F. McClatchey wanted Talmadge to retain. Sanford described Setze as "a man with a large family who really needs the post," and explained that "McClatchey and I are greatly interested in James W. Setze as he is our brother-in-law."[60]

With the completion of the stadium, the gala dedication game, and the end of Sanford's presidency of the Southern Conference, the focus turned away from sports and in the direction of Sanford's plans for the university and, more important, the creation of a true university system.

Many of the ideas for a statewide educational organization directed by a board of regents had germinated during the late teens and into the twenties. Initially Sanford's forum for expounding his views about these ideas was limited to the campus of the university. By the second year of his deanship, however, he was corresponding with administrators on the campuses of other state colleges, sending a draft of "an act to create a State Board of Higher Education." Sanford described it as the "newest movement in higher education" and insisted that it was needed to govern junior colleges and four-year colleges and to act as an accrediting agency. He wanted it to "have power to prevent overlapping and wasteful expenditures of State money." He cited the existence of engineering and commerce schools at both the university and at Tech as examples of the current duplication problems and asked, "why should new institutions be created to gratify a political faction when the state is not able to support what already exists?"

Sanford described, without the use of the title *chancellor*, "a high class executive secretary" to act on behalf of a board whose members would serve without pay. His projected job description called for "a man of education, talent, with ten years of college experience." Such a figure "would be the most important educational officer in the state from the standpoint of higher education." In Sanford's view "he would be to the colleges what Duggan [State Superintendent of Schools] is to the public school, but would be removed from politics."[61] Just how to make this last qualification a reality was not explained. It is difficult to imagine that Sanford did not have himself in mind as he described the new post.

The 1927–28 report of the dean of the university reiterated Sanford's concerns about needless and wasteful duplication of services in Georgia in higher education, especially the growing junior college movement. On the one hand he dismissed junior colleges as a somewhat beneficial entity: "Perhaps it may not be uncharitable to say that one of the merits of these new institutions will be keeping out of college, rather than leading into it, young people who have no natural taste for higher education." [62] Sanford quoted Harvard's Dr. Lowell, who saw junior colleges as beneficial diversions for students who otherwise might try four-year colleges but "are the types that would probably be misfits in the American College after a year or two drop out or be a drag on the rest of the class." [63]

What Sanford feared, however, was the tendency he saw in Georgia for such two-year colleges to become four-year degree-granting colleges. This he viewed as "a serious blunder in [his] judgement, whether considered from the viewpoint of the best interest of higher education or of the bright young men. The State of Georgia cannot support the present system of higher education and yet nothing seems to be done to stop the overlapping system and the creating year by year of additional institutions to be starved."

As Sanford reached toward the future of the state's higher education system and his own professional future, he found it necessary to continue to fight the critics who found fault with the stadium project and what was perceived as an overemphasis on sports. Both he and Chancellor Snelling addressed the nay-sayers of stadium building in the 1927–28 chancellor's report. Snelling's opening sentence in the section of his report on "Athletics-Stadium" fully reveals his posture: "An interest or activity that appeals to the popular imagination and wins the sustained interest of people generally while it makes for physical development, mental alertness and honorable self-denial, must exert a valuable influence, especially upon young people, notwithstanding defects that attach to it." [64]

Dean Sanford's section on "Athletics" also dismissed the critics in an opening shot: "From time to time articles both in the daily press and in the leading magazines attack intercollegiate athletics, particularly football. The main indictment against intercollegiate football is overemphasis. Certainly there is overemphasis, but not nearly so much by college students and college faculties as by the American people." [65]

Sanford took to task "those professors in our faculty who are still living in the past and who are not in sympathy with the changes that have taken place in college life in the last quarter of a century." Football, he insisted, had found its place in American collegiate life and it was a proper place.[66]

Laurence Veysey's study of the rise of the American university at the turn of the century addresses the role of football as part of the larger evolution that took place in American higher education about the time S. V. Sanford was beginning his career in Georgia. Veysey's work focuses on the eastern, western, and midwestern institution, virtually ignoring the South. This omission may be considered a silent description of higher education in that region. The South was, as in so many other institutional matters, a lagging region, not fitting the patterns in the other regions of the country. Much of Veysey's description of events outside the South became valuable for the region a decade or so after the fact elsewhere. This interpretation has value for understanding Sanford and what was, for some, "the football issue."

Football, which in the 1890s hit the mainstream (nonsouthern) universities, fit the contours of the shifts in American higher education. The new wave of universities faced the reconciliation of the traditional, the romantic, the insular, with change, new students, the practical. Football "was both romantic [with its heroes] and real [physical]." There was in football "the frenzy of solidarity."[67] The game emphasized the practical rather than the abstract powers, asserting itself as "the archetypical expression of the student temperament and for a time threatened to make the purpose of the American University expressive in a single short sentence."[68] Three decades beyond this experience outside the South, S. V. Sanford, in the late 1920s, for good or evil, consciously or unconsciously, understood this rationale and accepted it as a defensible creed for the University of Georgia.

Choosing to report on the stadium separately, Sanford defended its value in bringing people to the campus who would see the needs of the university. "The Stadium," he anticipated, "here as elsewhere will no doubt prove to be the incentive or pacemaker for better and bigger things."[69]

It would be an error to think of the mid- and late twenties as simply a bipolar world for Sanford, an athletic forum in balance with a growing interest and effort in the direction of a refined state higher education system. Life was never that simple for S. V. Sanford. A sampling of university committee membership rolls reveals that during this period (1926–30), Sanford served on the following: absences, athletics, curriculum, general lectures, schedule, student social activities, student publications, scholarship records, academic records, university extension, and public relations.

Illness was the repayment for Sanford's overextension. A number of letters to Sanford refer to his health during the late winter and early spring of 1928. His health problems continued into 1929. George Woodruff wrote from Columbus that he was sorry to hear of recent bouts of "acute appendicitis." Woodruff encouraged him to take care of himself and insisted that he turn the details of all the football games in Athens over to Stegeman: "With your many other duties I am truly afraid that if you attempt to attend to the details of Ga-Yale and Ga-Tech games for next season, it will prove to your decided detriment." Woodruff expressed his enthusiasm for having Tech and Yale in Athens "but when I think of what may be the result as far as you are concerned it dampens my enthusiasm to a great extent. These games are worth a great deal to Georgia, but they would not be worth anything if all that work caused you to have another breakdown." [70]

A letter written to Sanford two days later by Dr. F. Phinizy Calhoun of Atlanta seconded Woodruff's concerns: "You are too important to your family and the University to take any chances and a reasonably [sic] amount of care on your part will keep you well and strong. Don't forget that your health just now is the most important thing in your life." [71]

As the twenties ended, part of Sanford's health-threatening pace peaked; the stadium was completed and dedicated, and Sanford's quarter-century chairmanship of the university's athletic committee ended as did his leadership of the Southern Conference.

The new decade dawned on great change and challenge for the

university, higher education in Georgia, and S. V. Sanford. The long-discussed and much delayed reorganization of public higher educa-tion came with the election as governor of Georgia of Richard B. Rus-sell Jr., whose campaign had promised efficiency in government and the reduction of the number of agencies and boards that competed among themselves for depression-trimmed state resources. Russell's victory was the signal for Sanford's rise from dean to university presi-dent, success as unifier of the university, and ascension to head of the University System in the first half of the new decade.

SEVEN

Chancellor-in-Waiting
1930-1934

Dick Russell's 1930 election as governor of Georgia set in motion Steadman Sanford's elevation to his last position in the University System, that of chancellor. Russell, thanks to the severe impact of the depression, was armed with a mandate to reorganize state government, make it more efficient, and cut costs. The disorderly arrangement of public higher education was a prime target of the Reorganization Act of 1931. Thanks to legislative studies in the late twenties there already existed an outline for a new system: a board of eleven regents with broad powers and the authority to organize Georgia's public higher education as they saw fit. Charles Snelling was nominal executive officer of the system, operating with the title chancellor of the University System of Georgia. Sanford was named president of the University of Georgia, taking an old title. In his brief time as chancellor, Snelling's role was minimal. The real leadership came from the newly created board, notably regent Hughes Spalding of Atlanta. Spalding and Philip Weltner, who replaced Snelling from mid-1933 until Sanford was appointed in July 1935, in turn depended on President Sanford to address the most pressing crisis in the new organization: the fragmentation of the university at Athens.

At one point Sanford complained to Spalding that the board had been hasty in selecting Snelling. It seems obvious, however, that the presidency of the university, at this critical point of transition, was more important than the chancellorship, and that Sanford's success in Athens would pave a clear path to his headship of the entire system. Given these circumstances, the period 1930–35, the last two years of Sanford's deanship of Franklin College and his interval as president of the university, was clearly preparatory to the chancellorship.

Sanford's children were enjoying their early years of establishing their families and careers by this time. In the early thirties Shelton and Charles were both married and living in Savannah; Charles was resident manager of the investment department of the Trust Company of Georgia at its Savannah office in the Liberty National Bank and Trust, and Shelton was practicing medicine in a civil service position. Homer Reynolds was married and in the insurance business in Atlanta.[1] Elsewhere on the family front Grace was enjoying her club work and becoming a statewide figure herself, thanks to her presidency of the Georgia Federation of Women's Clubs. Her biography, published in conjunction with that office, makes notice of her involvement in the United Daughters of the Confederacy, the Colonial Dames, and Daughters of the American Revolution. Among her interests were entertaining, motoring, theater-going, and traveling. She was a Sunday school teacher of the Athens Methodist Episcopal Church, and a member of the National Democratic Congressional Committee for Georgia.[2]

Several months before the first official meeting of the newly created Board of Regents, Hughes Spalding wrote Sanford regarding the composition of the new board, addressing the letter to the home address on Cloverhurst. At this point Sanford apparently harbored the hope that he would be appointed chancellor, and Spalding was his most important ally in this ambition. In informing Sanford of the list of proposed regents, Spalding said he was not telling anyone else (except Marion Smith) and "If there is any such thing as an inside track, I wanted you to have it."[3]

Given the appointment of Snelling as chancellor, it might seem that

Spalding had failed in his mission. A closer examination of the situation, however, reveals that Sanford's appointment in Athens as president was more critical at this juncture for the success of the transition to a new university system organization and for Sanford's future as the leader of that new system.

Governor Russell's reorganization of state government was still in the process of being put into place when U.S. Senator William J. Harris died in 1932 and Governor Russell successfully ran to replace him. Russell appointed the first members of the Board of Regents, one from each of the congressional districts: Hughes Spalding, Cason Callaway, Richard B. Russell Sr., M. D. Dickerson, A. Pratt Adams, W. J. Vereen, T. F. Green, Martha Berry, W. D. Anderson, and George C. Woodruff; Philip Weltner was named member-at-large. But it would be Russell's successor, Governor Talmadge, with whom the board had to deal.[4]

The January 1, 1932, meeting of the Board of Regents, chaired by W. D. Anderson of Macon, gave the head of the system the title chancellor and named Charles Snelling. They also created the position of president of the University of Georgia and named S. V. Sanford to that position.

The correspondence between board member Spalding and president of the university Sanford continued with great regularity. As soon as Sanford assumed his new position, Spalding began to communicate information and requests which seem to go beyond what might be considered the ordinary dealings between a board member and the president of a single institution in the system. It was still in a day of "man-to-man" business and politics. These men knew and respected each other and shared ambitions and disappointments freely along with occasional complaints and demands. Spalding had taken a special interest in the early history of Georgia and found that university history faculty member E. Merton Coulter was a promising source of publication in that field. Spalding urged President Sanford to make sure Coulter had relief from his course load in order to pursue his Georgia history research. He closed a January 1932 letter: "Do not overlook to make arrangements next fall so that Professor Coulter can have a leave of absence."[5] As the months passed matters much more pressing and critical to the success of the new Board of Regents occupied Spalding's mind and became the focal point of his requests and demands of Sanford.

The *Red and Black* of January 22, 1932, profiled both the new chancellor and the new president of the university. It is interesting that the piece on Sanford is the longer and more laudatory.[6] Long-time benefactor George Foster Peabody wrote Sanford early in the first months of his presidency to extend congratulations and to express the hope that he would "have the same measure of support for [his] energetic efforts that [he was] able to develop in connection with the athletic equipment, and, perhaps not less effectively but even more, as to putting Georgia on the map."[7]

Sanford's role in university sports and his high profile in association with the football team and the building of the stadium had, for many who knew him, defined his career at the university to this point. The presidency, however, brought an end to the most active part of that earlier stage of Sanford's career at Georgia. Among his friends were many who shared Ralph McGill's sweet sadness in this transition. McGill, in 1932 a sportswriter for the *Atlanta Constitution,* wrote of Sanford: "No man ever wielded more genius for organization and direction than he. Southern athletics owe him a great deal. Sanford as Athletic Chairman was willing to stay up all night and talk football. In the mighty task of managing a great University Georgia could not have found a finer more capable man as President yet I will miss him in football."[8]

Early in its existence the new University System made a shift in strategy regarding leadership among the elements of the system based in Athens. Initially, plans called for retention of strict identities for the Teachers College, the university, and the College of Agriculture, led by Jere M. Pound, Steadman Sanford, and Andrew Soule respectively. It is not altogether difficult to believe that the apparent change of direction toward "integration" of the university under Sanford had been the plan all along, awaiting the appointment of the board and the revealing of the agenda of its leading figures, Hughes Spalding and Philip Weltner. This alliance, along with Weltner's early appointment to replace Anderson as chairman of the board, assured the continuation of Sanford's "inside track." The domination of board policy by Spalding and Weltner assured a tough initial job for Sanford in Athens, but a smooth path from there to the chancellorship.

Communications between Spalding and Sanford during 1932 and 1933 fit into two distinct categories; at least the letters to Sanford from Spalding do. When the communications were of a general and official nature Spalding addressed Sanford at the campus; when there were more private or privileged letters they were addressed to the Cloverhurst address, Sanford's home. This pattern suggests an awareness of the delicate nature of the special relationship between the two men.

Early in 1932 Spalding sent to Sanford, Andrew Soule, and M. L. Brittain, president of the Georgia Institute of Technology, a copy of the rules and regulations adopted by the Board of Regents in their initial January 1 meeting. Spalding instructed Sanford to show these items to Chancellor Snelling and "go over them completely with him." Spalding also asked for "suggestions" about the regents' by-laws. Evidence of Spalding's devotion to Sanford's success and future may be seen in the fact that Spalding shared with Sanford copies of his confidential communications with then chairman of the Board of Regents, W. D. Anderson of Macon. Within two weeks of the initial meeting of the board, Sanford was privy to Spalding's strong statement to Anderson that "Andy" Soule must be kept in check and not allowed to dominate matters in Athens by means of his narrow interpretations of federal laws as they affected the distribution of federal funds for higher education.[9]

For years there had been discord regarding the relationship of the University of Georgia and the units of the university, that is, the agricultural and mechanical branches, especially in regard to the distribution of funds. The branches or units wanted to lay claim to funds as independent units but to declare graduates of their programs as graduates of the University of Georgia. Early in his tenure as president of the university Sanford wrote his mentor/benefactor and former boarder Hughes Spalding as to his personal desire to keep the name of the university off diplomas except as used in conjunction with the new "University System of Georgia."[10]

In earlier years Andrew Soule's heavy-handed domination of matters in Athens had been witnessed by Sanford from a subordinate role as faculty member and dean. As president of a university at the point of being redefined, Sanford unloosed his pent-up frustrations. By the spring of 1932 Hughes Spalding had an earful of difficulties in Athens. Sanford asserted that President Soule did not pay his fair share of administrative costs in Athens, that he "worried [Sanford] to death about these diplomas," and that he always wanted concessions "but will give none." Regarding the county-supplied labor under Soule's supervision, Sanford wrote Spalding, "I have had the convicts for a week, and he [Soule] calls me every hour to send them back to work on his campus. It is this eternal nagging that ran Chancellors Barrow and Snelling crazy."[11]

A file copy of a note from Sanford's secretary to Lloyd Grandy in Sandersville, Georgia, dated April 7, 1932, apologized for a delay in some matter. The explanation defined the vortex that was Steadman Sanford's early months in his new role as president of the university: "Dr. Sanford is terribly busy at present with the reorganization of the University of Georgia."[12]

Hughes Spalding saw President Soule as the chief obstacle to a successful reorganization of the university and thus a major impediment to a true university system. By April Spalding had focused on the debate over the use of the name of the degree-granting institution as the issue with which to make his move to end Soule's obstructionism: "If the State College of Agriculture cannot [stand] alone," Spalding wrote Sanford, "it should be integrated with the University of Georgia. It seems to me that the sooner the Regents find it out the better." The die was cast.[13]

In mid-April Spalding writing Sanford again at his home, but showing copies to board chairman Anderson and fellow regent Philip

Weltner, addressed directly the fate of the College of Agriculture. At the time of the writing, Spalding stated that he was not sure of that fate but expected that the regent committees on education and law seemed to have the responsibility for taking direction of the matter. He said he and Weltner would discuss it before the next board meeting and reach "some kind of decision." It is difficult to believe a decision had not already been made. Spalding asked for confidentiality, "as we do not wish to stir up political activities on the part of the Heads of any of the Institutions." [14]

Apparently Spalding and Weltner decided on a strategy quickly. On April 20 a notice was sent to Sanford, Soule, and Jere Pound, president of the teachers college in Athens, to meet with Chancellor Snelling, Spalding, and Philip Weltner on April 26, three days before the next scheduled meeting of the full board. [15]

The spring 1932 actions of the board in defining the respective roles of the three institutions in Athens were apparently acts of imperfect reform. Sections 33, 33a, and 33b of the by-laws of the Board of Regents were amended at the April meeting of the board, on the recommendation of the Committee on Education and the Committee on Law. Section 33 as amended identified the University of Georgia as being composed of Franklin College, Georgia State College of Agricultural and Mechanical Arts, and Georgia State Teachers College. Section 33a, however, defined as the "official head" of each element a "President." Genuine integration called for something beyond an alteration of by-laws. [16]

In June W. D. Anderson resigned from the Board of Regents and Hughes Spalding replaced him as chairman. [17] As chairman, Spalding pressed forward, urging Sanford to work out real integration. Two letters, one from Sanford to Spalding dated June 20, 1932, and one from Spalding to Sanford dated June 23, 1932, reveal the tensions and problems inherent for Sanford in putting an old, if irascible, colleague in his place, and for Spalding in understanding the apparently glacial pace of change in the setting of academic politics and manners. Sanford wrote of Soule: "He is a wonder in many respects but lacks the spirit of cooperation. At heart he means well, but gets himself in many difficult situations. He lacks tact and good judgement and needs someone to direct in a firm manner." [18] Spalding, if nothing else, approved the "firm" direction of Soule and saw Sanford as responsible for that process. While Sanford's letter maintained that "integration is taking place" and that Soule was "coming along since he realized his predicament," [19] Spalding's patience was growing short.

Soule had been called on the carpet by the board in April. A special meeting of the board was called for May 10, where Soule defended himself against charges of being uncooperative and dispelled talk of fiscal improprieties regarding the use of federal funds in the agricultural college. In the face of the possibility that he would be fired, Soule promised his full support for the wishes of the board despite his well-known and admitted objections to a truly unified university. Soule was reelected, but the summer was proving a stormy continuation, at least in the eyes of an eager Hughes Spalding, of old evidence of obstructionist actions on Soule's part. Spalding's exasperation is obvious in his June letter to Sanford: "You have the most responsible position in the whole University System, and you have the most difficult situation to handle. One of your associates will run over you, if you let him. The other one is your good friend, but I am doubtful if he knows how to serve you best. . . . You have got to be cold-blooded and businesslike and shove all opposition aside. . . . You will have to tell Dr. Soule what to do and must make him do it. You will have to tell Dr. Pound what to do, how to do it, and then you must see that he does it. This is a big job for any man, and you must play the part of a hard-boiled executive." [20]

Spalding assured Sanford of the backing of the board and emphasized personal support: "Philip Weltner and I, and the rest of the Board, will back you up in this to the limit. I am frank to say we will be disappointed if you do not run the three integrated institutions, at Athens, just like you think they ought to be run, irrespective of opposition. You should know you are right and then execute your plans. You are in a position to do more than anybody in the System. You have the ability to do it, you know how to do it, and if you do not knock the opposition down to start with, it will nag, annoy and worry you until you will lose your efficiency. You can do anything you want to do in Athens, except commit murder, and we will back you up 100 percent. Personally, I will back up your committing murder 100 percent, and so will Philip and George—all I ask you to do is be certain to kill the right man." [21]

Sanford's sanity may well have been preserved that summer only by way of his trip to Chicago in June as a delegate to the National Democratic Convention. "I have just returned from Chicago where I had a great time," he wrote Earle Cocke, secretary-treasurer of the Board of Regents early in July. Sanford was pleased to have had a chance to get "an outlook on national politics." He was also grateful for the temporary relief from the details of University System business. "I have had so much work to do integrating these institutions," he wrote Cocke, "that I felt it would be less costly and less embarrassing to my family if I went to Chicago rather than go to Milledgeville." He closed assuring Cocke that he was "much refreshed and ready to begin duties again." [22]

Hughes Spalding wrote Andrew Soule in early August, ostensibly about his support for the improvement of grounds and campus beautification. "The Regents are determined," Spalding's letter insisted, "that the three institutions at Athens must cooperate and work together. We will never get anywhere until everybody reaches the conclusion that this is an accomplished fact." [23] A blind copy of the letter was sent to Sanford.

Amid the swirl of dispute, obstructionism, and uncompromising demands on all sides, President Sanford completely revised the university *Bulletin* in keeping with the aims of the regents. Regents Weltner and Spalding were effusive in their praise of the resulting product. "You have wrought well and not only deserve appreciation but have it in full measure," wrote Weltner. "It sets a new tempo for the Old University." [24]

The welcome distraction of national politics resumed after Labor

Day. Sanford, an ardent Roosevelt supporter, was locally involved in fundraising for the party and writing the usual form letters regarding support for FDR. Hughes Spalding, however, continued to pepper Sanford with almost daily letters regarding "the situation in Athens," "important matters, and a great many things that you and I should talk about."[25]

The primacy of Spalding's role in Sanford's world, personally as well as professionally, made it difficult for the Atlanta lawyer to be given anything but priority attention. The October 1932 dedication of the Harold Hirsch Law School building involved a tightening of an already close working relationship between the two men. The invitation list, weighted heavily with lawyers, bankers, businessmen, and political and educational leaders, was a cooperative product of the two. They didn't seem to miss a single important connection.[26]

The rewards for his efforts were sweet for Sanford and he was generous in his compliments for partner Spalding. He thanked Spalding for his "kind words relative to me and my work at the dedication. Many times my wife and children have remarked, 'the good Lord never made a more lovely and considerate person than Hughes.'"[27]

In spite of the mutual admiration, Sanford was comfortable in complaining to Spalding about the ongoing troubles relative to the university; Spalding, for his part, was not above pinning Sanford down about pet irritations. The way in which the university library was being managed was a special Spalding concern. "From what I hear," wrote Spalding, "it is being very efficiently mismanaged." Stealing a newly minted FDR phrase Spalding said, "It seems to me that the library should be entitled to a new deal." He then reminded Sanford that while the law school was in excellent shape, there were areas other than the library that needed attention. "It will involve the wielding of the axe," warned Spalding, "and we can't afford to be buried in mediocrity for sentimental reasons." Spalding told Sanford he wanted him to "get the axe sharpened up because you will certainly have to use it before long."[28]

President Sanford let his hair down a bit at the end of October,

writing regent Spalding in defense of the status of the library and be-
moaning the university's financial situation. "The forces have been
against me but I now have them in hand thanks to you and Weltner."
He claimed that he did not wish to reflect on the chancellor but "I
inherited an institution run down at the heels and one that is financially bankrupt." [29] Given such conditions it would be too much to
expect the university library to be in the best of condition or able to
have staff sufficient to most effectively administer its collections. The
business of axe sharpening, he felt, might well have been attended to
by his predecessor. Spalding, in his reply, advised Sanford to take a
break and get away from the campus and its pressures. Spalding, however, suspected he wouldn't because "you do not want to leave Athens
because in your absence Dr. Soule will preside at faculty meetings."
Spalding advised that he "give that a trial. It will make you all the more
appreciated." [30]

Reductions in state support for higher education had begun in the
late 1920s and double-digit salary cuts were imposed on faculty with
the threat of more cuts to come before the end of 1932. This situation
especially complicated Sanford's position vis-à-vis President Soule in
Athens. Soule, long a beneficiary of federal support for agricultural
programs, had kept the portion of his budget devoted to salaries at
45 percent, while Sanford and his predecessors operated with personnel costs of around 75 percent of budget. When budget cuts were issued Soule could make them, at least up to a point, without having to
drastically cut into salaries. Sanford was not left that relative luxury.
More dissension and complaint ensued. [31] Spalding responded that
Sanford should reduce his own budget in the personnel side until it
neared 65 percent, leaving him more room for maneuver in the event
of further cuts. [32] Meanwhile, it was becoming more obvious that true
consolidation and integration, if it was to mean improvements in the
fiscal management of operations, would require a radically new feature, lump sum appropriations to the regents from the legislature.

In the name of efficiency of operations, cutting of duplicate programs, and needless internal competition, the case was to be made to

bring about this dramatic change and with it the power to eliminate institutions. For a state where long traditions supported individualism of institutions and localism protected inefficiency, these changes were so unheard-of as to be thinkable only under the most pressing of economic circumstances. The depression provided those circumstances.

Nineteen thirty-two ended in a flurry of regents' business for Sanford. Much of it was encouraging; some of it possibly alarming. Sanford wrote Weltner concerning the budget. It was in this element of the business of consolidation that Sanford felt that "not much [had] been accomplished." [33]

The communication chairman Weltner sent to "Heads of All Institutions" dated December 25, 1932, seemed to provide the answer for which Sanford hoped. Weltner explained that the upcoming General Assembly would "make a searching inquiry" of the system in view of the regents' request for a lump sum appropriation for the system rather than separate allocations for institutions. Weltner described the change as an "outward manifestation of the inward change." While this was addressed to units beyond the campus in Athens, it must have seemed directly aimed at President Soule. Weltner reasoned that each of the institution heads "must have pondered the part you are to play in days to come." Will you "circularize" the legislature in behalf of your institution? Seek to get direct appropriations? "Each of these expedients," he allowed, "is subversive to what the University System was intended to become. My own recommendation would be that we voluntarily abolish every vestige of an educational lobby." [34] Given the support he had been assured by Weltner and Spalding, it seems obvious that this was good news for S. V. Sanford.

While the inside support of Weltner and Spalding was assuring, it could also have its down side, as at the very end of 1932 when Hughes Spalding unilaterally removed the dean of the law school of the University of Georgia. Dean H. M. Edmunds was caught up in health and financial difficulties, and there was pressure to replace him. Spalding took things in hand. Spalding wrote Chancellor Snelling and President Sanford that he had met with Edmunds and that in order to prevent "a source of embarrassment to the University of Georgia and the System," he had offered $2,500 in paid leave. Edmunds had accepted, and Spalding had granted the leave and paid him off. "I hope you two gentlemen will not think that I was presumptuous in handling this matter," wrote Spalding, "write me if you approve or not."[35] The responses of Snelling and Sanford are not available, but Harmon Caldwell, soon to be dean of the law school, wrote Sanford in distress, asking that the matter of the leave for Edmunds be reconsidered and assuring the president that Edmunds would get his act straightened out.[36] Applications for the vacant position were pouring in before the dawn of the new year.

Nineteen thirty-three opened to more gloomy financial prospects for the University System. A statement of the liabilities and unpaid appropriations revealed almost one and a quarter million dollars of unpaid appropriations at the system level at the end of 1932. For the university there was approximately $150,000; for Georgia Tech there was more. On the other side of the ledger, Tech's obligations stood at only a little over seventy-six thousand dollars while the university's amounted to more than a quarter of a million dollars.[37]

Money problems worked in two directions on the university. While state appropriations declined precipitously, there were increases in tuition income, thanks to the growing enrollment. The lack of jobs was a driving force in motivating more young people to attend college. Among those growing numbers of students, however, was an increasing volume of cases of personal financial difficulties. To Sanford's larger fiscal concerns were added the individual appeals of scores of parents whose sons or daughters faced having to leave the university unless Sanford could come to their rescue in some fashion. In a single week early in the new year, Sanford received appeals from Brooklet, Rochelle, Forsyth, and Greenville, Georgia, parents who faced such difficulty.[38]

Revenue sources were drying up and the state faced a crisis of meeting allocations on all fronts. Sanford had lived through a long period at the university during which he had come to believe that the support of the institution was truly more from the alumni and friends than from the state anyway. He had seen the only building take place with their support and realized that in this period of special difficulty, new sources of support must be considered. It is not surprising that he came to favor and fervently seek not only new sales taxes, but Roosevelt's New Deal programs as additional means of keeping the university not only alive, but growing.[39]

Sanford was certain that continued fine-tuning of the consolidation in the system and at the university would allow for cost savings through "a more efficient" operation. In his notes on this subject to Hughes Spalding, he outlined practices which, if he was allowed the power to carry them out, would be fiscally beneficial. Among them was the elimination of overtime for full-time employees, close examination of and justification for expense accounts, and twelve-month contracts that precluded special, additional contracts for summer school work. He also favored a form of wider income distribution by means of allowing no more than one member of a family to be employed by the University ("except under unusual circumstances").[40]

Despite the Christmas Day 1932 admonitions of chairman Weltner, Sanford could not resist working the crowd at the capitol in the interests of his university. Patron Hughes Spalding wrote Sanford in late January: "I quote you as follows from the January 21 issue of *Atlanta Life*. 'President S. V. Sanford of the University of Georgia was among those present in the legislature corridors this week. Informally, smoking a cigarette, he was holding conversation with all and sundry just outside the doors of the Senate.'" Sanford's January 1933 files include a form letter containing the following: "The Board . . . respectfully requests you to refrain from legislative activity."[41]

Cautionary notes from Weltner or Spalding about his visibility in the halls of the legislature may have temporarily interrupted one approach to effective participation in the changes being wrestled with over the young system, but Sanford had a large inventory of tactics to which he could turn. Sanford advised Spalding in late January 1933: "You should ask five of us to meet with you and Earle [Cocke] for planning purposes." He suggested not letting the invited individuals know who else was to be part of the meeting. Among those who should meet was a member of the legislature "who lives in Governor Talmadge's district." The president was "sure we should have as many of the Talmadge fanatics on our side as possible." Early in the new governor's administration there were pockets of resistance to the regents and even hints of the abolition of the board. Talmadge had mildly supported this opposition during the campaign.[42]

Sanford's activities on behalf of the system and the regents were not all limited to letters of advice from Athens. In a note from Sanford to W. W. Stancil, superintendent of the Fitzgerald schools, the president allowed that he had "been spending most of his time in Atlanta looking after the bills introduced by the Regents."[43] He wrote state Senator Andrew J. Tuten to thank him for the "service you rendered us."[44] Tuten had only in the previous month called for Hughes Spalding's resignation from the regents. Sanford saw such people as adversaries to be won over rather than enemies with whom to continue losing battles. Pragmatic politics left few outside of S. V. Sanford's circle of friendly communications and contacts. Sometimes, as in the case of Sanford's campaign for a general sales tax in support of education, he resorted to broadcast-style mailings of booklets or copies of speeches from his office at the university. In more recent times this use of his office might have caused difficulties, but not in the climate of the politics of depression-era Georgia.

Robert Hutchins, president of the University of Chicago, wrote to Sanford: "Let me congratulate you again on the wonderful progress you are making in the development of your System. I have seen nothing as encouraging anywhere in the country."[45] Despite such praise from distinguished figures, Spalding felt it necessary from time to time to caution Sanford about being too easily within reach of the clutches of members of the legislature. "We must stay away from members of the General Assembly," he advised; "they want to trade help for jobs, and if that ever starts, the University System will be doomed."[46]

Spalding's anxieties peaked in mid-March 1933. Worsening economic prospects, the specter of even more radical salary cuts, and the board's inability to use Chancellor Snelling effectively in working through these and other problems resulted in a hard letter to Sanford. "Plain language," Spalding asserted, "is necessary on account of the very critical situation in which we find ourselves." He called for cuts "to the bone" and the reduction of the university organization "to a mere skeleton." "It is not beyond the realms of probability," cautioned Spalding, "that the University System may be compelled to be temporarily discontinued."

Spalding urged Sanford to get his report and recommendations in final form. "If I lose your friendship and affection it will be a matter of deepest concern to me, but after Philip and I have been forced to take all the responsibility, I feel like it is my duty to see that this job is done as it should be." He concluded the letter with a reminder that the regents were giving "at least 90 percent of their time and thought to the situation at Athens." Spalding found that "absolutely unfair to the other institutions in the System."[47]

The same day Sanford received Spalding's communication, he got a letter from Philip Weltner, briefer by far, but firmly establishing April 1, 1933, as the deadline for Sanford's report.[48] The report and recommendations were in hand in time for the mid-April board meeting, which indeed completed the integration of the university and the reorganization of the system. The recommendations were in part a response to Sanford's recommendations, in part from a consultant study's suggestions, but most from the prevailing views of regents Philip Weltner and Hughes Spalding.

The tensions and demands of the spring were eased temporarily for Sanford when he was able to enjoy his role as host with Mrs. Sanford of a large luncheon at Memorial Hall on the university campus in conjunction with the Ninth Annual Religious Welfare Conference. This was a traditional university event cosponsored by the YMCA and YWCA. Bishop Francis J. McConnell of the Methodist Episcopal Church from New York was the featured speaker, and Dr. and Mrs.

Sanford extended invitations all around Georgia for their luncheon honoring McConnell. If Sanford felt buffeted about by the regents as president, he could and did exercise a more comfortable certainty of authority. A note to all faculty requested "that no member of the faculty, for any reason whatsoever be absent on the occasion" of McConnell's address.[49]

Sanford may be excused for this uncharacteristic exercise of naked authority. He was no doubt overreacting to what he described to Spalding as the "depressing effect upon members of the faculty" that resulted from a late March notice Sanford had to send out to university faculty explaining the necessity of "severe reductions in salaries" as the only alternative to reductions in positions.[50]

The recommendations of organizational consultant George Works of the University of Chicago and his committee were used to support the regents' requests for extended powers vis-à-vis lump sum appropriations and the power to eliminate as well as to reorganize institutions. It was, however, probably the fiscal exigencies of the depression that most persuaded the legislature to agree to the regents' proposals. Given the latitude they had sought with the ongoing advice of the Survey Committee and with considerable help from Sanford, Weltner and Spalding proceeded to change the face of public higher education in Georgia. The trimming of the fat at specific institutional levels continued apace, but after the regents had secured the authority to do so, the real cutting of excess began with the elimination and consolidation of units in the system.

The April 1933 meeting of the Board of Regents marked a real starting point for the University System of Georgia. Chancellor Snelling's retirement was announced; Andrew Soule's presidency of the College of Agriculture came to an end; Jere Pound took an assignment as president of the University System school in Valdosta; the number of state schools was reduced by the abolition of eight, one of which was the medical department at Augusta—revived later in the year by Governor Talmadge. By the end of the year the number of senior state public colleges was fixed at seven: the University of Georgia, Georgia

Tech, Georgia College for Women at Milledgeville, Georgia State Women's College at Valdosta, South Georgia Teachers College at Statesboro, the Medical College of Georgia, and Georgia State Industrial College at Savannah. North Georgia at Dahlonega, West Georgia at Carrollton, Georgia Southwestern in Americus, Middle Georgia at Cochran, and South Georgia at Douglas made up the five junior colleges of the system. Abraham Baldwin at Tifton as an agricultural school; Georgia Normal and Agriculture College at Albany, a surviving secondary/college level black institution; and the black agricultural college at Forsyth rounded out the fifteen system institutions.[51]

Effective July 1, Philip Weltner became chancellor. J. D. Bolton was named treasurer and comptroller at the university. Several programs on specific campuses were either ended or transferred. The Evening School of Commerce, previously a part of Tech, was separated to become a more-or-less free-standing unit focused on adult education. The civil engineering program at Athens was transferred to Tech and the commerce program at Tech was ended.

None of these changes, of course, came without continued strife, disagreement, or delay, and shaky cooperation at the university and elsewhere in the system. For the most part, however, S. V. Sanford might justifiably have taken pride in the portion of the regents' report for 1933 that claimed: "The three separate institutions which formerly existed at Athens . . . are now one institution with one executive head. The confusion, jealousy and the habit of working at cross purposes is a thing of the past. . . . The University of Georgia is functioning smoothly and harmoniously. . . . A great work has been done at Athens."[52]

The April actions of the regents suddenly freed Sanford to return his focus to matters more usual for a university president. Sanford found himself back responding to requests for appointments from people who frequently failed to indicate why they needed his time and attention. He was back answering grammar questions from far and wide, helping an aging alumnus enjoy Alumni Day by the giving of his special attention, aiding in the replacement of a diploma lost to a fire, soothing an angry hotel manager who was demanding restitution for room damages caused by rowdy university football players, or continuing his old practice of diplomatically responding to job seekers who sought his support in getting some appointment or other.[53]

With early June graduation on the horizon, Sanford wrote Chancellor Weltner: "I'm too busy to do all you ask right away. I must handle the problems of this University from now until June 5."[54] In dealing with requests from Governor Talmadge, Sanford was a bit more circumspect. He wrote Talmadge in May promising to send "our landscape folks to Irvinville to preserve that historic spot where Jeff Davis was captured," as per the governor's request.[55]

Economic problems did not end with the resolution of system reorganization difficulties, but there was hope on the horizon. President Roosevelt was inaugurated in March 1933 and began developing some of the revolutionary policies of the first hundred days of his administration. Sanford expressed his optimism for the future under the new Democratic leadership and the New Deal that Roosevelt had promised. "Franklin Roosevelt," Sanford wrote Hughes Spalding less than a month after the inauguration, "will show us a new era in our economic condition in twelve months. You may not have that much faith in our President, but I have."[56] Philip Weltner had been chancellor little more than a month when he received Sanford's five-page proposal for borrowing $350,000 from the Reconstruction Finance Corporation for dorm construction.[57] This southern educator born in the fading years of the "old Yankee Reconstruction" had at last found for the term "Reconstruction" a redeeming interpretation. Sanford was off and running for Georgia's fair share of New Deal benefits. President Bruce Payne of Peabody College in Nashville wrote to his "fellow sufferers in this depression," including Sanford who shared "a certain bond of sympathy generated by our common poverty." Payne found encouragement in what he saw happening in Georgia and requested of Sanford: "if you do find the pot of gold at the end of the rainbow somewhere in Georgia, please send for me."[58] His correspondent had not found the pot of gold in Georgia, but he was on the trail of it in the vicinity of Washington.

The bridge between seeking funds for the university and seeking funds and other forms of support for the larger system was one Sanford frequently crossed. In point of fact, it is difficult to distinguish between his two concerns, university and system. The success of one, of course, ensured the success of the other, and if Sanford's objectives at first appear confusing, they were, on closer examination, logically of a whole. Such was the case in the first year of the regents, and so matters continued, especially regarding the growing interrelationships of state agencies and the federal government as the New Deal created ground-breaking economic opportunities and not a few political and bureaucratic complications. In a sense Franklin Roosevelt's programs were the catalyst for the "nationalization of Steadman Vincent Sanford" as attention to Washington became a part of the routine.

Long-time friend and demanding overseer of system reorganization and university integration Hughes Spalding returned to his familiar pattern of frequent letter-writing. Only the nature of the subjects changed. "I suppose you will find out from the number of letters you are getting," wrote Spalding to Sanford in June 1933, "that I am back on the job and am again sticking my nose into everything." He was. The range of Spalding's interests was broad enough to include passing along complaints from the mothers of students regarding dorm living and dining hall fare, to the condition of the Confederate Constitution that was in the university library. Spalding, a prominent lay leader of the Catholic Church in Atlanta and recipient of Papal honors, went so far as to express to Sanford his concerns about the religious or spiritual welfare of the students at the university. The comments were made with apparent good humor but indicated that the chairman of the regents felt the university had a special responsibility regarding these matters. Spalding felt some pressure from critics among Georgia's citizenry who rejected the university as a "Godless institution." Spalding admitted he didn't think the university was

Godless. "Presumably everybody in Athens and all the students believe in God, but a great many have a damned poor way of showing it. We want to make our schools popular with everyone, including even religious fanatics."[59] He continued, expressing his dissatisfaction with suggested means of resolving his concerns, and closed: "This is a rambling letter, Dr. Sanford, and these things are not set in my mind with any continuity, but they are there, and they are right. . . . Of course you want everybody to be a Baptist, and Mrs. Sanford wants everybody to be a Methodist; Mrs. Spalding wants everybody to be Presbyterian, and I want them to be Catholic, so whatever they are, I want them to believe in the Church of their choice, to stick up for it, and to fight for it, if necessary. That is what makes good Christians and good citizens."[60]

Late in the summer of 1933, the Sanfords took a two-week vacation to visit their sons and families in Savannah. Steadman Sanford wrote that he needed a vacation "not because of my physical condition, but because of my mental condition. I have stood the strain as long as possible." He reported his satisfaction at what had been accomplished, but felt he had "overtaxed [his] strength" and "done too much work." Despite continued unhappiness with Soule, he felt he had the support of "95 percent of the people and 99 percent of the faculty."[61]

Spalding's resignation from chairmanship of the regents came early in 1934. Before ending his two-plus years as a mainstay in the development of the system, Spalding, along with law school dean Harmon Caldwell, joined President Sanford in beginning the long process of lobbying on behalf of federal building funds for the system. Sanford had on many occasions remarked that during his thirty years with the university "the State had not appropriated a dime for buildings on the University campus."[62] The delegation of university advocates who started their marches on Washington in the first year of the New Deal were determined to make up for lost time.

The regents' initial effort in Washington resulted in a $3.5 million loan from the Public Works Administration. Sanford soon came to be considered something of the regional expert on matters related to seeking such funds. University heads from around the South conferred with him on the details that the Georgia trio worked on through the end of 1933. In October Sanford wrote George H. Denny, president of the University of Alabama, that the best hope seemed to be for President Roosevelt to exercise some discretionary powers. "The President," he observed, "is very sympathetic with the idea that PWA funds be allowed for loans to higher education building projects."[63]

The President's support did come with the condition that the Supreme Court of Georgia allow the legality of the regents having the power to borrow. The court so ruled in 1934 and the way seemed clear for campus planning and construction. In their annual report for 1933, published in late January of 1934, the regents reported on the initial stages of this effort and its anticipated approval. The complications of working around or through Governor Talmadge's anti–New Deal obstructionism were not as yet fully realized.[64]

In his pursuit of President Roosevelt's continued support, Sanford took advantage of the opportunity provided by the 1933 Georgia–New York University football games as a means of extending lobbying efforts. Sanford invited the president as an "adopted son" of Georgia. Roosevelt sent his regrets, but the point had been made.[65] Another potential ally in the business of getting federal funds for university construction was, however, in attendance for the game but "the conduct of the spectators made it difficult to enjoy the game." State Supreme Court Justice S. Gilbert Price wrote that he hoped he would have the opportunity to "talk this matter over with you for the betterment of our Beloved State University."[66]

The idea of wooing President Roosevelt to the "home field" did not go away. In November Georgia alumni leader F. Phinizy Calhoun of Atlanta suggested to Spalding that the university grant the president an honorary doctorate of laws. Sanford was delighted with the prospect of making a closer connection to FDR for himself and for the university. Sanford was adamant in his support of Roosevelt. He would "not admit that anything for which Roosevelt stands will be a failure." Furthermore, reasoned Sanford, "as soon as the WPA comes to our rescue in buildings then we can look toward attracting more men of national standing."[67]

A long letter to son Charles in Savannah around Thanksgiving of 1933 is revealing of Sanford's values and frame of mind as that busy year neared its close. The letter began with a glowing account of the family fondness for the city of Savannah, its beauty, culture, and "fine traditions." Ever mindful of "the store," he added, "By the way, it has done more for the University than any other city in Georgia." His recent travels to several midwestern schools had left him with the impression that "there are worse sections than the so-called benighted South." Conditions in Chicago indicated that the University of Chicago and Northwestern University might be forced to consolidate "to conserve their endowments which are fast shrinking." He considered consolidation a "progressive measure" that promised hope, but he feared that "all people seem to prefer a laissez faire policy to a constructive policy of business acumen." Naturally, he saw a parallel in Georgia's own recent "progress." He credited Weltner and Spalding and expressed pleasure at having played a part in it all. "We are asking for a large sum of money from the P.W.A.," he wrote. He might "not get a dime" but felt confident in the plans he had submitted and confided that important sources had praised it as "ideal." He anticipated that the success of the project would "put a new and active spirit in the alumni. If I am successful I shall leave behind an enlarged university—one the people will some day appreciate either in depression or prosperity." Sanford declared "a new day has dawned" and that his policy, despite the traditions that preceded him, would be to "profit by the experience of the progressive universities."[68]

A few days later Sanford was back in Washington at work on the PWA project. Hughes Spalding sent him a telegram at the Mayflower Hotel advising that George Peabody would be in Athens shortly, but for Sanford to remain in Washington "if you can do any good at all with respect to the University System project." Spalding suggested consulting Senator Russell and wrote the senator that he had asked the university president to call on him and consult him about the "advisability of asking Senator George to join in meetings with federal officials." [69] Despite Spalding's plea to Senator Russell to "please stay in Washington until the project is approved," both Russell and Sanford were home for Christmas, and the details of approval were not yet worked out.

Subsequent trips to Washington occupied much of President Sanford's time in 1934. In many respects the continuing pressures of depression-generated economic woes dictated the script the entire year and for Sanford's future beyond 1934. With the declining appropriations from the legislature, the New Deal looked more and more promising as a means of getting building done on the campus. The complications, however, in pursuing this "pot of gold" were found both in Washington and back in Georgia. Those complications helped determine the fate of Sanford's two greatest allies on the Board of Regents, Spalding and Weltner, both of whom, at least indirectly, left the board out of frustrations surrounding the Washington bureaucratic morass and the Talmadge politics.

The president's office in Athens was without Sanford's presence a great deal during the year 1934. Letter after letter indicates his secretary's explanations that the president was "out of town," "in Washington for a few days," "out of the city for a few days," "attending to University business in Washington," and so forth. Sanford apparently enjoyed the activity, the lobbying with the congressional delegation from Georgia, matching wits with frustrating brain trusters, and seeking the support of subcabinet connections. Spalding often joined in these Washington trips before his resignation from the board early in the year; Chancellor Weltner also made trips with Sanford. Regent Cason Callaway was another ally whose company Sanford especially enjoyed. Senators George and Russell saw the university delegation probably more often than they might have preferred. Sanford, now approaching his mid-sixties, was an untiring trooper through it all. When Harmon Caldwell, dean of the university law school, expressed concern about missing so much time from the campus on trips to Washington, Sanford declared, "I would be willing to close down the University to get possession of a million dollars." [70]

When Hughes Spalding's patience for the process and his lack of support from fellow regents ran out in February 1934, he wrote Sanford in a "Personal and confidential" letter, "in all this PWA work I did not have one iota of assistance from any Board member. No institution head, except you, showed any interest or did anything, and I had to put our two Senators on the spot to make them move a hand."[71] Spalding left the board, but continued his correspondence with and concern for Sanford, his family, and his future in the system.

President Sanford saw himself as the only system administrator actively working for the PWA money: "My experience and position make it necessary for me to take an active part in getting funds. I feel heads of the Junior Colleges have confidence in my aiding them, and I am glad to work for them. Confidentially, I can not see why our friend at Tech has not lifted his hand to help in this great project. I have spent my time and effort on the PWA. I would willingly give my life to see my state have a higher education system that would command the respect of Georgians and the nation."[72]

For Sanford there were two levels of problems in the process of gaining federal support for higher education. At the state level there was Governor Talmadge's anti-Roosevelt posture. At the federal level, secretary of the interior Harold Ickes was the troublemaker. Sanford saw Ickes as an obstructionist whose devotion to considerations of race made for difficulties in working on behalf of southern-based projects, which traditionally ignored minority needs. Sanford was unsparing in his criticism of Ickes. In letters to both Spalding and Weltner he expressed his distaste for the secretary with unusually negative candor. He wrote Spalding that he hoped "that when I enter the Pearly Gates that Secretary Ickes will not be on guard."[73] The greater difficulty was the Talmadge battle with Franklin D. Roosevelt and the New Deal. When PWA loan approval seemed near, Governor Talmadge moved to block the use of federal funds by introducing bills in the legislature that would prohibit the University System from receiving loans, thus eliminating the PWA loan.

The governor's campaign met the opposition of Chancellor Weltner and board chairman Marion Smith, one of Talmadge's appointees to the regents. The battle between FDR and the governor was played out in the halls of Georgia's General Assembly where Weltner's role inspired the governor to drive him out of the chancellor's office. The legislative battles between board and governor led to appointments of men dedicated to ridding the chancellorship of Weltner. By mid-1935 Weltner chose to resign, paving the way for Sanford's chancellorship.[74] Sanford's statement to Hughes Spalding the year preceding Weltner's resignation pondered: "If he [Weltner] should resign I do not know where we could find a man to take his place." It is not beyond reason to believe that both the sender and recipient of that line knew better.[75]

As the Thanksgiving holiday neared, Sanford's attention turned from the politics and economics of the university toward his family. Mr. and Mrs. Sanford enjoyed the letters they received from their three sons. Charles especially could be counted on to write letters of encouragement when some matter had caused his father distress. He wrote from Savannah commenting on a recent controversy at the university involving the decision to charge for the radio broadcast of football games. The university had been taken to task for charging advertisers for the broadcast, and Charles, a bank executive, comforted his father with his own analysis of the social/political/economic circumstances which he felt had contributed to such apparently unreasonable responses to sound decisions. His analysis early in the New Deal has come to be considered a fundamental criticism of Roosevelt policies more than a half-century later. This may be as near as he would come to being critical of FDR with his father. "I think the government in its human effort to protect the less fortunate has been misunderstood by a large number of people to the extent they make unreasonable demands upon people and expect their desires to be granted." He cited the example in his own bank where an individual felt he should not be held accountable for his loan debt because "conditions had changed since he took out his loan."[76] Charles brought a banker's eye to the situation; his father might have seen it all in terms of a teacher's heart.

EIGHT

Chancellor Sanford

1935-1940

In the summer of 1935 Sanford was elected chancellor of the University System of Georgia, replacing Philip Weltner, who had resigned. In the spring Charles, his second son, married. During that same year Sanford's name was bandied about as a possible candidate for governor of Georgia. The heavily Democratic Congress, elected in an off-year landslide supporting Roosevelt and the New Deal, promised ever-increasing federal aid to higher education, and there was a general spirit of activism, which Sanford optimistically embraced. Officially, the year marked the end of Sanford's career at the university, a thirty-two-year marriage of man to institution. Unofficially the bonds were not broken. The Sanford household remained in Athens at 359 Cloverhurst.

As the end of his presidency drew near, Sanford was somewhat bitter about the scars left by reorganization. "Since the reorganization by the Regents," he wrote in the fall of 1934, "I have not had a bed of roses." He observed sarcastically, "As you know I am responsible for the death of Dr. Soule and for the critical illnesses of Chancellor Snelling and President Pound and for all the men and women not only in the University but the University System who have lost their positions."[1]

The level of Sanford's distress may be seen in his uncharacteristically defensive posturing to a friend: "My only salvation has been that I have so far been successful in whatever I have attempted. All admit that the University is far superior to what it was when I inherited it. This is my compensation for the unjust criticism made by those who have always been antagonistic to any progress. So long as real progress is being made, I can stand criticism and I can say reverently as was said of old, 'Father forgive them for they know not what they do.'"[2]

The private words and thoughts of Sanford were, however, carefully and thankfully kept from public view. In his written comments in the *Pandora* for 1934–35, Sanford endorsed the view of the chairman of the Board of Regents, which credited the system with newly established efficiency and cooperation. There is some hint of his feeling in Sanford's observation that "while this is [the] expressed opinion of Chairman [of the Board of Regents] Smith, it also seems to be the judgement of the most thoughtful and constructive citizens of Georgia."[3] There seems to be the implication that there were Georgians who are not "thoughtful or constructive citizens."

Eugene Talmadge was elected Georgia's governor for three two-year terms during the decade of the thirties. As president of the university and chancellor of the University System, Sanford had to balance keeping Talmadge folks happy and maintaining the support of Talmadge's numerous adversaries. Sanford's diplomatic talents proved him able not only to survive this tension but to carry out his complex and politics-ridden responsibilities. Of necessity much of the story of the chancellorship of S. V. Sanford is a tale tightly wound to "Talmadge Politics" in Georgia.

By the early fall of 1934, Talmadge had been assured a second term as governor, having handily carried the Democratic primary for the party nomination, an accomplishment tantamount to election in those one-party days of Georgia politics. In his first term Talmadge had kept his own counsel regarding his support for President Roosevelt, but following his second victory word was out among close confidants that he was going into a second term ready to challenge those policies of the New Deal that were at odds with his own particular view of conservative, yet populist, limited government.

President Sanford was required to deal delicately with this and many other political, social, fiscal, and philosophical differences with Talmadge. One of Georgia's most distinguished observers of mid-twentieth-century political and social change in the region, Ralph Mc-Gill, apparently adjudged Sanford's efforts masterful. In September of 1934, he telegraphed the university president that he had just read a recent public introduction of Talmadge by Sanford: "It is a masterpiece of oratory and good sense. Congratulations."[4]

The *Atlanta Constitution*'s September 11, 1934, report on Sanford's introduction of the governor carried such leads as "University Head Lauds Talmadge" and "Sanford Picks Governor as True Friend of Georgia Education." The chancellor was reported to have had "warm praise" for the improvements in education during the governor's first term. Talmadge's appointments to the Board of Regents were singled out for praise by Sanford as was the governor's work for good roads and his moves to provide for teachers' salaries. The specifics of Sanford's text, however, included some hints of a less-than-perfect relationship with the governor: "My friends, Governor Talmadge is a man to count on. If he is your friend he will die for you; if he is your enemy then leave him alone. . . . I believe today just as I did last April that Governor Talmadge deserves a second term. We may not agree with the way he does things but we admire honest efforts."[5]

Sanford gave Governor Talmadge one of his favorite blessings: "He came to the University as a student about the same time I came as an instructor. He is one of my boys." Contrary to the reporter's interpretations elsewhere in this article, Sanford did not claim that he had taught Talmadge nor did he swear to the quality of "his boys."[6]

A 1995 interview with Eugene Talmadge's son, who also served as governor and U.S. senator from Georgia, shed no special insights as to the senior Talmadge's evaluation of Sanford. When asked of his father's estimation of Sanford, Senator Talmadge couched his response in the same style his father or Sanford would have employed: "high regard." From the Sanford camp an observer of the scene in the late 1930s asked not to be quoted regarding Sanford's candid estimation of the governor.[7]

When the legislature convened for its biannual session in January 1935, Governor Talmadge presented, via his supporters, a bill "designed to kill" the University System's PWA support for a building program. Chancellor Weltner immediately circulated, in a confidential notice, a copy to the heads of all system institutions and asked that they identify the legislators in their respective regions and try to inform them of the facts of the situation regarding the bill.[8] The battle was joined, and Weltner's time as chancellor was marked for termination by the Talmadge crowd.

A written exchange between President Sanford and the governor came in March after Talmadge's recommended budget had failed in the legislature. Sanford claimed he had "tried to help" but stated: "My views did not prevail. I have great faith you will work it out as you have been able to do before." The governor thanked Sanford for his "interest and cooperation." These letters both seem devoid of anything more than pro forma communications, lacking sincerity on either side.[9]

If Talmadge and Sanford covered their differences with courtly niceties, Chancellor Weltner and the governor were all but ready to resort to fisticuffs when the chancellor decided to resign in March. Weltner officially resigned at the April meeting of the Board of Regents but had announced his decision just as the legislature adjourned. All over Georgia interested parties were speculating as to his successor. Steadman V. Sanford was among those recommending and being recommended.

Sanford wrote regent Dickerson of Douglas, Georgia, on April 1 that, though Weltner's motives were honest, the public "will assign politics as the cause for his resignation," and that would be bad for the University System. He went on to praise the progress made under the regents and despaired that the momentum of "solidarity of the System which now prevails" might be lost. "I hope," he wrote, "the Regents will select a Chancellor as soon as possible," in part to end the "many wild rumors afloat." He seemed to be describing himself as he claimed that all he was "anxious about is that some person acceptable to all the Regents, old and new [i.e., Talmadge and anti-Talmadge] be selected at the earliest possible date to prevent restlessness, speculation, and wild rumors." He added, "I stand ready to serve the Regents in any capacity in which they think I can render the best service. My interest is in the University System, and not in myself."

Sanford closed the letter explaining that this was a "personal and confidential letter to [Dickerson]. Only to Chairman Smith have I suggested that a Chancellor be selected as soon as possible."[10] That same day he wrote a practically identical letter to regent R. P. Burson of Monroe, Georgia. A response from Judge Dickerson a few days later expressed agreement on the matter of a timely appointment of a chancellor and urged Sanford to rest assured that Dickerson was his friend.[11]

In April Sanford was named as Weltner's successor, to start work July 1, effective with Weltner's date of resignation, but officially September 1 to conform to the regents' fiscal calendar. An undated newspaper clipping says that "Governor Eugene Talmadge was the first to shake [Sanford's] hand." There was speculation that the governor had offered the position to his confidant on the Board of Regents, Sandy Beaver of Gainesville, but it was reported that Beaver had chosen to support Sanford.[12]

Governor Talmadge wrote the new chancellor that he had "heard only splendid things from all over the state and gratification over your election as Chancellor." He said, "I am glad to add my word of congratulations and know that it is honor well merited and that you will continue to serve the people of Georgia to the very best of your strength and ability."[13] Talmadge also said he was sorry he couldn't "run over to see" Sanford. It is revealing that this letter was so casually dropped loosely into a scrapbook while there are several carefully clipped and pasted items of praise for Sanford's appointment in one of the many family scrapbooks in the collection at the University of Georgia. It is somewhat frustrating that in his leisure Sanford enjoyed making and filling these scrapbooks but invariably clipped the items so as not to reveal either the source or the date. In one book devoted to items clearly surrounding events of 1935 are undated clips that lavished praise on the choice of Sanford as chancellor: "Best choice that could have been made, happy selection, ideal choice, useful life in education, outstanding educator, no better hands, no man in the state is in closer touch with the alumni of the University nor more beloved by them than Sanford."[14]

Of all the items in that particular accumulation of clippings, the one that seems best to capture the essence of Steadman Sanford's unique talents as he assumed the leadership of the University System is an undated editorial from the *Atlanta Journal:* "But even more important than [Sanford's] knowledge and experience, are his human contacts throughout the State, his instinctive friendliness and knack of dealing with people, his resourcefulness and work-a-day wisdom in the management of affairs, and his wholehearted loyalty to every interest in every unit of Georgia's education program,"[15] in brief, the personal equation.

It was critical that Sanford be able to represent all of the system and beyond that to carry forward a higher education program with the proper understanding, sensitivity, and concern for public education in the state at the elementary and secondary level. This was necessary not only for reasons of articulation but because of the possibility for the University System to be seen by the public, and especially public educational leaders, as a competitor for meager state funds. No man had a better claim than Sanford to the confidence and support of the public school establishment in Georgia during the 1930s. His ties were anchored in his own forty-plus years of teaching students, teaching teachers, and cultivating a network of school leaders around the state. Sanford's presidency of the Georgia Education Association began in 1935, before his appointment as chancellor, a clear indication of the esteem in which education colleagues held him.[16] Shortly after he began his new job, Sanford participated in the Annual Educational Conference of County School Superintendents of Schools and Laymen, a long-time forum of importance for maintaining a network of contacts among this significant and influential group of Georgians.[17]

It is important to recall as the chancellorship period commenced that those "human contacts" which so well equipped Sanford for his job were based on not only individual and personal connections, but significantly, on the strength of his association with several of the most influential "subcultures" of Georgia during the first half of the century. In that period before the changes in the post–World War II American South, S. V. Sanford, by birth, possessed the two most fundamental characteristics of potential leadership, the "correct" race and gender. To those significant factors was added his potential for leadership through his family connections. For S. V. Sanford "family connections" boiled down to one man, his paternal grandfather, Shelton Palmer Sanford, educator. It is indicative of Steadman's ongoing devotion to the reputation of his grandfather that he linked himself to Shelton Palmer Sanford in laying claim to his own role in Georgia education on the eve of assuming the chancellorship, declaring "my grandfather and I for 96 years have labored for" a greater education for Georgians.[18]

Given race, gender, and family connections, plus the facts that Steadman Sanford initially followed his grandfather's career path, successfully pursued higher education for himself, and became a teacher, it seems obvious that by the time he joined the faculty of the university in 1903, his ambitions were beyond those of most Georgians of that period. Had he been content to simply stay on the traditional career course, however, Sanford may well have never achieved the level of importance we now attribute to him. The University of Georgia and higher education in general in Georgia would have been much poorer for the loss. Sanford chose the broader path, one that moved beyond the confines of the educational profession and linked him to other important sources of influence in his society.

Influence in Georgia in the period 1900–1940 as always before and since was measured to a significant degree by wealth. For those like Sanford, who were not destined to pursue the traditional fortunes won in commerce, the second measure of influence was their ability to exercise their personality in the determination of how those who did possess fiscal resources chose to distribute their wealth. Political careers often gave those without their own wealth the position to exercise such influence. At a community level, prominence established through connections in churches, social relationships, and fraternal organizations provided a nonpolitical avenue for the nonwealthy to reach a certain level of influence. Sanford, apparently very consciously, determined to achieve influence from outside commerce or politics by means of the strength of his association with what might be called the "third level" sources of power: professional affiliation, religious affiliation, membership in fraternal organizations, veterans' organizations, and sports-related interest groups, as well as his special connection with one of the most important elements of influence in Georgia at that time, the press and especially the weekly small town newspapers. With God, the flag, education, and the press behind him, S. V. Sanford would have been hard pressed to fail in doing whatever he desired. Also, it never hurt that the sons of some of the most important lawyers in Atlanta roomed in his home as college students. To this delightful mix Sanford was known occasionally to add a fistful of hard-to-get football tickets or a brimming basket of luscious Georgia peaches.

Among these important tools, Sanford's relationship with the press deserves to be singled out for attention. Just when Sanford's special affinity for association with newspapers first began is impossible to determine, but as early as the 1890s he was highly successful in making use of the Marietta newspaper in keeping the public apprised of the activities that drew his energy, the schools and the local militia unit. When he moved to Athens he made a more formal and significant connection via his development of the journalism program. As a teacher of journalism Sanford made a special effort to provide a level of practicality for students which enabled them to reasonably expect to become members of the working press, usually in Georgia on the staff of a small weekly paper. The process put Sanford and his students in a position to establish an unusually broad network of contacts with editors and publishers around the state. A critical ally for Sanford in establishing good working relationships with the journalists around the state was the Georgia Press Institute.

The Georgia Press Institute was organized in 1928 by Emily Woodward, editor-owner of the *Vienna* (Georgia) *News* and at the time president of the Georgia Press Association. Woodward, dean John Drewry of the School of Journalism, John Paschal of the *Atlanta Journal,* and Sanford were close professional friends, and the records of the meetings of the Press Institute, most of which were held in Athens at the university, are replete with the highly visible roles these individuals played in bringing quality professional opportunities to newspaper people in Georgia. Year after year the annual meetings of the institute brought leading writers and newsmakers as speakers and leaders of workshops. Long after he no longer taught journalism courses, Chancellor Sanford retained his ties to the Press Institute.

One of Sanford's greatest fans in the fourth estate was Ralph McGill, the long-time Atlanta sportswriter who went on to become the Pulitzer Prize–winning editor of the *Atlanta Constitution.* The journalist and Sanford had become friends and traveling companions in the course of McGill's coverage of university football games. When Sanford became chancellor, McGill was delighted. "There are not enough honors for Dr. Sanford," said McGill. "There is no office which would be fine enough for Dr. Steadman Vincent Sanford." McGill described their game travels together and concluded that while the chancellorship was "a high honor, he still belongs to us who write of football—we discovered him first!"[19]

At the April 10, 1935, meeting of the Board of Regents Chancellor Weltner's resignation was accepted "with regrets." George Woodruff nominated Sanford to replace Weltner and regent Howell seconded the nomination. The election of S. V. Sanford as the system's third

chancellor was unanimously approved. While Sanford did not officially take office until September he was called on by the board to
recommend candidates for the presidency of the university as well as
for the subsequent vacancy in the deanship of the law school. Harmon Caldwell was Sanford's top recommendation for the presidency,
but as a courtesy he offered the names of McPherson, Bocock, Park,
Hooper, and Payne, all well-established university figures, as qualified men. The board accepted Caldwell as their choice and followed
Sanford's recommendation of Lucien Goodrich for Caldwell's replacement in the law school. Goodrich declined and Alton Hosch, another
Sanford recommendation, was named dean at a July board meeting.[20]

Sanford managed to slip away for a brief rest. As he wrote to regent
S. H. Morgan of Savannah: "I am leaving town for Denver to attend
the National Education Association. My real purpose is to get ten days
rest. I have reached the limit and realize that I must stop at this particular juncture."[21]

In the summer of 1935 Sanford was deep into the major tasks of his
early tenure. He had to provide extensive information on behalf of the
regents to the various federal agencies in conjunction with the Federal
Emergency Relief Association and the Public Works Administration.
In the midst of this Sanford began his ongoing tour of the system's
institutions, reporting in July on his "recent inspection trip to Georgia
Normal and Agricultural College at Albany." From that visit the new
chancellor recommended the reappointment of President Holley for
that institution and approval of his recommended budget. The need
for this individual approval of a budget was the result of a spring
decision by the board to approve the proposed budgets of only the
white system institutions, "referring the three Negro institutions to
the Committee on Education." In May the board was on the verge of
accepting the possible recommendation from that committee that the
black schools be closed "as said committee may determine." Sanford
successfully helped discourage that action.[22]

Discrimination against the black institutions of the University System was, as in virtually all southern institutions in that period, a fact
of life. Black schools at all levels in the state were relegated to a dis-

tinctly second-class position. African American students in elementary and secondary schools in Georgia got the hand-me-downs at every turn, from the textbooks which the white students had almost worn out to last consideration for any sort of budget enhancements. Salaries for administrators and teachers alike were lower at all levels for African Americans in Georgia. Sanford, however, while certainly no iconoclast, exhibited a certain sensitivity in matters relating to race. Charles Gowen of Brunswick, Georgia, a legislator and subsequently an unsuccessful moderate Democratic candidate for governor, said in a 1995 interview that he had been impressed with this quality of the chancellor. Gowen recalled that he was member of a committee from the legislature which visited campuses of the system with Sanford. The chancellor always went to special pains to guard the personal feelings of African American faculty, staff, and students from what might have been otherwise careless conventions of some of the members of the visiting committees.[23]

Steadman Sanford's dilemma as an essentially nineteenth-century man faced with twentieth-century issues and controversy is nowhere more apparent than in matters of race and gender. He might have, in his functions as chancellor as observed by Charles Gowen, been attuned to the personal feelings of African American Georgians. Tempting as it might be to use this point to make the case for Sanford's liberalism within a traditional system of race and gender values, it would be misleading to do so. Charles Gowen spoke of his memories of Chancellor Sanford from the perspective of the late twentieth century. Gowen himself, like Sanford, was considered a man of moderation in race. That moderation, however, is a relative term in Georgia politics for much of the heart of the twentieth century. Sanford, like Gowen and the better-known Ellis Arnall, was by today's litmus tests merely a moderate racist. Any of these gentlemen, and thousands more like them all over the country, were at best thoughtful and kind to blacks tête-à-tête. They were not coarse men, but beneath their manners were value systems planted firmly in the Georgia of the previous century. Gowen and Arnall lived long enough to face the move from civility to conscience. Post–World War II Georgia at long last had to deal with the twentieth century in more challenging terms, initially most visibly in matters of race and eventually in gender concerns. What path Steadman V. Sanford would have taken in the face of such a challenge cannot be known.

As seen in the earlier treatment of the coming of coeducation at the university, Sanford's role exhibited no special progressivism. Gender issues were addressed on a legal level in part vis-à-vis the success of the suffrage movement. Events would prove more generally what some, especially women, perceived at the time, that the Nineteenth Amendment was an act of imperfect justice; Sanford was spared that late-twentieth-century moral challenge. In personal matters, gender, as long as it was of the dominant race, was never a great challenge to Sanford's personal equation. The personal equation, however, was a nineteenth-century device, and time was running out on that past.

Early in 1936 there was a brief flurry of speculation about Sanford being a gubernatorial candidate. J. C. Meadows, then dean of the law school at the university, wrote Sanford pledging his support should the chancellor decide to run. Steadman Sanford was smart enough not to be tempted by such talk, and nothing came of the suggestion, which was apparently first advanced by regent Morgan.[24]

Sandy Beaver was elected chairman of the Board of Regents in March 1936, and Miller S. Bell was chosen as vice-chairman. For much of the year Beaver, Bell, and Sanford worked with Governor Talmadge on matters related to funds for the system. As state and federal funds became available, an extensive building program ensued. The volume of business that needed board action grew to the point that in April it was determined that the board should meet monthly rather than quarterly. Before the summer Chancellor Sanford had been given the support of R. H. Driftmeier from the university to employ architects and engineers and assign them as necessary. The monthly meeting of the board became largely informational regarding the increasing number of building projects.[25]

In the summer he was a delegate at the National Democratic Convention but revealed to Grace in a telegram from Philadelphia that the sessions "lacked the enthusiasm of the Chicago Convention [of 1932] since there is no contest." [26] It seems that even though Sanford was a great FDR supporter, he might have enjoyed some spirited challenge within the proceedings.

On his return to Georgia, Sanford occupied much of his time with visits to campus building projects around the system. Such visits became an expected part of the routine of Sanford's chancellorship. Even after the flurry of construction he made it a point to familiarize himself with each campus, and he apparently enjoyed having the communities in which they were located get to know him better, too. It was not unusual in the late thirties for Sanford, usually driven by a staff member, to visit Valdosta or Carrollton or Americus, to tour the campus, address the faculty, address the students, speak to at least one civic club, and have an interview with the local newspaper. If a corner of the state had somehow missed knowing Steadman Sanford from his earlier pursuits, interests, friendships, and connections, the last ten years of his life provided a great opportunity to correct that deficiency. Ralph C. Moor, a secretary in the board office, drove Sanford on many of these trips. Moor recalled that all along the way the chancellor made a point of stopping by to visit members of the legislature who lived in the areas through which they were passing. [27]

With all his new responsibilities, the chancellor enjoyed increasing opportunities to travel with his wife. Freed from the daily demands of the presidency and the complexity of his earlier years of deep involvement in the athletic affairs of the university, the chancellor and his wife enjoyed the most elaborate holidays and vacations of their marriage in the late 1930s before wartime curtailed leisure travel. They visited Key West in April 1936 and were in Montreal late in August the same year. We know about their trips only because of the records left as a result of Sanford's tendency to keep up with what was going on "back at the office" via telegram, letter, and occasional picture postcard. [28]

Steadman Sanford rarely failed to convert an experience to some practical end on behalf of the cause of education in Georgia. His travels, even as holidays, provided him with some of the inspirations he brought to his role as chancellor. From his earliest days on the faculty at the university Sanford had been alert to innovation from outside the state. One of his great strengths was his receptivity to the possibility that improvements might come from looking broadly for ideas and examples of success, even outside the South. He had always held in special regard the eastern Ivy League institutions and the great midwestern universities. Sanford did not seek to make the South another region, but he sought to make the most of the South even by means of appropriating some of the ideas of other regions. His hope was to leave the South a better place, without turning his back on the core of the region's traditions.

To what extent did Sanford's admiration of institutions of higher education outside the South result in specific, concrete reform of the University of Georgia or the University System? Little other than occasional gridiron battles was brought to Athens directly from the Ivy League or the Big Ten. More apparent was Sanford's success in gaining a reputation by way of association with those institutions. Sometimes the reputation gained was the university's or the system's; most often it was S. V. Sanford's. His energy in "getting" left the impression that Sanford was a go-getter rather than a caretaker. In this respect much of what he did to build the University System during his chancellorship puts his accomplishments in a league with the successful late-twentieth-century leaders in higher education. That building success was based in large part on a combination of willingness to look in new directions for support and to keep uppermost in the minds of Georgians the value and importance of higher education in the state. Sanford excelled in both areas.

In October 1936, Sanford wrote the editor of the *Macon Telegraph* concerning one of his ideas for putting a new spin on the role of the University System of Georgia. The Macon paper had carried an article on the promotion of Georgia hams. Sanford believed that not only hams but all Georgia products deserved such promotion and suggested that he saw in this a role for the University System.[29]

While technically the third chancellor, Sanford was the first with the talent, inclination, and opportunity to define the system on behalf of the interests of the State of Georgia in its broadest terms. The letter to the Macon paper is illustrative of this inclination and opportunity.

What Sanford suggested in the letter was to "get the University System to use and promote Georgia products." He saw the results not only in the advance of Georgia products, but also in "extending the value of the System to all Georgians."[30] That concept, hardly in keeping with the traditional functions of higher education in Georgia, by the late twentieth century has become a central principle for the state system of higher education.

Near the end of his first full calendar year as chancellor, chairman of the Board of Regents Sandy Beaver took issue with Sanford's continued residence in Athens rather than in Atlanta, site of the office of the board and the chancellor. Beaver, in the October 6, 1936, board meeting, said that he had wanted Sanford to "sever at once his connection with University" in the interests of the larger system. Beaver said that Sanford's "remarkably consecrated devotion" to Athens and the university had kept him from insisting on such a move initially. "It is the opinion of your Chairman," said Beaver, "that the time has now come for this severance to be effected." Beaver thought it was appropriate to suggest to Sanford "the propriety" of moving from Athens to Atlanta. Beaver felt that Sanford's presence in Athens "will probably prove embarrassing to President Caldwell by preventing complete autonomy." Beaver also feared that other system institutions might feel discrimination on the part of Sanford in favor of the university as long as he resided in Athens. "We called him," continued Beaver, "to the larger field of usefulness as Chancellor of the University System for the reason that we needed him to do for the system as a whole what he had done so brilliantly for the University." Beaver's view of the chancellor's role was one of coordinating academic matters and the "selling" of the system throughout the state, working with the legislature for more funding, and making a detailed study of the units of the system.

The last recorded mention of Beaver's concern was his closing comment: "I suggest the Board not order but request the Chancellor give consideration to the advisability of now leaving Athens more or less permanently."[31] We may assume that Sanford did "give consideration." Further, we know from subsequent history that while S. V. Sanford received mail in care of the Henry Grady Hotel in Atlanta on occasion, he and his wife continued to live at 359 Cloverhurst, Athens, Georgia.

Sanford's last public appearance on a system campus during 1936 was the December 15 dedication of a boys' dorm at Georgia Southwestern College in Americus, where he spoke on that which he, probably better than anyone else including Sandy Beaver, understood and appreciated, "The University System of Georgia, Its Aims and Province." The people in Americus had no problem with the chancellor's home address. The people of Milledgeville who heard Sanford at a dedication there in January 1937 felt the same way. Sanford's home was all over Georgia.

What role, if any, Governor Talmadge had in Beaver's effort to get Sanford to move to Atlanta is open to speculation. It may have been in part an effort to reduce Sanford rather than to enlarge him that motivated Beaver, and it may well have been Beaver's obligations to Eugene Talmadge that contributed to such a motive. At any rate, Beaver had been a Talmadge appointee to the board and as chairman was always considered linked to the governor. Beaver's role then diminished in some respects after 1937 when the newly elected governor Eurith D. Rivers took office. Marion Smith was appointed the governor's regent for the state at large and Beaver resigned as chairman in deference to the tradition and to Smith's chairmanship on behalf of the new governor.

Outgoing Governor Talmadge had inspired something of an organized opposition to himself in the state during his second term (1935–36), thanks to his anti–New Deal and anti-Roosevelt actions. The governor's battles had been fought mostly with the legislature and in the House his opposition centered on the leadership of House Speaker Eurith D. Rivers. It is impossible to say how well Talmadge would

have done in a direct contest with Rivers for the governor's office because Talmadge was prohibited by the Constitution from offering for
a third consecutive term. The Talmadge crowd supported Charles D.
Redwine against Rivers while Governor Talmadge entered the race for
the U.S. Senate seat held by Dick Russell. New Deal supporters Russell
and Rivers both won, and Georgia began what came to be called the
"Little New Deal" of Rivers's two terms in office (1936–40). Chancellor Sanford enjoyed the four-year respite from the threat of turmoil,
which was the style of Georgia politics any time Eugene Talmadge was
in charge. Gene, however, would be back. Meanwhile Chancellor Sanford enjoyed a relatively issue-free interim, busying himself with the
pleasurable tasks to which he was long accustomed: working, traveling, and talking on behalf of the University System.

A great innovation in Sanford's promotion of higher education was
his appearance on WSB radio a number of times during 1937. Although he said he was "extremely nervous before an invisible audience," he was, as ever, at no loss for words. John Paschal, a long-time
friend and associate from the Georgia Press Institute, was manager of
the *Atlanta Journal,* which owned and operated the WSB radio station.
It was Paschal "my loyal friend" whom Sanford credited with his radio addresses, a series of fifteen-minute "talks" about the University
System, its origins, evolution, current activities, and plans.[32]

The more traditional venues for Sanford talks that year included
the Georgia Baptist Convention and the first annual Georgia Beta
Club Convention, which took place in Atlanta in April 1937. The Beta
Club address merits special attention. This organization was composed of the brightest, most promising high school students from all
around the state. Their potential future importance was not lost on
the chancellor. The message included the essence of much of his view
toward American society of the late 1930s. He called for the students
to have "faith in your fellow worker and to co-labor with him in rais-
ing the general level of society." He called for "faith in our form of
government" and asked that they "seek to purge its imperfections."

Sanford said that with "faith in God and the triumph of right no man can set limits to your achievement." It was good "New Dealism" throughout.[33]

At North Georgia College in Dahlonega that summer the chancellor expressed his delight that "we have one unit in the University System that fosters and promotes military tactics, not because I believe in war but because I believe in peace." Such a unit, he said, "inspires patriotism, creates intense love of country, exemplifies democratic ideals, and awareness of feelings of national unity."[34] Given the calm before the storms in Europe, matters of military preparedness joined with sentiments for national unity make Sanford's comments seem precognitions.

The old days and former accomplishments were never far out of Sanford's mind and routine. Sometimes a student from his teaching days in Athens or a contest fan who had heard of Sanford's puzzle prowess would contact the chancellor with most unchancellorlike requests. Mrs. Monroe A. Butler of Watkinsville wrote Sanford asking for help in solving the "Old Gold Picture Contest." She had been told that "both of you [Mr. and Mrs. Sanford] are experts at this sort of thing." Mrs. Butler said she was a contest finalist but was "pressed for time" and "wonder if you will consider helping me. The lure of big money makes me just that bold." Butler offered to "share any prize." Sanford responded, too late for the contest deadline, but in a kindly way cautioning Butler not to be too hopeful in view of his own information that 40,000 people had been identified as "finalist."[35]

In October 1937, a former student wrote Professor Sanford to request a makeup test. In a letter that would bring a smile to anyone who has taught, Mary Fletcher explained that she had been sick and missed Sanford's final exam in English fiction and would like a chance to finish and get her course credit. She missed the exam in the late summer of 1923.[36]

Often reminders of the old days went back even much further than Mary Fletcher's illness. In September 1937 the Marietta Male Academy held a reunion, which Sanford of course attended. Following the reunion Sanford wrote several of the men who had been his students when he began his career at the Male Academy. "Of course Marietta is very dear to me in many ways," he wrote. "There I found my wife, companion, and helper, our four children were born there and one lies there." He wrote of the reunion as a "wonderful gathering of old boys of Academy days," calling it a great "love feast." As if he found it impossible to dwell exclusively in the past, Sanford took the opportunity to comment on his own desire to "give to Georgia an ideal University System that may serve the youth of Georgia and be a model for other states to imitate."[37]

Building projects constituted far and away the most time- and energy-consuming work of the regents and Chancellor Sanford during the two administrations of Governor Rivers. That fact, however, did not deter Sanford's pursuit of his "ideal System." For some years there had been talk of introducing a doctoral level program at the university. The chancellor worked hard to promote that important step for higher education in the system. During 1937 the regents approved a study of suitable areas of study for the degree and determined that biology, chemistry, history, and education were the best options. Many of the leading faculty in these areas had come to the university in Sanford's time as dean or president and he had special reason to be involved in gaining this next level of recognition for his system.[38]

In addition to Sanford, the staff of the 1937 Board of Regents consisted of L. R. Seibert, board secretary; W. Wilson Noyes, treasurer; and the office support of two male secretaries. The great volume of construction-related business was acknowledged by system assistance from outside the regents' office. In academic matters, however, Chancellor Sanford, with only two or three other staff members, was charged with seeing to the details of projects such as curriculum studies, in addition to keeping up with the progress and problems of each of the system units. The minutes of the Board of Regents meetings provide a glimpse of the range and volume of Sanford's tasks. Virtually every set of board minutes contains the phrase: "resolved, Chancellor

Sanford is authorized and required to take all proper and necessary actions in order that this recommendation be carried into effect as herewith adopted." [39]

One of the chancellor's assignments was to make a study of black education in the state. The charge involved, more than a deep analysis of these institutions, a general inventory of programs and facilities, along with statistical profiles of the black schools. Sanford felt the task important but beyond his single-handed capability. He requested that the board authorize him to seek the assistance of various experts on the matter within the system. [40] There was no way of knowing that with the return of Eugene Talmadge to the governor's mansion in 1941, race would become the flash point of political maneuvering in the University System. Some of those Sanford identified as "expert" in the matter of black education would become the target of Governor Talmadge's controversial "purge" of the system in 1941.

The assignments coming from the board might have tied Sanford to his desk in the regents' office in Atlanta, but the notion of a desk job interrupted only by annual lobbying visits to the legislative chambers was unacceptable; Sanford was forever "on the go." In a meeting of the board in late 1937 he described the in-state traveling aspects of his work. "I have an advantage over the majority of the Regents since my duties as Chancellor compel me to be a circuit rider, visiting the junior colleges at Dahlonega, Carrollton, Americus, Forsyth, Albany, Douglas, Cochran, and Tifton, and the senior colleges at Atlanta, Athens, Milledgeville, Augusta, Valdosta, Statesboro, and Savannah and the experiment stations at Griffin, Tifton, and Blairsville. To visit each of these units, confer with the heads, hold a conference with the faculty, speak to the student body, and address civic bodies is a severe tax on one's mental and physical strength and yet it must be done." [41]

It might have taxed his mind and body, but according to those who traveled with him he relished it all. Sanford's campus visits, however, represent only a portion of his schedule in the late 1930s. A family view of the chancellor's routines is provided in a sketchy daybook that Grace Sanford maintained in 1937 and part of 1938. While much of what she recorded has to do with her own activities, it is obvious that she and her husband, his work, their children, their families, and their jobs were all intertwined in the closely knit Sanford family. The Sanfords were enjoying their first grandchild, Charles S. Sanford Jr., who was born in 1936, and the accounts for 1937 are replete with understandably gushy praise for "our fine grandbaby, he is wonderful." [42]

Beyond the expected devotion to the latest addition to the family there is abundant evidence that both Grace and Steadman enjoyed the company of their adult children. Their youngest, Homer Reynolds, lived with his wife in Atlanta, and the older Sanfords frequently joined them for lunch at Rich's Tearoom or for dinner at the Commerce Club or the Piedmont Driving Club. With both Charles and Shelton in Savannah, it was not surprising that the Athens Sanfords beat a fairly regular path along "Tobacco Road" to the coast, frequently for holiday gatherings. [43]

Few weeks passed without the chancellor making a couple of bus trips from Athens to Atlanta for his work at the office. Usually Grace drove him over for a day during which she shopped or visited with family and friends. A room was always available for the chancellor at the Henry Grady Hotel and sometimes either he or both of them stayed over for some special evening function in Atlanta. Frequently Sanford would take the 8:00 A.M. bus from Athens to Atlanta, returning by bus about 8:00 P.M. or catching a ride with someone returning to the university from the capital. The first week of 1937 was fairly typical, with Sanford making two trips to Atlanta and one to Milledgeville, working in Athens on Friday and devoting his weekend to writing a report for the regents. The Sanfords, despite maintaining separate denominational affiliations, regularly attended church together, occasionally took in a "picture show," and frequently took a Sunday afternoon drive out of Athens "to get some fresh air." [44]

When the legislature was in session the Sanford routine would shift to a more Atlanta-based operation. Grace was proud of her husband's talents in dealing with people and winning them over to his side. Her diary entries for March 1937 include several comments on his success with wining and dining and generally charming Georgia lawmakers. [45]

The Sanfords joined Charles and his young family at Tybee Island for a vacation in July 1937. Grace Sanford reported in her diary that the chancellor had been called by regents chairman Smith "over long distance" to report on an unexpected glitch in a federal building application and that "as a result he caught the night train for Atlanta."[46] Late in the summer, on Steadman's birthday, Grace lamented, "I wish he could stay with me today," but Sanford had to be in Atlanta to attend to more building matters.[47] At sixty-six Steadman Sanford was still going strong, with the end of his labors nowhere in sight.

In the spring of 1938, a convention of Spanish-American War veterans was held at Gainesville, Georgia, and Chancellor Sanford was invited to speak at the memorial service at the First Baptist Church on the Sunday evening opening of the convention. Sanford enjoyed the opportunity to be among long-time comrades and as usual his comments were well received.[48] Gainesville, an hour's drive from Athens, was home to a number of Sanford's friends, and he and Grace sometimes included drop-in visits on their Sunday afternoon outings. Among those friends was Edgar Dunlap, well-known Democrat and Roosevelt supporter of significance on the state level. Dunlap was among those who influenced President Roosevelt to visit Gainesville following the devastating tornado of April 1936. He was also an important supporter of Senator Walter George of Georgia.[49] In the small world of politics in Georgia and in the nation's capital, the paths of Senator George, Edgar Dunlap, President Roosevelt, and the chancellor crossed in the summer of 1938.

In July 1938 the Board of Regents of the University System of Georgia passed a resolution authorizing the "conferring of an honorarious [sic]degree of Doctor of Laws on Franklin Delano Roosevelt."[50] The board authorized Chancellor Sanford and Governor Rivers to request that the president visit the campus of the university during the summer session. A proper ceremony was to be held at Woodruff Hall and it was to be "of the strictest academic nature." As usual S. V. Sanford was put in charge.[51] Sanford had no trouble handling his end of the arrangements. He did not, however, count on the various twists and turns of the New Deal and local politics which the president chose to inject into events on that important day. Thursday, August 11, 1938, was the day that the president was to accept his degree in Athens. The occasion was scheduled for the morning so that he might travel from Athens to Barnesville, Georgia, for another event that afternoon. Senator Walter George had not supported the New Deal to the president's satisfaction. George was running for reelection in 1938, and the president chose Barnesville to ask Georgians to support his hand-picked candidate to unseat George. Lawrence Camp had been Senator Russell's campaign manager in 1934 and almost by default he was anointed by FDR. Few leading Georgia Democrats believed George could be beaten or that the president should interfere, especially Edgar Dunlap, George's campaign manager.

Roosevelt's Barnesville comments were not well received among his Georgia friends. In the end George handily defeated the rest of the field. Sanford's friend Edgar Dunlap was fired from his New Deal post for refusing to go along with the president, and the glory of the day was considerably diminished for S. V. Sanford. Under the lead "Democracy," the *Gainesville Eagle* reported: "Last Thursday morning the University of Georgia gave President Franklin Roosevelt a doctor's degree. That afternoon at Barnesville Doctor Roosevelt prescribed for the people of Georgia. The prescription made some happy, others sick, and still others mad as the devil. . . . He seems to think that the people must send ninety-six Charlie McCarthies to Washington and let Roosevelt pull the strings. The *Eagle* will vote for George. It prefers being buttheaded to wooden headed." [52]

Not everyone forgot the glory of the occasion at Athens on the morning of August 11. A relative from Macon wrote Sanford that he was sorry he did not see him in Athens after the ceremony. "We were very glad indeed to see you deliver the degree to the greatest man in the world today, do hope he will accept the third term am sure they will or ought to offer it to him." [53] Most Georgians seemed to separate their devotion to Roosevelt from what they considered his misplaced sentiments about Senator George. Barnesville did not ruin Georgia for Roosevelt; it simply took a lot of the shine off the events of the morning in Athens and clouded the chancellor's day.

Sanford took some time off following the awarding of Roosevelt's degree. The board had recommended a vacation of "at least a month" and Sanford happily complied. On his return to activity in the late summer and early fall things were soon back to normal. Sandy Beaver came out strongly in opposition to accepting federal funds for system dorm building. He cited his opposition to the extensive construction in process already, the declining student-age population, and his objection to dorm living "unless under strict military discipline." [54] His views did not, however, carry the day. Federal support of building in the system continued. The prospect, however, of the return of Talmadge as governor to energize the sentiments that Beaver advocated loomed ominously. Meanwhile the end of the year was busy. Sanford reported building dedication activities on ten system campuses between November 29 and December 15, 1938. He planned to attend them all. [55]

The second administration of Governor Rivers (1938–40) witnessed a return to depressionlike fiscal pressures. The costs of Rivers's Little New Deal drained the state's resources beyond anyone's expectations and as the second term neared its end, cost-cutting was back as the order of the day for the chancellor and the Board of Regents. Early in 1939 the board stated that "we face a real tragedy as far as the state's institutions of higher education are concerned." The tragedy revolved around a doubling of students in a period of nine years and a reduction in appropriations of 55 percent. The only recourses seemed to be to add more students to classes that were already overly full or to increase matriculation fees, both daunting prospects in what were still tough economic times. [56]

Some found the state of the system puzzling. Thanks to federal assistance there was an unprecedented building program, but at the same time there were salary shortfalls. Chancellor Sanford found himself with the difficult task of explaining this contradiction on his many visits around the state. Although he seemed always able to put the best face on any situation, even he let his frustrations show through occasionally. Never one to bite the hand that fed him, by 1939 Sanford was criticizing federal red tape. The *Atlanta Constitution* quoted him as blaming "jealousy between agencies" in the federal bureaucracy for "impairing efforts by the University System to aid Georgia farmers." He decried the lack of departmental coordination in the face of increasingly desperate needs in the system.[57]

The fiscal crisis resulted in serious reconsiderations of tenure policy and talk of novel approaches to merit pay. By the summer the board addressed issues which related to the money bind that many potential students in the system faced. Increasingly, students sought to complete their initial entry into higher education at the two-year units near home where there were cost advantages. There were problems, however, when these students attempted to transfer to a senior institution only to discover that many of the courses would not count toward their degree in the four-year schools. As much as he loved the university in Athens, Sanford could not ignore the obvious problems this situation created for students who started elsewhere but faced difficulty in attempting to transfer to Athens. The chancellor, who earlier as president of the university opposed the growth of the two-year units, became their advocate. After outlining the problem before the board, Sanford proposed a resolution for the "further coordination of the curriculum of the various units" in order that "students who complete the junior college course may transfer to a senior unit without the loss of time or academic credit."[58] The fact that almost fifty years after his death this problem has yet to be satisfactorily put to rest should not detract from Sanford's farsighted concerns for education for Georgians all around the state.

In the latter part of 1939, Sanford reported good success in spreading the word of the system and its efforts to better serve the citizens thanks to the "splendid cooperation which the Atlanta newspapers, the newspapers of the state, and the radio stations have given to the Board of Regents in the dissemination of research findings and other things about the University System." Sanford and the board were especially grateful for the positive view thus created in that it helped smooth the way for a modest, but essential tuition increase, which was slated for introduction in 1940.[59]

During the fall of 1939 the University of Georgia Press was established. A university press was one of the signs of national higher education status to which the university aspired under the combined encouragement of President Caldwell and Chancellor Sanford. The building of such new bridges to a significant national academic reputation, as well as the purchase of the DeRenne Library, another Sanford project, testifies to the somewhat less well-known side of Sanford's labors for his university and the system.[60]

In 1939 war erupted in Europe. Despite the immediacy of more local issues and problems, Chancellor Sanford realized war's potential implications for Georgia, Georgians, and the business of their education. During the summer Sanford spoke to the directors of Georgia's experiment stations. In his talk he acknowledged "a race going on at the present time—between those who would keep the world a jungle and another which would give it order and justice. If the latter succeeds in overtaking the former and we are all saved from future catastrophe such as we encountered in 1914, it will be done by education."[61] A few days later Sanford received a postcard from his friend Walter B. Hill at the University of North Carolina at Chapel Hill. Hill very pointedly asked: "Are you willing to help the Poles? You helped the Cubans in 1898 and the Belgians in 1917 did you not?"[62] Hill knew his card would provoke Sanford to thought. Sanford's own experiences and those of the nation during his lifetime had left him, like many Americans, with ambivalent feelings about the role of Americans in world affairs. It might be safe to say that where FDR stood vis-à-vis the world situation in 1939, there stood also S. V. Sanford. Both men would take other steps as time passed.

The decade closed in anticipation of the return of many old issues, the continuation of others, and the prospect of brand-new problems and rewards. For S. V. Sanford the forties were to be his eighth decade on the scene. For America and the world the forties were to be the final decade of an old world. For Sanford in his seventies the trauma of the decade took its toll.

NINE

War at Home and Abroad
1940-1943

At the end of Sanford's first half decade as chancellor there was much of which he deserved to be proud. Since 1935, the regents had enjoyed the benefit of more than five million dollars in building funds, almost half of that from federal sources, most from Roosevelt's PWA programs. The regents and Chancellor Sanford spread these funds across the whole University System, but the program had the most dramatic impact on the campus in Athens where seventeen new buildings were constructed and several old structures were remodeled.[1] Despite the relatively limited volume of work on campuses like those at Valdosta and Americus, it was every bit as important to local pride and to the system's status that one or two buildings were added in those locations.

With American entry into the war, military training on system campuses became significant. By the end of the war, the likelihood of continued federal involvement in higher education during peacetime was obvious. The enactment of the G.I. Bill in 1944 would assure a boom on American college and university campuses for years to come. S. V. Sanford had every reason to anticipate an unlimited future of federal largess. Given his impressive track record in securing available funds from such sources, there was little reason to question his optimism.

For Chancellor Sanford the forties began with full expectations for continued successes. Up to that point he had enjoyed and shared political philosophy with his governor and his president. Governor Rivers had carried on his Georgia version of the Roosevelt program in the Little New Deal and the chancellor and the Board of Regents were as busy as the governor in translating the Roosevelt program into accomplishments for Georgia.[2] The strains of Eugene Talmadge's anti–New Deal postures in the mid-thirties were almost forgotten. There was, however, the very real prospect of Gene's return in the gubernatorial campaign year of 1940. On the national scene, Sanford was reasonably comfortable in anticipation of an unprecedented third term election for Roosevelt. Sanford, however, could not have anticipated that the next battle with the reelected Governor Talmadge would have little to do with national politics or Roosevelt. Matters on the national level would rapidly shift from New Deal programs to defense issues. Gene Talmadge was, however, not without an issue.

In March 1940, Sanford's old friend Hughes Spalding wrote to say that Mr. Charles Naegele, who was painting a portrait of the chancellor, was almost finished but needed to schedule at least one more sitting. This portrait depicts Steadman Vincent Sanford at the apogee of his career. He was almost sixty-nine years old. He had lived in eight dynamic decades of American history. His health would shortly suffer a serious setback. He had been, up to this time, never thought of as being any particular age. He was about to suddenly become an old man.

At the beginning of what would be his last five years, Sanford had the pleasure of seeing the creation of another of the University of Georgia's distinctive academic-intellectual traditions, the George Foster Peabody Award. Peabody, a native of Columbus, Georgia, had been a long-time supporter of the university who provided its most significant private individual contributions in the first half of the century. Sanford and other university supporters had courted and consulted with Peabody over the years. When Peabody died in 1938 it seemed logical to pay special homage to this important benefactor. The Board of Regents approved the final form of that tribute in April 1940.

The George Foster Peabody Award was to be administered by the Henry W. Grady School of Journalism "in the same way the Pulitzer Awards are handled by the Journalism School of Columbia University."[3] It may have seemed ambitious to attempt to put this newly created recognition in a category with the Pulitzer, but Sanford and the other supporters in the journalism school at the university proved to be not one bit too immodest, as it turned out. The Peabody is today considered the most distinguished of awards in broadcasting. The George Foster Peabody Radio Award, as it was initially known, was to be awarded beginning in 1941 for "the most distinguished and meritorious public service" rendered by each of three American radio stations, one local, one regional, and one national. The award was also to go to "a national chain." It was the purpose of the award not only to recognize excellence, but to "perpetuate the name of George Foster Peabody, benefactor and life trustee of the University of Georgia and friend of the education profession everywhere."[4] The regents of the University System were to bestow the award upon the recommendation of an advisory board to be set up and maintained by the University of Georgia and composed of the chancellor "and eleven other outstanding American citizens who have demonstrated in notable degree their interest in public affairs." The first awards were to be made in 1941 for programs broadcast in 1940.[5]

Within a month of the board meeting at which the Peabody Awards were formally established, Sanford's poor health led to his confinement in bed at home in Athens. Board of Regents chairman Marion Smith informed the board of the "serious illness of Chancellor Sanford" on May 10, 1940. Smith said that Sanford's attending physician "had pronounced the Chancellor's illness to be critical." The complaint was "bordering on pneumonia" and the doctor had ordered him to take a "rest of not less than one month from all activities of the Board of Regents."[6]

The notice of Sanford's illness in the newspapers brought a flood of

letters. Presidents of system institutions wrote expressing their concern: Guy Wells from Milledgeville, M. L. Brittain from Georgia Tech,
Marvin Pittman from Statesboro, and others. Members or former
members of the Board of Regents conveyed their sympathy and occasional asides and advice. Edgar Dunlap of Gainesville cautioned
Sanford to get well because he might be required to "take another
company of Georgia soldiers to the European war" in light of what
he was reading in the papers lately. Georgia Tech president Brittain
advised Sanford to "take things more easily, cut out speeches for a
while."[7]

Sanford was out of commission for almost four months. As soon as
he was well enough to travel, he and Grace went to the Georgia coast
where they visited with their children as Sanford rested and recuper-
ated. There were dozens of letters to Sanford or Grace about her husband's health during the spring and summer. After the first round of
contacts from his colleagues, Sanford began to hear from his broad
constituency around the state. W. M. Hubbard wrote to "Mrs. Dr. Sanford" that he was "praying daily" for Sanford and for the "restoral
[sic] of his health." Hubbard, who apparently worked in public relations at the system school in Fort Valley, Georgia, allowed he could
not "see how the University System neither Georgia can get along
without our dear Chancellor Dr. Sanford." Hubbard was willing to go
beyond prayer and offered to send "him some more chickens from
my yard any time desired." In the touching and telling manner of that
day Hubbard signed his letter W. M. Hubbard "Negro."[8]

John Donald Wade, at the time chairman of the English department
at the university, one of the state's most distinguished scholars and
an expert in southern literature, wrote Mr. and Mrs. Sanford in late
May that he was pleased to hear "cheering news" of Sanford's health.
"Heaven knows it has been grateful to me to have it so ... particularly
in a time when the world at large is so terrifyingly uncheering."[9]

As time passed and Sanford improved, the notes became more informal and newsy. Chip Robert wrote that he was interested in Sanford's views on the "present crisis, inasmuch as you helped settle the
Spanish American War in such a great way."[10]

The war was a topic to some degree in almost every letter during the late summer of 1940. President Frank Reade from the system college in Valdosta wrote Sanford that his father, an Englishman, was "distressed about the war." The events in Europe were creating cases of "nerves" all over. The writer finally got to the apparent point of his letter: "all of which bring me around to *you* and how you have stood the past five years without going into screaming fits nobody in the University System can understand." He continued to plead for Sanford to remain away from work for at least *three more months.* "You have," he wrote, "done fifteen years of work in the past five years. We need you back in good shape when the General Assembly meets early in the winter." [11]

Sanford appeared at the Board of Regents meeting in July, but under orders to continue to rest until September. One particular item on the agenda in July probably reinforced Sanford's will to be there and to return to the job as soon as possible. At that July 12, 1940, meeting the new chairman of the board, Cason Callaway, negotiated the formal amendments to the by-law which allowed for the appointment of a vice chancellor. Dr. J. Curtis Dixon had been enlisted to cover the work of the ailing chancellor some months earlier at the behest of Callaway. Dixon's position as vice chancellor was formalized at an annual salary of $6,000, beginning July 1, 1940. Sanford had not wanted and felt he had not needed such an assistant. Back on the job the chancellor made sure he did not have that burden for long. On a more positive note, that same session approved the newly created Ph.D. programs in history and American literature, firsts for the university. Sanford was also pleased that the Peabody Award board which he had recommended had been approved, and that he was to inform them and invite them to be members. [12]

When Sanford returned to work in September it was just in time to prepare for the inevitable tensions of the coming year; Gene Talmadge had just been elected to his third term as governor of Georgia. More than a year before the 1940 gubernatorial race, Talmadge had gathered his closest supporters and begun politicking in a quiet way. By 1940 a grassroots movement was in place. Given the growing disillusionment with Governor Rivers, hints of scandal, the cost of his programs, and the near bankruptcy of the state, the situation seemed ideal for Gene's return to power. No small factor working in his behalf was the sense of crisis which the war in Europe had created. Talmadge was seen as a man of action in a time that might demand a decisive leader. He was also a man of simple answers to complex problems. The voters' mood seemed to enhance Talmadge's chances.[13]

By the time of his resounding victory in September 1940, Talmadge appeared even to his old nemeses, the Atlanta newspapers, a mellower fellow, willing to recognize the past errors of opposing the New Deal and dedicated to a platform of addressing real needs in Georgia. According to Talmadge biographer William Anderson, "a cautiously optimistic state press seemed to think that possibly Gene's time as a leader had arrived." In an effort to ensure a cooperative legislature, Gene worked for its support in advance and "the 1941 legislature opened to more soothing words than had been heard in years."[14]

In the months between the election and the beginning of Talmadge's third term, Chancellor Sanford enjoyed several personal and professional recognitions. In December he and Dr. Frank K. Boland were the only Georgians elected to the initial founders board of the Phi Beta Kappa Association. The association, established at the Harvard Club in New York, chose only seventy individuals nationwide.[15] That same month outgoing Governor Rivers, in his last meeting with the Board of Regents, singled out Sanford for special recognition: "If I had to select a man in Georgia to whom the State owes most at the present . . . then there would be no question in my mind as to whom we should honor the most . . . Chancellor Sanford."[16]

American society and its values had changed considerably since young Professor Sanford suited up for the war with Spain almost fifty years earlier. The experience of World War I and the disillusionment that followed it had created a less-than-unified American point of view vis-à-vis the situation in Europe as the forties began. Sanford looked to President Roosevelt for guidance in those months of agonizing debate. The old comfort of national unity, a windfall of late-nineteenth-century American history, was no more. Sanford and his generation longed for the clarity of that other century, but the unsettling experiences of an earlier world war, an economic depression, and the revolutionary programs of Roosevelt's New Deal all conspired to deprive Sanford of the security of his past. These last years of Sanford's life were to be increasingly uncomfortable as what had essentially been a continuation of the previous century faded and the reality of the twentieth century dawned.

At the April 8, 1941, meeting of the Board of Regents, old-time Talmadge supporter and advisor Sandy Beaver of Gainesville was elected chairman of the board. Beaver, a university-educated native of the Augusta area, had become a wealthy and influential figure through his role as an entrepreneurial educator. Beaver had purchased a failing private secondary school and by the late thirties built from that base and another modest military boys' school a profitable institution, Riverside Military Academy, with campuses in Gainesville, Georgia, and Hollywood, Florida. Beaver was first named to the Board of Regents by Governor Talmadge in 1933, and he continued to serve until 1952 with the interruption of a single year during those years. Beaver would preside over the most traumatic events in the history of the regents to that time, what has come to be called the "Cocking Controversy," the "Talmadge Purge of the Regents," or as Talmadge's biographer William Anderson entitled it, quoting a regent's description, "One Hell of An Incident." [17] It is something of a puzzlement that Chancellor S. V. Sanford, arguably the best-known figure in the University System of Georgia and its chief executive, was to play a role all but invisible to the public in these matters. Examining and understanding Sanford's low profile in these events is part of appreciating the dilemma of a nineteenth-century man caught in a twentieth-century controversy.

Race was not an issue in Georgia before the changes set in motion by events of near mid-century. Georgia, like the rest of the American South and much of America at large, was a segregated society in which African Americans occupied a distinctly disadvantaged second-, if not

third-class status. It may be accurate to say that white women occupied the second-class place. Such was the case in matters of daily business, work, recreation, worship, politics, education, or any realm considered to be a social, cultural, political, or economic domain. There
was no issue as to inequality; it was the norm and was protected by
the formal machines of citizenship as well as tradition. S. V. Sanford
was as much a product and part of this reality as Gene Talmadge or
any other white male figure of prominence or of no consequence. The
reality, however, was under siege. Not all the establishment saw or
understood the invaders. Those who saw it understood it in terms of
their own paranoia.

Before 1941 Gene Talmadge was not especially racist nor was he
even vocally a segregationist; there was no need for it. During his third
term, however, Talmadge recognized the invaders and took steps to
halt their march. Roosevelt represented a new and threatening direction in society, a direction of intrusive values, especially disconcerting
to a southern leader well grounded in the structures of the past. Talmadge, without regard to the matter of race, had been initially uncomfortable with the New Deal, but, in the face of economic pragmatism, he had suppressed his animosities. When he returned to
office in 1941, it was on the heels of a fiscally straining Rivers administration experiment in a Little New Deal for Georgia and after several
years of having had the microscopes of the academic social scientists
focused on the South. Roosevelt and the social engineers whom Talmadge saw as his spawn were fair targets again. In his earlier administrations Gene had done battle with New Deal programs and with
agency heads who seemed out of touch with the reality of tradition in
Georgia. When New Deal dollars came they sometimes were delivered
by critics of Georgia's social order, its educational system, and its racial situation. Governor Talmadge had attempted to dampen Chancellor Sanford's early enthusiasm for federal dollars for building in an
earlier manifestation of his fears. This time Governor Talmadge took
more direct action.

Among Governor Talmadge's initial targets were Walter D. Cocking
and Marvin S. Pittman. Cocking was dean of the university's Col-

lege of Education and Marvin Pittman was president of the Georgia Teachers College at Statesboro. Before the squall of controversy subsided almost a year later, several other individuals had been swept up in the tide of Talmadge's purge of the University System.

Dean Cocking had earned the respect of both President Caldwell and Chancellor Sanford. The Iowa-born Cocking with his Ph.D. from Columbia came to Georgia in 1937 from Tennessee, where he had been commissioner of education since 1933. At the University of Georgia Cocking exercised forceful leadership, hired new scholars, and took on serious curriculum revision.[18] His brusque personality and his identification as an outsider offended some, but Caldwell and Sanford valued his efforts and in 1938 enlisted him to head up the study of the status of higher education for African Americans in Georgia under the auspices of a Rosenwald Fund grant. Cocking's role in the dismissal of university staff member Sylla Hamilton initiated the dean's persecution by the governor. Hamilton contacted the governor with the accusation that Cocking had advocated racially integrated schools. Additionally, Talmadge stalwarts in the community of Athens suggested Cocking was socializing with blacks.[19] Cocking quickly became an item on the governor's hit list.

Marvin Pittman was targeted by the governor because of reputed political activity in the Statesboro community. Talmadge's informant in Pittman's case was a disgruntled professor who disapproved of Pittman's progressivism and resented the promotion of some of his colleagues. Pittman, like Cocking, had a Ph.D. from Columbia, but he was a native of Mississippi. He was director of laboratory schools at Michigan State Normal College when he was hired as the president of the South Georgia Teachers College at Statesboro in 1934. Pittman enjoyed a busy and successful regime of building and improvement, and in 1939 the regents changed his institution's name to Georgia Teachers College. Talmadge was irritated at his loss of the Statesboro community in the fall 1940 governor's race. He took the reports that Pittman, who was demeaned as a racial equality advocate, had supported another candidate as reason enough to remove him.[20]

In the logic and rhetoric of Governor Talmadge, Cocking and

Pittman personified the outsider, the foreigner, the critic of southern and Georgia traditions, and thus the establishment. They appeared to threaten a value system the heart of which was based on clear separation of the races and subjugation of one to the other.

More has been written about the Cocking Case than about any other topic of higher education in Georgia until the desegregation of the university system in the 1960s. Virtually the entire attention of the Board of Regents for most of 1941 and 1942 was devoted to matters related to the case. Consequently, it would seem Chancellor Sanford during that time was also consumed by the matter. Among Sanford's scrapbooks are at least three devoted to "Talmadge and Negroes" or similarly identified collections of newspaper clippings from May 1941 to January 1943. It is odd that amid all the newspaper accounts represented by clippings in the scrapbooks, there are few accounts of the role of the chancellor in the matter.

"The matter" after all is said and done was simply this: On May 30, 1941, when Chancellor Sanford recommended the reelection of the heads of the units of the University System, Governor Talmadge, as a voting member of the regents, announced "after careful consideration, the committee on Education and Finance approved the recommendation of Chancellor Sanford except in the case of President Marvin S. Pittman of the Georgia Teachers College at Statesboro." Talmadge justified the rejection on the basis that "President Pittman had engaged in local partisan politics and that it would be for the best interest of the University System not to re-elect him as President." The governor proceeded to state that he had been informed that Dean Walter Cocking of the College of Education at the University of Georgia "had made a statement that he wanted to see the time when a school of Negroes would be established at Athens so that Negroes and white boys and girls could associate together." Talmadge then announced he "would remove any person in the University System advocating communism or racial equality." Talmadge's subsequent motion that Dean Cocking not be reelected was adopted by a vote of eight to four.[21]

The governor's action did not come without previous discussions with University System administrators. Chancellor Sanford, according to a detailed account of the Cocking affair, "early in 1941 discussed the whole [Cocking] situation with him [Governor Talmadge]." Reportedly, Talmadge wanted resignations from Cocking and several others in the system, but Sanford, "to avoid a confrontation, did not disclose publicly the happenings at the meeting. Neither did he act on the Governor's suggestions, hoping no doubt that by a delay the problem might correct itself, or that Talmadge might change his mind." [22] In his history of the university, Professor Thomas Dyer reported that university president Caldwell heard of the Talmadge-Sanford conversation and approached Sandy Beaver, who carried out an informal investigation of Cocking in Athens and concluded that the rumors about Cocking were unfounded. [23] Robert Preston Brooks's account says that Talmadge asked his friend Beaver to look into the case. In this version Beaver came to Athens and "held long interviews with those concerned in the matter, including President Caldwell, Chancellor Sanford, Dean Cocking, and others." Brooks, in whose office these hearings were held, reported that Beaver "became convinced that there was no substantial basis for Mrs. Hamilton's charges." According to Brooks, Beaver thought Talmadge, when given his conclusions, would drop the matter. [24] The events of May 30 proved otherwise. That Beaver, who is considered a heroic adversary of his friend Talmadge in this controversy, and Sanford, who is seen by some as ineffective and not devoted to justice in the matter, occupied virtually the same position at this point is significant for the long-term evaluation of Sanford's role in these and subsequent events.

The May 30 board meeting was held in Athens on the campus of the university; during a recess for the ceremony dedicating the new fine arts building, President Caldwell was informed of the events of the early session. Caldwell immediately tendered his resignation. Caldwell's response has been called by one historian of these events the "forthright action," which "saved the day." [25] When Sandy Beaver read Caldwell's letter of resignation to the reassembled board meeting he also suggested that Cocking be given an opportunity to respond to the charges against him. Beaver, despite his long-time connections to the governor, was obviously distressed over the turn of events, especially since he, like Chancellor Sanford, believed they had allayed Talmadge's fears about Cocking. Beaver's suggestion was adopted with only Governor Talmadge and regent John J. Cummings voting in the negative. In an odd turn of events, Governor Talmadge moved that, given that Cocking was to be allowed to respond, Pittman should also be reconsidered. This motion passed unanimously. The board scheduled a June 16 meeting in Atlanta to more fully examine "alleged communistic and racial equality utterances."[26] Caldwell's resignation was retracted.

The June 16 meeting convened in the governor's office at 10:00 A.M. Various accounts of these events indicate that the meeting was to be a public one, but the minutes from the May 30 meeting do not make that clear. At any rate, the meeting devolved into an executive session to discuss the reemployment of Cocking and Pittman. All members of the board were present.[27] During the five hours of the meeting, Sylla Hamilton testified to Cocking's advocacy of race mixing, but no corroboration was offered. A large number of Cocking supporters testified. Cocking was reappointed by a vote of eight to seven with chairman Beaver not voting. "Talmadge was visibly upset." The length of the meeting precluded acting on the Pittman case, so another meeting was called for July 14.[28]

In the relatively short interval between the June and July meetings, Governor Talmadge took steps to ensure a reversal of the board's action. The *Atlanta Constitution* reported on June 21 that the governor had notified Cocking to be present at the July meeting.[29] It was obvious that Talmadge had a plan to ensure a more supportive vote at the next meeting and did not intend to allow Cocking to escape his wrath.

The governor's plan was simple. He called on Sandy Beaver, E. Ormonde Hunter, and Miller R. Bell, all his appointees to the board, and none of whom supported him in the June meeting, to resign under the pretense that as University of Georgia graduates they had violated a supposed limit to the number of graduates of any single system institution on the board. All three refused. Next Talmadge asked another opponent on the board, Clark Howell, to step down. As a regular anti-Talmadge member of the regents, Howell had some time before told Talmadge he would resign if their differences presented problems for the governor. Howell honored his pledge. Another non-supporter, Lucien Goodrich, also resigned. Meanwhile the governor blatantly changed the termination date on regent Miller R. Bell's appointment. Bell had been appointed to replace his deceased father and was designated in Talmadge's appointment of him to serve until 1947. Talmadge simply changed the date on the appointment document to make the termination date 1941. Miller was out. Three of the eight who voted against Talmadge's position in June in an eight to seven split were gone before the July 14 meeting, replaced by Scott Candler, Joe Ben Jackson, and James S. Peters. The replacements could be counted on to vote on behalf of the Governor.[30]

Accounts of the July 14 meeting of the regents depict it as a nadir of leadership in higher education in Georgia. Chancellor Sanford's absence has been pointed out and criticized by some, but given closer examination of the setting and circumstances, Sanford's explanation to the press that "there wasn't any use" being present makes sense.

The governor pressed one of his recent appointees, James S. Peters, to serve as Cocking's prosecutor. As Peters lamely tried to satisfy his patron, Talmadge reportedly yelled his directions to Peters: "Hit the chair and holler." Both Cocking and Pittman were dismissed, the vote being ten to five. The remaining five of the original Talmadge opponents cast their votes for Cocking and Pittman while the old Talmadge supporters and his three new appointees acted according to the governor's script.[31]

Other dismissals followed: two staff members at the Statesboro school who were ardent Pittman defenders, the chair of an academic department in Statesboro charged with "communist" and "pro-German" leanings, a Cooperative Extension Service employee who had crossed a Talmadge appointee, Professor P. D. Bush of North Georgia College who had pro-Talmadge enemies in Dahlonega, and J. Curtis Dixon, vice chancellor of the University System.[32]

The matter of Dixon's dismissal, a sometimes overlooked facet of the "Talmadge Purge," provides a pivot on which turns a closer analysis of the role of S. V. Sanford in these events up through the July 14, 1941, meeting. The most thorough study of the Cocking case, James Cook's "Politics and Education in the Talmadge Era: The Controversy over the University System, 1941–42," found little to admire in Chancellor Sanford's role during those critical months of 1941. Cook said that despite the chancellor's conviction that Pittman and Cocking were "excellent educators" and the fact that he had recommended their reemployment, "he failed to support them in their time of greatest need."[33] Cook dismissed Sanford as, while "dedicated to public education, old, infirm, and dispirited." Sanford's absence from the July 14 meeting was cited by Cook as if that constituted proof of his ineffectiveness and unwillingness to support the side of right. Cook believed that Sanford's position was "critical" in the conflict, with his "considerable prestige throughout the state." "In this controversy his opinion," posited Cook, "would have been influential with the public and even with the Regents, but after May 30 his voice was silent."[34]

Cook drew heavily on the recollections and testimony of J. Curtis Dixon. Dixon, it will be recalled, was appointed as vice chancellor of the University System during the previous summer when Sanford had been ill. Cason Callaway, chairman of the Board of Regents at that time, had contacted Dixon in June 1940 about taking on what the regents envisioned as the responsibilities of this soon-to-be-created position. According to Dixon's testimony, "Mr. Callaway and other of the Regents felt that Dr. Sanford was getting along in years and should be relieved of all detailed duties of the Chancellorship."[35]

According to Dixon, Callaway saw the proposed vice chancellor devoting "his time and attention to the development of the University System's program of education and to the improvement of the business administration of the System." Sanford would be left free to "devote his entire time and energy to the political and public relations aspect of the job." In a parenthetical aside in his testimony at this point Dixon interjected, "little did he know the Chancellor!"[36]

Dixon met with Callaway at the board office on June 13, 1940. Callaway informed him that he had been elected vice chancellor, assuring him that the action was "approved by Dr. Sanford, the Chancellor, and was unanimous." According to Dixon, Callaway had done all this by phone with the chancellor and board members. Dixon said that since Sanford was absent due to illness Callaway requested that he start work immediately.[37]

During the remainder of the summer of 1940, Dixon said he kept in contact with the chancellor who was recuperating at Savannah Beach. Through phone calls and letters the two, he said, worked out an outline of the vice chancellor's job. In his September 1941 statement, Dixon moved directly from these events in the summer of 1940 to the Talmadge purge a year later. Dixon reported that he realized he, too, was to be fired when regent Peters, acting as prosecutor for Talmadge, included in his evidence against Cocking on July 14, 1941, "a list of names of those who had attended a meeting of the Council on Rural Education of the Julius Rosenwald Fund." Peters, "from this list of forty names, read two—W. D. Cocking and J. C. Dixon."[38] The Rosenwald Fund had long since come to mean "outsider meddling," "race-mixing," and "foreign ideas" in the lexicon of the Talmadge crowd. Seeing Cocking doomed, Dixon knew that he, too, tarred with the Rosenwald brush, was on his way out. In an executive session later that same day Dixon was fired.[39]

Professor Cook's study faulted the chancellor, who he said "was in a position to prevent the purges." Sanford "chose a safe course rather than confront the governor, while bolder spirits defended the University System." Cook contended that "Sanford evidently valued his own job more than the reputation of the University System . . . for he did not lift a finger to support them even though he regarded several of them as outstanding educators." Cook weakens his own logic when he places the great weight of his evidence against Sanford on the chancellor's failure to attend the July 14 meeting of the regents. "So careful was Sanford in avoiding a commitment that he did not even attend the public hearing which ousted Pittman and Cocking." Cook asserts that Sanford's "renown" and "respect" in Georgia "might well have aroused the public and the Regents to such a point that Talmadge could have been persuaded to abandon his effort to control the colleges." Cook believed Sanford "contributed substantially to the purges," in his "unwillingness to protest against activities that he knew were wrong."[40]

The influence of Dixon on Cook's analysis seems clear from a strikingly similar indictment of the chancellor in the typescript of Dixon's testimony: "It is particularly significant that: (1) In the Athens meeting of May 30, the Chancellor did not utter one word in defense of Cocking or in advocacy of the professional procedure which should be followed in the election or discharge of a faculty member; (2) in the meeting of June 16 in the Governor's office the Chancellor again did not come to Cocking's defense; (3) in the public hearing in the House of Representatives, July 14, the Chancellor was conspicuous by his complete absence from the Hall; (4) In the executive session of the Regents in the Governor's office, later in the afternoon of July 14, the Chancellor again did not have anything to say when Bush, Davis, and I were fired."[41]

Dixon correctly perceived that Chancellor Sanford was not enamored with the notion of a vice chancellor. Two regents staff members who worked in the office of the Board of Regents in late 1939 and into 1941 recalled that around the office it was a shock to Dixon that he was not assigned a private office and secretary and that he was assigned a corner of the board room and shared, as did the chancellor, the secretarial support with others in the office. "Steadie did not want a vice chancellor," recalled Ralph Moor, "and although he always treated Dixon with courtesy, he never gave him any assignments nor did he relinquish any of his own activities to him."[42] Ben Gray Moore, another office staff person, characterized Dixon as having a "tremendous ego." Dixon, he says, spent a lot of time writing to and talking on the phone with his colleagues outside Georgia. He didn't fit into the culture of the board office and early on realized he had "made a terrible mistake in taking the job."[43]

Sanford's views of the value of Dixon to the operations of the chancellor's office were reflected in the budget proposed for 1941– 42 by the chancellor; it did not include Dixon. At the time Talmadge began his purge, Dixon's fate had already been determined to S. V. Sanford's satisfaction. He was to be gone.

Cook said of the relationship between Sanford and Dixon: "despite Dixon's cooperative efforts, friction soon developed between the two men and it became more acute when Sanford returned to work" (following his absence due to illness in the summer of 1940). Chancellor Sanford himself admitted to his displeasure with the appointment of a vice chancellor. In November 1941 under questioning by a committee assigned by the Southern Association of Colleges and Schools to investigate the University System situation, Sanford was completely open with his position. He said: "I am a very peculiar individual. I want to do all the work myself or none. I have rejected offers for assistants for the past four years. I didn't want any because they are only in my way. They [the Regents] finally decided to send me Dixon. He was a fine man but I realized his experience was not in the type of work I needed. He is fine—would be valuable to someone who wants to transfer some of his work. I didn't need the position of Vice Chancellor in the office. There is nothing irregular, just my wish in the matter." [44]

Dixon obviously knew how Chancellor Sanford felt about him. Whatever the motive behind his dismissal, Dixon is correct in the assumption that Sanford did nothing to save him from that fate. The difficulties between Dixon and Sanford are admitted on all sides. Dixon's assessment of Sanford's role in the larger issue of the Cocking dismissal should be considered with that in mind.

Chancellor Sanford's uncharacteristically low profile throughout the storms of 1941 deserves further analysis. Cook admits that Sanford was "politically astute, wise to the ways of Georgia politicians in general, and to Talmadge in particular." [45] His conclusion that Sanford "knew that if he spoke out against the Governor, he would become expendable," however, does not match up to Sanford's actions. There is no indication that Sanford did anything out of order, unsupportive, or cowardly in the May 30 meeting. He recommended Cocking's reappointment despite his knowledge of the governor's suspicion of Cocking. Had he been a toady of Talmadge, as suggested by Cook, would he have done so? Cook says Sanford "chose a safe course" and that "bolder spirits," suggesting university president Caldwell, "defended the University System." We do not and cannot know what course Sanford would have taken if Cocking and Pittman had been fired on May 30. They were not fired then and while it seems appropriate to give credit to President Caldwell for threatening to resign and to Sandy Beaver for moving for a reconsideration of the firing of Cocking, it does not logically follow that Sanford should be discredited for his role at the May 30 meeting. He recommended Cocking and Cocking was not fired; thus Dixon's, and by implication, Cook's criticism of Sanford's actions, or lack of them at that point, seems misdirected. There may have been no higher ground for Sanford to take.

Looking into the progress of the events beyond May, Cook and Dixon fault Sanford for not coming to the defense of Cocking at the June 16 meeting. The facts are these: Cocking was well defended by many at that meeting; the Talmadge side had but one witness; Cocking, once more, was not fired but rather confirmed by a vote of eight to seven. Sanford had no vote to cast; President Caldwell did not threaten to resign again, nor was there a need to. What value would there have been in the chancellor taking some dramatic stand which would have at best been an echo of the good sense that had prevailed anyway, especially since he faced a future of working with not only the regents who supported his original recommendation, but with those who opposed and with the governor? Thus Sanford appears unblemished after what might be considered round 2.

By round 3, July 14, "the fix was in." Talmadge had succeeded in replacing his opponents on the board with supporters. The power Cook attributes to Sanford through his "renown and respect" to "arouse the public and the Regents to such a point that Talmadge could have been persuaded to abandon his efforts to control the colleges"[46] was a myth under those circumstances. Surely S. V. Sanford was astute enough to realize the folly of betting the whole pot against a stacked deck. Sanford didn't feed cards to Talmadge; he merely sat out the hand. S. V. Sanford literally sat it out in the hallway outside the governor's office while Talmadge stooges cast their ballots as directed. Sanford's influence over that vote would have been nil.

An undated newspaper clipping in one of the several Sanford scrapbooks devoted to this episode starts with the lead "Disappointed Over Action, Sanford Admits": "Steadman V. Sanford, Chancellor of the University System of Georgia said he was a mighty disappointed man yesterday when the Board of Regents followed the lead of Governor Eugene Talmadge and voted ten to five not to re-employ Cocking and Pittman. After the public trials the Board of Regents went into an executive session in the Governor's office and from this conclave Dr. Sanford was excluded. Sitting alone in one of the big red leather chairs just outside the Governor's door the Chancellor twisted and untwisted a scrap of paper. 'I didn't attend the trials,' he said, 'there wasn't any use.'"[47]

The *Macon News* reported on July 16, 1941, that Sanford was trying to see what could be "salvaged." The comments came as the chancellor was leaving a meeting with the governor. Across the state the press took Talmadge to task for his actions. The *Atlanta Journal,* in its July 21 edition, published a long selection of attacks on the governor taken from newspapers in Macon, Walker County in northwest Georgia, Madison in middle Georgia, Cuthbert in southwest Georgia, Elberton in northeast Georgia, and from Gainesville, Thomaston, and Brunswick.[48] One of the Sanford scrapbooks contains fifty-three pages of newspaper clippings devoted exclusively to the anti-Talmadge reactions. There is no indication that Sanford was reluctant to share his disapproval of the governor's action. It also appears obvious that the chancellor enjoyed the attacks on the governor which the Talmadge purge had engendered. This hardly seems to indicate a passive, unsympathetic role for the chancellor.

Amid the flurry of events in mid-July, the Southern Association of Colleges and Schools announced a probe into alleged "political interference" in the University System.[49] Sanford, an old hand in dealing with matters that involved the effect of sanctions by such agencies, must have been ambivalent. He would do all he could to prevent actions against the system which would jeopardize accreditation, but he must have privately enjoyed the prospect of seeing Talmadge's indiscretions called to account in a way that was guaranteed to arouse the ire of many Georgians.

At issue was the possibility of the Southern Association withdrawing its accreditation for programs of the system. At risk would be the status of the credentials of those system students about to graduate, especially the status of graduates of 1941 who were seeking military commissions on the basis of their completion of accredited programs.

The Southern Association withheld action pending a hearing to be conducted in Atlanta in November. In October, meanwhile, another organization, the Southern University Conference, dropped the University of Georgia from its membership following its own inquiry into the matter, which included interviewing several regents, Chancellor Sanford, and President Caldwell in Birmingham.[50] This organization did not have the power of accreditation. It was a regional group devoted to "the promotion of excellence in collegiate work at the upper and graduate level in the south." Among the citizenry the lack of a clear understanding of the differences between the Southern University Conference and the Southern Association of Colleges and Schools worked to the advantage of anti-Talmadge forces.

The most focused reactions during the fall were those of system students, especially those on the university campus in Athens, where approximately fifteen hundred gathered to burn the governor in effigy.[51] Several hundred student protesters motored to Atlanta to present a petition on the capitol steps. In the rising tide of indignation, attorney general Ellis Arnall saw his opportunity to challenge Talmadge in the upcoming governor's race of 1942. Before the end of 1941 Arnall was a declared candidate, and his cause was the sanctity of a system of higher education in Georgia, unblemished and undiminished by the evils of political interference.

The tide of events late in 1941, including Sandy Beaver's persistent campaign to get Talmadge to back down in order to preserve accreditation for the University System, led to an unusually candid admission by the governor that he had perhaps acted hastily. Biographer William Anderson, citing communications between Beaver and the governor, credited the Gainesville educator with being the chief influence in getting Talmadge to admit his error. Additionally Anderson felt that Talmadge "buckled under the enormous public outcry to save the schools regardless of the cost."[52] Before the end of October, Talmadge admitted wrongdoing in a speech apparently written by Beaver, and in the November 1, 1941, meeting of the Board of Regents Governor Talmadge was quoted as saying: "I have inadvertently run afoul of the great higher educational system. I here now heartily concur in every proper and logical safeguard that has and can be made to 'protect the system.'"[53]

An investigative committee of the Southern Association of Colleges and Schools convened at the Ansley Hotel in Atlanta on November 3, holding hearings for two days. Members of the Board of Regents, as well as Chancellor Sanford, were questioned and offered the opportunity to make a plea for continued accreditation. Despite his promise to "do anything," the governor acted in ways at odds with the spirit of compromise which even his own advocates on the board held up to the Southern Association. Sanford and the regents promised reform, but in the background was the suspiciously lingering smell of brimstone coming from the governor's office. Talmadge, in keeping his distance from the placaters and their promises, doomed the efforts of those appearing before the early November hearings. For their part, even those who worked on behalf of continued accreditation appeared less than candid in admission of the problems of political interference and its potential in the system. There was talk aplenty but nothing to ensure that Governor Talmadge would not immediately revert to form as soon as the blessings of the association were restored.

The investigative committee was composed of O. C. Carmichael, chancellor of Vanderbilt University; Alex Guerry, vice chancellor of the University of the South; and Richard C. Foster, president of the University of Alabama. Under questioning by these men, Chancellor Sanford freely admitted that there had been irregularities in the proceedings leading to the firing of Cocking and Pittman, that the system by-laws had been violated, and that appointments had been made contrary to his own recommendations. It was, however, the chancellor's contention that despite the wrongful dismissal of "only a few people" the system was "functioning acceptably." Sanford contended that the villains of the piece were not University System people: "No charge of dishonesty can be brought against the Chancellor, the heads of institutions, or members of the faculties." He dismissed the Georgia affair as "a sporadic case, growing out of conflict of ideals and strong convictions among personalities." In the end Sanford called for understanding and mercy. In suspending accreditation for system schools, Sanford maintained, "the innocent would be the sufferers": the students, the graduates, the ranks of teachers, doctors, lawyers, and engineers to be. "Will you," Sanford asked, "permit the University System of Georgia to go on with the training of teachers, working in cordial cooperation with the other great educational agencies of our Southland in the effort to cure our many social, economic, and financial ills?"[54]

At the conclusion of his remarks to the committee, Chancellor Sanford promised: "If the committee of three from the Southern Association will tell us specifically what must be done to save the situation, I am confident the requirements will be met, however drastic they may be. In our opinion the Southern Association can render more effective service to the University System of Georgia by standing by us as a protector in this, our hour of peril."[55]

The committee was not convinced of the board or the chancellor's liberty to carry out such promises in light of Talmadge's record. In December the Southern Association, on recommendation of the November committee, voted unanimously to remove the white institutions of the University System of Georgia from the list of accredited members. The effective date was postponed to the fall 1942 term to allow graduating students to complete accredited programs. There were rumors and hopes that in part the delay was to give Georgia time to take some concrete actions that would assure the system protection from political interference. The pending governor's race loomed large as a motivation for such hopes.

Writing of the 1942 Georgia elections, Talmadge biographer William Anderson insists that the contest was not between liberal and conservative candidates (Ellis Arnall and Eugene Talmadge); that is, it was not a "blow to racism," "because all of the candidates were racists at heart." Anderson posits that two racists opposed each other: "one identified with closing the colleges, the other with keeping them open and accredited." [56] Arnall, taking advantage of the student and public outcry on behalf of saving the schools, based his whole campaign on education. He depicted Talmadge as Georgia's Hitler and promised to protect education from political interference by reducing the power of the governor over departments within the state government and by making the Board of Regents a constitutionally independent board. For his part Talmadge played the race card as never before in an attempt to drown out Arnall's call for educational independence. The campaign, however, was for Talmadge a series of missteps and disasters, complicated by the specter of former Talmadge stalwarts seeking their own political ends from the shadow of a former hero who looked to be in trouble.

On the eve of the campaign year and shortly following the ouster vote in the Southern Association, Chancellor Sanford had written to the "Presidents, Faculty, and Students" of the University System asking for "unity and loyalty" in the time of crisis. The letter was drafted in reference to the December 4 vote of the Southern Association, but dated on Monday, December 8, 1941, a day when Americans everywhere were recovering from the jolt of events of the previous day. In Stevens Pottery, Georgia, Sanford Branscomb began his fourth month on this earth. His mother had named him for Chancellor Sanford. "I am starting out a little son whom [*sic*] I hope will do honor to the name," the baby's mother wrote. "I wanted to tell you about it in appreciation of what you have meant to the lives of the youth of our state and what you mean in the present time of political turmoil." [57]

The early months of 1942 were largely occupied with matters of the nation at war. The governor's race would not officially begin until the traditional July 4 kickoff. The minutes of the board and Sanford correspondence files reveal a period of quiescence relative to the accreditation matter. During the spring the chancellor carried on a successful campaign of opposition to the sentiment for a wartime suspension of football. Sanford was reelected chancellor at the June 25 meeting of the board while the controversy that would feed the fires of the campaign of late summer simmered beneath the surface. [58]

On August 27, 1942, Sandy Beaver resigned as chief of Governor Talmadge's staff and as a regent and came out for candidate Arnall. Within days Sanford issued a statement to the press regarding the accreditation matter. The *Atlanta Constitution* of Sunday, August 30, 1942, carried a page one article headed "University Collapse Feared by Sanford."

Sanford, saying he had remained silent as long as he could, reviewed the whole controversy. "The time has come," he said, "when I must make a statement of facts in justice to the University System over which I have the honor to preside and to myself. Education must see that men today be free to differ without fear, to think without danger, to resist prejudices that coerce and appeal to hatred. The school, the college, and the University must be a nursery of intelligence, liberty, and Americanism."

Chancellor Sanford recalled his long personal and family ties to the University of Georgia, going back to his grandfather Shelton Palmer's days in Athens in the 1830s, and followed the history of improvements in Georgia higher education up through the period of consolidation under the University System a century later. Next he outlined the role of accreditation and the significance of the recent actions taken by the Southern Association of Colleges and Secondary Schools. The chancellor pointed out the current dramatic decline in enrollment at the university and around the system, attributing it at least in part to the pending loss of accreditation. Both Cocking and Pittman were without guilt, Sanford maintained, relative to the accusations of their advocacy of interracial education. Calling forth again his ancestry, Sanford held up Jeremiah Sanford of Revolutionary War days and his father during the Civil War as part of the legacy that he protected in his own dedication to the preservation of the principles of American and southern tradition. With pride he pointed out that his own son was "with the first division at the Battle of the Marne," and two of his three sons were presently in the world war, one in foreign service, another in training. "I have never endorsed and will never endorse any instructor in any institution in the University System of Georgia who teaches the co-education of races or miscegenation or any doctrine, directly or indirectly, contrary to the traditions of the South."

The chancellor defended President Caldwell and concluded by forecasting: "Tuesday, September 1, 1942 [the date of effective disaccreditation by SACS], will be a bad day for the youth of Georgia. I have exhausted every effort to get the constitutional authorities of Georgia to do what is necessary to restore the accreditation of the institutions. We worked with the Southern Association to no avail. An unaccredited system of state supported institutions of higher learning is of little value." [59] Seen as one more nail in the coffin of Gene Talmadge's campaign to outdistance Ellis Arnall in the governor's race, Beaver's actions and Sanford's statement helped ensure an Arnall victory. Arnall drew 174,757 popular votes, Talmadge garnered 128,394. More important, in that time of the rule of the County Unit System, Arnall won 261 county-unit votes to 149 for Talmadge. [60]

Arnall's victory was also a victory for the University System. Even before taking office in 1943, the governor-elect worked hard to pave the way in the state legislature for constitutional protection for the political independence of the Board of Regents. The Southern Association would be meeting again in late 1942 and would have the opportunity to reconsider the Georgia situation in light of proven moves to reform. In lining up the proposed legislation and constitutional amendments and securing guaranteed support among the members of the legislature, Arnall, with the help of many others, seemed to have convinced the accrediting agency. By the end of January 1943, the Executive Committee of SACS announced the restoration of accreditation to the University System, effective September 1, 1942, thus avoiding a penalty for those who had been system students during the period of 1941–42.

On January 12, 1943, the day he took office as governor, Ellis Arnall had introduced in the General Assembly bills directing the submission of a constitutional amendment creating an independent Board of Regents. The legislation passed in both houses without opposition. Under the new definitions there was to be a fifteen-member Board of Regents, one from each congressional district and five at-large, appointed by the governor for staggered terms of seven years.[61] The governor was no longer to be an ex officio member of the board. Arnall appointed a board that included many former members, notably Sandy Beaver. Marion Smith was elected chairman of the board and Beaver vice chairman.[62] S. V. Sanford's remaining time working with the board promised to be a salutary period.

The events of 1941–42 put a spotlight on the University System and the nature of Talmadge politics. Steadman Sanford did not occupy center stage because his brand of management, his style of administration and leadership, and his use of the personal equation were no match for the coarse spectacle of Ole Gene in full bellow. Politics were at work in higher education in Georgia, gritty, more complex, diverse, twentieth-century versions for which Sanford's nineteenth-century based skills were less well suited.

TEN

The Last Years
1943-1945

In the spring of 1943 Steadman Sanford appeared before his aging comrades at a convention of Spanish-American War veterans meeting in Augusta, Georgia. The chancellor and his audience were remainders of a passing generation, a passing century, and a passing America. The early 1940s was a period of generational shift, a benchmark on the timeline of the American experience. World War II marked the line between the remainders of the nineteenth century and the defining events of the American century, the twentieth. Steadman Sanford and his contemporaries would close the nineteenth century as they faded from view and from life in the aftermath of World War II. America's course beyond this point would be directed by those who had known Sanford only as the chancellor or the legendary president of the University of Georgia, rather than as the youthful, ambitious "Steadie" of Covington and Mercer or Captain Sanford of Marietta, as an elder statesman rather than a comrade.

In his comments before the veterans in Augusta, Chancellor Sanford reflected on the current wartime situation as viewed from the perspective of the experience of the Spanish-American War of 1898, half a century earlier. It was the earlier conflict, said Sanford, that had set the stage for America's world role in the 1940s. Sanford credited the 1898 war with ending the strain between North and South, the establishment of alliances in Europe, the beginning of tensions with other European powers, the establishment of the United States as a "nation among nations of the earth." It had proven our prestige by naval power; given us the Panama Canal as well as "safety zones" in the Pacific; "elevated, broadened, and vitalized the manhood of a rising generation of American." Most important, as a message for our current foes, the Spanish-American War experience had "served notice upon the world of a homogeneous race of soldiers and sailors destined to carry the flag of this great Republic to lands perhaps as yet unnamed and certainly able to hold it against all who might dispute its right of way."[1]

Nineteen forty-three began with events which allowed Chancellor Sanford and the regents to direct their full attention to the business of the university in relation to the world war. The local battles among chancellor, regents, governor, system personnel, and the general public at long last came to an end. The January 26, 1943, meeting of the Board of Regents marked the conclusion of the Talmadge purge. Governor Ellis Arnall, a newly appointed board, and new constitutional guarantees of political independence assured the chancellor and the citizens of Georgia that their public higher education system was free to address the demands created from that larger conflict, America's critical role in the world war.

On the recommendation of Chancellor Sanford, Marvin Pittman was reappointed president of the Georgia Teachers College at Statesboro. The board voted unanimously to follow the recommendation. President Caldwell appeared before the board to report that although he had been offered his old position, Dr. Cocking, now in a federal job, would not return to the university. At the March meeting, Chancellor Sanford read a letter from the Southern Association of Colleges and Secondary Schools detailing the reinstatement of system accreditation retroactive to September 1, 1942.[2]

Chancellor Sanford had been ill and unable to attend Governor Arnall's inauguration. The governor wrote the chancellor a note expressing his regrets and wishing him improved health. For the remainder of his chancellorship Sanford would be comfortable with the leadership which the moderate Arnall provided from the governor's office. In turn, Governor Arnall took special interest in the University System. No doubt this was, at least in part, a result of the very critical role the issues of higher education in Georgia had played in his victory over Talmadge.[3]

The most pressing issue facing the system according to Sanford was the decline in enrollment, especially at the University of Georgia. The chancellor said that it was causing him "great concern" and he expected more decline to come. It was obvious that the Talmadge controversy was not driving students away, as might have been suggested before the crisis had been resolved, but rather the war was the culprit. Sanford believed that the only salvation was for the system to "induce the government to place some students at the University in the Army, Navy, or other war training programs." Sanford admitted such a move might put pressure on campus housing, but he felt housing in the Athens community could be used for regular upperclassmen, if necessary. He requested the authority to use the Coordinate College to house military-related programs. The regents concurred and charged Sanford with making contacts in Washington that would facilitate such a move.[4]

In April the regents urged Sanford to "visit Washington at the earliest possible date and remain there as long as he deems necessary in order that additional Army and Navy units may be obtained for the institutions of the University System."[5] By this time there were naval preflight and signal corps units in Athens at the university and other units at Georgia Tech, Georgia State College for Women at Valdosta, Middle Georgia at Cochran, the Medical College at Augusta, at North Georgia in Dahlonega, and in Tifton at Abraham Baldwin Agricultural College.[6]

Ever mindful of not only the present demands but also future needs, Chancellor Sanford worked to bring programs and funds to the system for military-based programs and pursued the disposition of surplus equipment left at system locations from defunct New Deal programs such as the National Youth Administration. In July he reported on his progress in securing athletic training equipment for West Georgia College.[7] Looking forward to the war's end, Sanford was among the first to speak to the issue of postwar planning for the education of returning veterans, a group which would prove to be history's greatest boon to American higher education.[8]

The chancellor also busied himself in critical areas beyond those directly related to the military. Nursing education had long been a Sanford concern, and he was pleased to announce in the summer of 1943 that the nursing education program was being developed in cooperation with hospitals and schools in Atlanta, Augusta, Columbus, Macon, and Savannah under the recently passed Public Law 74, the Bolton Act.[9]

Earlier in the spring lingering tensions between Chancellor Sanford and J. W. Holley, president of Albany State College, resulted in a focus of attention on the black institutions within the system. What began as a stirring of discussions about having a separate chancellor for the black institutions probably motivated Sanford's activities in this arena during 1943. Holley had taken a most vocal stand in support of Governor Talmadge during the Cocking controversy, and the governor had encouraged Holley to think he might be named to a newly created position as chancellor for the system's black institutions. President Holley had not been pleased with the final turn of events, and without the protection of Governor Talmadge's favor, the time seemed appropriate to redefine roles among the black schools and in the process rid Sanford of one of his ongoing irritations, Dr. Holley.

Sanford suggested to the board in April that the three black units of the system should have "well-defined educational objectives." The chancellor then proceeded to outline a plan. For the oldest of the schools, Georgia State College at Savannah, the plan called for a concentration of training in agriculture of the coastal plain region of the state. The anticipated graduates would be teachers, county agents, and home demonstration agents, all of whom were segregated for service to their own race. Training at Savannah should also be available in general education and in the trades and vocational education. The long-term plan for Savannah called for nursing and law programs at some future date. At Fort Valley the focus would be on the preparation of teachers for rural (black) schools, in vocational education, and as county and home demonstration agents. It was proposed that advanced graduate work might be offered there in cooperation with Atlanta University, the major private black institution in Georgia. For the college at Albany there would be programs of training for teachers in elementary and high school, in home economics, and in vocational education.[10]

In part, Sanford's proposal was designed to convey to the black community the importance that the system placed on those institutions as well as his personal concerns for them. However, the plans themselves represented little change from what was already in place. The fact that advanced study was suggested for Savannah and Fort Valley, but not for Albany may be interpreted as a "message" to President Holley. More direct, however, was the chancellor's recommendation that Holley be named president emeritus and assigned duties "as may seem wise to the Chancellor." Sanford suggested that "new blood is needed" and the board, following the chancellor's recommendation, made Holley president emeritus, and named Professor Aaron Brown as president of Albany State.[11]

Given that Holley was a long-time, high-profile black educational leader in Georgia, the board and the chancellor must have been conscious of the necessity of putting the best possible face on what was considered by Holley and his supporters as his "firing." One study, "The Black Public College in Georgia: A History of Albany State College, 1903–1965" by B. Carlyle Ramsey, says that Holley was shocked when he learned of his "early retirement." Holley was depicted as a "casualty of Georgia's politicized system of higher education."[12]

Chancellor Sanford further recommended to the regents' Committee on Education that "the same educational opportunities should be provided for the Negroes as for the white," suggesting a special $5,000 infusion of funds to these institutions. "This action," held Sanford, "would convince the Negroes that the regents are their friends and are trying to give them equal educational opportunity as rapidly as possible." [13] As cynical as that may sound today, it represented the prevailing attitude of the most progressive of southern educational leaders. The wider majority view of the white population had little understanding of any state support of higher education for blacks.

The year was punctuated with system-related trips for the chancellor. While Washington was the most common destination, Sanford also had the opportunity to get a reading on national matters in higher education from trips elsewhere. In October 1943, he attended the meeting of the National Association of State Universities in Chicago. From this meeting, Sanford wrote Seibert back at the board office in Atlanta that he was eager to get home to meet with Governor Arnall and "the man from Washington who controls state priorities—universities, prisons, and roads, all state supported institutions, good and bad." From his own observations, Sanford felt Washington types failed to distinguish between state and private institutions to the disadvantage of state schools, leaving the latter "in a hard way." It was Sanford's opinion that "there are too many Harvard, Yale, and Princeton men on the payroll." [14]

As for the chancellor, he looked forward to the end of the war and having the University System of Georgia in the best possible position for what he correctly anticipated as a dramatic period of change in American higher education. In October 1943 he requested from the Board of Regents the authority to appoint a committee for the study of a plan for the postwar operation of the institutions of the University System. [15]

Late in 1943 Sandy Beaver wrote Sanford about the chancellor's recent trips to Washington and New York. Beaver was confident that the trips had been "productive of good results" for the system. After reading Sanford's position paper, "Post-war Cooperation Between Industry and Agriculture," Beaver declared in a postscript that it "contained more information than any one man is supposed to possess." [16] It was obvious that Sanford was keyed into the vast change that wartime industrial growth would bring about after the conflict ended. As the product of an essentially agricultural state, Sanford was alert to the absolute necessity of providing a meaningful link between the new leading economic force in America and the changing nature and role of agriculture in American economic life. The backbone of Georgia's traditional economic base could ill afford not to be an influential partner in postwar industrial America.

Chancellor Sanford's political directions in these few remaining years of his life were clouded by the exigencies of the war, and in the end, the personal loss Sanford felt at Roosevelt's death. According to his grandson, Charles Sanford, there was a division in the family in the matter of politics during the forties. The oldest son, Shelton, like his father, was a Roosevelt devotee while middle son and banker Charles did not hold FDR in such high regard. Shelton for most of his career was a physician in the employ of the federal government and never established a successful private practice. Charles and Homer Reynolds Sanford were making their mark in the business world, as banker and insurance–real estate broker, respectively. Postwar change was to plant the seed of Republicanism in an old-line Democratic family. Though S. V. Sanford was a strong Roosevelt devotee, it would have been interesting to see how he might have responded to the full view of a Truman-led Democratic party and subsequent mid-century party directions.

Steadman Sanford and his household never really enjoyed wealth, often a dependable barometer of political inclinations, but the Sanfords nonetheless enjoyed many of the pleasures associated with the privileged classes. In 1943 Sanford held stock valued at $16,803.72. Among his modest holdings was Coca-Cola common, which accounted for about half the total value; New York and St. Louis Coca-Cola bottling companies, U.S. Steel, Studebaker, Trust Company of Georgia, Eastern Airlines, Radio Corporation of America, General Electric, Nehi Bottling, Pennsylvania Railroad, and Montgomery Ward accounted for the rest.[17]

The Sanford household in 1943 enjoyed a comfortable upper-middle-class existence: membership in the local country club, membership in both the Doubleday and Book of the Month clubs, subscriptions to *National Geographic* and *Newsweek,* local and Atlanta newspapers, extensive domestic travel, chiefly in conjunction with the chancellorship and thus not at Sanford's expense. Apparently not great sticklers for keeping household accounts, the Sanfords had to be reminded of past-due auto insurance and overdue local tax bills. About the latter Sanford wrote Albert Davidson, Athens tax collector: "I am seldom in the state. I have neglected private affairs for official affairs." [18]

The family made modest but wide-ranging charitable contributions to the Baptist and Methodist churches in Athens, to the Masonic Home of Georgia, and to various war relief agencies. Both Steadman and Grace Sanford continued to enjoy membership in patriotic organizations, his favorite being the Spanish-American War Veterans and hers the Colonial Dames and Georgia Federation of Women's Clubs.[19]

As was the custom, the Sanfords enjoyed the largess that befell people of their public station. A complimentary weekend at the Cloister with its accompanying "package" was as much a part of the routine as were chickens from a yard in middle Georgia, melons from summer fields, or the gift of six shirts for which Sanford thanked Guy Jackson of the Department of Agriculture in the fall of 1943.[20]

At the end of that year, Sanford wrote a note of thanks to the McGregor Company, an Athens office supply and bookstore, to thank them for the gift of Raymond Nixon's *Life of Henry W. Grady,* "one of the few books I did not have." The Sanfords enjoyed a special relationship with long-time connections in Athens like the McGregor Company. In his thank-you note Sanford remarked that he and his wife had been recalling the firms that they had done business with in the forty years they had been in Athens: "very few are still in business— we congratulate McGregor Company." [21] Grandson Charles Sanford fondly recalled that firm from his visit to his grandparents when he was a young boy. It was a standing rule that he could charge any book he wanted at McGregor's, no questions, no limit. More than fifty years later Charles Sanford looked back on that as one of the indications of the value the Sanfords placed on reading.[22]

Cloverhurst continued to be the site of numerous football week-end gatherings of relatives and friends from all around Georgia. The Sanfords entertained the regents at informal dinners at home, and when the weather permitted, casual garden get-togethers involved family, neighbors, and university faculty. They enjoyed the company of grandchild visits in the summer, the radio and newspapers late in the day, their weekly automobile outings on Sunday afternoons, war-time regulations permitting, and an occasional motion picture for relaxation. Their life was good.

Still, these were war years with their special troubles, some only minor and inconvenient, others tragic and life-changing. On the side of minor difficulties were such matters as that reflected in Sanford's December 1943 letter to the local Rationing Board in Athens in which he requested approval for "another [gasoline] C book." His work, he reminded the board, required extensive travel and he maintained he "never used the car if I can use other means of transportation."[23]

It was not, however, the complications of rationing that brought the real suffering of the war to the home front. Over his many years in education the chancellor had developed a strong attachment to thousands of draft-age men and volunteers he had come to know as students or as the children of his students. Sanford shared the tragedy of the loss of so many of these men in the war. Among his letters were many to mothers and fathers who had lost a child in combat. When he wrote Sanford usually related his own experience of loss and the folly of war and the role his sons were playing in the conflict. A con-dolence letter in late 1943 to Mrs. Mike Fleming of Hartwell, Georgia, is typical. In it Sanford lamented what he considered the "lost chance" for a "decent world" inherent in the mismanaged victory of World War I. He expressed his hope that the sacrifices the loss of her son represented "may be used more wisely" in the future. He recalled his own family's knowledge of grief in the loss of a child and shared with Mrs. Fleming that he had had sons in both World Wars.[24]

The course of the war by 1944 gave Americans increased hope for an early end to the fighting. The Red Army cleared the Germans out of the Soviet Union and pressed westward, and by mid-year the allied invasion sealed the fate of the western Axis powers. In the Pacific Japanese resistance persisted, but with the full force of allied powers focused in that theater there was optimism, despite continuing heavy losses in the island-hopping movement toward mainland Japan. Roosevelt seemed headed for a fourth term; for Sanford, 1944 began with a broad plan for the University System in postwar Georgia.

In the January 1944 meeting of the Board of Regents, the chancellor outlined his objectives for the system for the year. At the top of his list was the priority of educating the returning veterans, followed closely by increased appropriations for a long-overdue salary increase for faculty members. During all his tenure Sanford had considered the public universities and colleges of the state as partners in a seamless public education program which began in the elementary schools. In the postwar period, Sanford foresaw the need for enhanced teacher training in the colleges and universities of Georgia. Sanford called for the creation of an outstanding graduate school in the system and provisions for quality Ph.D. programs. For Georgia Tech the chancellor wanted an all-out effort to make it the "outstanding engineering school in the Southeast." Goals for the Medical College included specialized research in neurology and psychiatric care, venereal disease, and human nutrition. Sanford called for creating a special role for one of the junior colleges in preparation of students for senior engineering courses of study. The outline was rounded out with a request to develop more special scholarships; to "make the undergraduate work in our colleges for the Negro substantially that of the work for white students"; and finally, to "enhance cooperation between industry and agriculture," a pet theme of Sanford's late career.[25] From the perspective of a half century later the 1944 Sanford proposals have an amazingly familiar ring. The years would prove his plan a sound one, though one that would still be a work in progress at century's end.

Sanford called 1943 the most difficult year in his educational career. He had feared the war would reduce the demands for higher education significantly from pre–Pearl Harbor levels but was relieved to find that in the fall of 1943 there were 30 percent more men and women in the units of the system than there had been in 1942. "And so," he concluded, "what has been my most strenuous, most discouraging year, and my most tireless and determined year, has proved with your aid and cooperation to be the most successful year."[26] It must have been gratifying to Sanford to be able to enjoy the fruits of his tireless efforts in winning the appropriate considerations for the University System and education throughout Georgia. The saving of the system had been the successful linking of it to military training, and the chancellor had devoted the greater part of his energies to that effort.

During 1944, a consultant report to the system advised several administrative changes in the central office. In March the board authorized the chancellor to make use of President Frank R. Reade of the Women's College at Valdosta to "assist in some of the duties of his office." In July a new position of business manager was added to the board staff and Lt. Commander H. T. Healed was appointed to fill that position. The nature of the office was changing and the work was expanding and promised to grow even more rapidly in the coming years. Staff members who remember the operations of the central office before the war fondly recalled the intimacy of the operation when the entire complement consisted of Chancellor Sanford, executive secretary to the board L. R. (Sam) Seibert, and two male secretarial office managers. There was no private office or individual telephone line, even for the chancellor. Toward the end of the war, young staff members, long since drafted, carried with them the memory of Monday, December 8, 1941, when the whole office listened to the radio together. More than fifty years later one recalled how "very sad" the chancellor was, how he had said "I know this will be a long, hard war," and "how he felt for us."[27]

Sanford presented the regents with a five-year building plan for the University System in August 1944. The eighteen-item plan included building projects for all units of the system. The grand total request for $13.7 million to carry out these projects seems modest in late twentieth-century terms, but the request was a record for its time and really the first long-term, systemwide building proposal. While Sanford knew at the time it was something of a pie-in-the-sky request, he acted on his certainty about the direction of growth in the state's higher education programs. Just days before the Japanese surrender Chancellor Sanford, essentially a nineteenth-century educator, was exercising distinctly twentieth-century vision on behalf of what he still quaintly thought of as "the boys and girls of Georgia."

Sanford's last year was also to be the last year of his hero, FDR. In the election year of 1944 Sanford relished a fourth run for the presidency by Roosevelt. He wrote Marvin McClatchey, a nephew on Grace's side of the family, in January 1944: "President Roosevelt's latest speech on the state of the Republic was a masterpiece that made all the little self-seeking politicians tremble in their swivel chairs."[28] Sanford once again headed up the Clarke County Democratic fund drive for the upcoming election, successfully soliciting a quota of $1,136.00 in donations. Following the election the chancellor wrote his oldest and most thoroughly Democratic son, Shelton, cheerfully pronouncing "the old time GOP is forever dead!"[29]

It is difficult to reconcile Steadman Sanford's ardent Rooseveltism with some of the less-than-liberal comments that the chancellor made in the heat of rising fears of internal security threats and the related political "isms" that reared their heads late in the war and moved with increasing force into the end of the forties. Sanford's remarks at the Kiwanis Club Convention in the fall of 1944, in Auburn, Alabama, were widely reprinted in the press in Georgia. Taking as his text "Dangers Within," Sanford warned his audience of "forces at work here in the United States in the classrooms, press, and pulpit that would destroy our faith in our form of government and in our free institutions." Sanford blamed our vulnerability on our willingness "since World War I . . . to be too receptive to cultural and social traditions from foreign lands."

Sanford's most quotable accusations were directed at "the so-called respectable college professors." It must have been uncomfortable for some of his old colleagues or younger admirers to see in cold print his indictments of academic freedom as a "barrier" protecting those professors who were "doing [their] best to convince students under [them] that a clean life is a joke, that God is a myth, and that the ideals set forth by the Declaration of Independence are imaginary." In tones that found increasing currency in postwar America, Sanford declared: "we have the inalienable right to see that they [students] are taught the true principles of Americanism and nothing more." [30]

Sanford pointed proudly to his family's historic devotion to tradition. It was not uncommon for Sanford to remind his audience not only of his own wartime service in the Spanish-American War but also of his father's Civil War service and on back to the Revolutionary War participation of Sanford ancestors. In his remarks in the fall of 1944, the chancellor detailed the wartime roles of sons Shelton, Charles, and Homer Reynolds. Commander Shelton Palmer Sanford was serving in a United States naval hospital in California. Charles Sanford, president of the Liberty National Bank and Trust in Savannah, was also a lieutenant in the United States Coastal Reserves for the Savannah Battery, a volunteer post security force. Captain Homer Reynolds Sanford was in the 315 Air Service Corps, 14th Air Squadron, APO, New York, serving in China. [31]

The waning months of 1944 saw the usual flurry of exchanging little tokens of remembrance with friends and associates around the country. In September Sanford "sent . . . a large watermelon by express" to Major General Philips B. Fleming in Washington. "I hope it reaches you in good condition," he wrote, "for much time was spent in packing and crating." The football season renewed the annual ritual of mailing football tickets to the "needy."[32] On the receiving end the chancellor enjoyed "a lovely basket of fruit," courtesy of regent Cason Callaway. On a larger scale and in a more lasting form, the Sanfords enjoyed the gesture of the naming of a newly constructed women's dormitory at Georgia Southwestern College in Americus for Grace Sanford.[33] Kindness, friendship, recognition, and rewards came in both simple, small ways and in larger-scale acknowledgments.

On January 17, 1945, the Board of Regents reelected Steadman Vincent Sanford as chancellor of the University System of Georgia for the period July 1, 1945, through June 30, 1946. At that same meeting Chancellor Sanford read to the board a letter he had written secretary of war Henry L. Stimson, secretary of state Edward R. Stettinius Jr., and secretary of the navy James V. Forrestal. The letter recapitulated the role played by the University System during the war, beginning with the 1940 offer of the Board of Regents to support President Roosevelt "when it seemed evident the United States needed to be prepared for national defense." "Since Pearl Harbor," reported Sanford, "the institutions of the University System have aided in the training of 7,443 in the armed forces, and are at present, aiding 3,957 more." With peace in sight, "it is essential," he maintained, "that we have the power to prevent another war." He described as "fundamental to the preservation of America and its system of government," the acceptance of universal military training. Sanford spoke of the need to be prepared although "wars should be unnecessary."[34]

Building from this background and these assumptions, Sanford proposed a plan whereby students presently attending high school would go to college and, at the end of their freshman year, enter the army for three months and then return to their sophomore year of college. This pattern would be repeated for each year of college, resulting in a year's service during the course of their baccalaureate career. Additionally, he proposed an expansion of ROTC programs and closed by asserting that "sports, out of door sports, has saved the English and the American people in every war. Universal military service is nothing more than an enlarged program of our sports and should be required of all able bodied men."[35]

The board approved his letter and with that approval endorsed one of Sanford's leading postwar goals, the continuation and expansion of partnerships between the federal government and public higher education. A second postwar goal, increased attention to the improvement and expansion of higher education in the black institutions of the state, was proposed and adopted with the board's approval of the establishment of a graduate school at Fort Valley. Sanford was granted the authority to offer work leading to a master's degree in the field of education. While he would not live to see his own proposals implemented, Sanford was, at this early date in the scheme of things, anticipating the avenues, if not the final goals, of change in American higher education and American education in general for the next half century.

In February the chancellor met with the presidents of the three black system institutions to plan the groundwork for further improvements in those units and reported to the board the results of that meeting. The chancellor in consultations with the three presidents had concluded that rather than attempt new graduate programs initially, there should be cooperative programs with existing black graduate institutions, such as Atlanta University, and some provisions for out-of-state scholarships for programs elsewhere.[36]

In the spring Governor Ellis Arnall suggested that a survey of the system be taken before the further development of programs and the development of projected budgets. In April he appointed Sanford and regents Sandy Beaver, Miller Bell, and Marion Smith to a committee to conduct such a survey.[37] It was apparent that there would be a great deal of interest in all postwar governmental activities at the state level and the federal level and that chancellor Sanford would not necessarily be given carte blanche to pursue his particular vision of the future.

As winter wound down, Sanford hit the familiar road around the state and northward, speaking at the Polled Hereford Association Banquet in Valdosta in March and to the Ladies Memorial Association in Columbus for Confederate Memorial Day in April. After the Columbus talk, Sanford traveled to New York and Washington for ten days, working in particular to support universal military training.[38]

In Columbus the local newspapers carried in full the text of the chancellor's April speech in that city. It was high style Confederate Memorial Day stuff in the grand old tradition, a speech he might have made in 1898. He called the War Between the States "the struggle [which] dwarfed every other conflict known to modern history." Speaking of his forebears, he claimed that "the highest ambition that dominates my life is to be true to [my grandparents'] memory and lessons taught me by their heroic lives and be true to the state on whose soil reposes their blessed dust." [39] The nineteenth-century South was still in the air and somewhere in the heart of S. V. Sanford.

President Roosevelt's death on April 12, 1945, weighed heavily on the chancellor. As contemporaries they had witnessed the course of American and world events as rising young men at the turn of the century, as survivors of the tragedy of World War I and its aftermath of disillusionment, the depression, and the ultimate recovery born of another world conflict.

Sanford enjoyed suggestions that he shared leadership traits with President Roosevelt. He no doubt saw in Roosevelt a role model on a scale with his grandfather Sanford. A friend and protégé of the chancellor, John E. Drewry, dean of the Henry W. Grady School of Journalism, was an observer of Sanford's style for a period of more than two decades. In evaluating Sanford's career, Drewry commented on the similarities between President Roosevelt and Chancellor Sanford.

"What the President was to statesmanship on a national and international level, Dr. Sanford was to education on a state and regional plane," wrote Drewry. He credited both men with success based on "intelligence, and a remarkable ability for doing three things well." They both had the talent to "establish worthy objectives, dramatize the steps that led to the achievement of these goals and to win the support of those persons who would be most useful in the realization of what they were seeking." Drewry called them "directors of public relations—master promotion men who were familiar with all the devices of showmanship and propaganda." [40] Sanford would have proudly appreciated Drewry's observations.

The month following the president's death at Warm Springs, Sanford wrote his son and fellow Roosevelt devotee, Shelton, that he was going to miss the Washington of Roosevelt days. Not only was he personally devoted to FDR, he very pragmatically reasoned: "I am glad I got all the funds I did while Roosevelt held the reins." Beyond this the chancellor recognized the larger loss. "How this world will miss him in the post-war world." [41]

As their days together moved toward their end, Grace Sanford relished having "Dad" spending a day at home rather than rushing to the business of the board in Atlanta or to another speaking engagement somewhere in south Georgia. In the irregular diary she kept during the 1940s, Grace noted on May 19, 1945: "Dad stayed home and planted tomatoes, beans, and cauliflowers." [42] After fifty years of marriage she was still pleased to have him close by at home.

In June 1945 Grace and Steadman Sanford celebrated their golden wedding anniversary. Early in the month, the chancellor was, as usual, seeing to the future of the University System. He traveled to Washington to appear before the Joint Committee on Military Affairs. He was there to encourage postwar attention to military training. He wrote friend, fellow Georgian, and university law figure Alton Hosch, who was then serving in the Judge Advocate General's Department in Washington, that he wanted to visit him before the hearings and try out some of his comments on Hosch. "I have," he said, "been asked to give my views . . . and I shall be outspoken in my attitude toward the necessity of Universal Military Training." [43]

Before leaving for Washington the chancellor wrote the Clarke County draft board to make a plea to delay the induction of Ozie Cochran, "27, Negro, married, a chauffeur in my employ." Sanford reasoned that this delay would "contribute much to winning the war" since the University System's "many war units" were being served by the chancellor's being able to travel for the system and Ozie was critical to the process. "I will testify to keep military training," explained the chancellor. "I could write more but you know me and how urgent and important my work is and how much of my time is spent in an auto all over Georgia and other sections. All for the University System and war efforts and units in winning the war."[44]

Grace and Steadman Sanford planned to celebrate their golden wedding anniversary quietly on June 16, 1945. None of their children was able to join them, and in keeping with the times they had resolved to pass the day at home enjoying the company of their grandson Charles, visiting from Savannah, and a few local friends. In the middle of the afternoon they were surprised with the arrival of a delegation of friends representing all the schools of the University System and bearing a gift of war bonds valued at $1,725. Both Atlanta and Athens newspapers reported the party and gift as page one news. Their accounts, obviously provided by the same source for both the *Banner-Herald* and the *Constitution,* reported that "for once in a long and articulate lifetime Chancellor Steadman V. Sanford admitted that he was 'totally without words.'" Lloyd W. Chapin, registrar for Georgia Tech, spoke for the delegation, explaining that the bonds were the "University System's way of showing its love and affection for a man who literally had dedicated his life to the cause of higher education in Georgia." Chapin went on to say that "there are too many people in Georgia who love the Sanfords to let June 16, 1945, go unnoticed." Cake and several rounds of a "well known soft drink" were served. There were dozens of telegrams and individual gifts, and lots of roses, said to be the chancellor's favorite flower. The chancellor, by now having recovered his tongue and glowing with his usual humor, stuck a carnation in his vest to pose for a picture with Grace and grandson Charles. He joked to his wife as he handed her the bonds, "Here Grace, now you can take that trip around the world you've been planning so long."[45]

The picture-taking was complicated by Grace Sanford's reluctance to take part until "a shrewd sale by young Charles did the trick." When his grandmother demurred from the photo session he declared, "It won't be much of an anniversary picture with just Grandpa in it."[46] As usual Grace responded to his charms. Lots of pictures followed, including an especially fetching one of Steadman and Grace

Sanford and eight-year-old Charles. Grace had not been well of late, but the festivities surrounding the anniversary celebration seemed to reinvigorate her. The chancellor wrote Shelton that during the activities grandson "Charles had the best time of all of us," and that he was like a "tonic" for his grandmother.[47]

Sanford's summer 1945 letters to Shelton are the most complete source of his frame of mind in the last months of his life. One letter in particular from that period is wide-ranging in its topics. A revised state constitution was to be voted on August 7, and Sanford's anticipation of its ratification drew comments on that long-time player in various significant sagas, Eugene Talmadge. In these, probably his last written comments on Talmadge, Sanford reiterated his candid views. "He has always been against progress," he said, "but nobody except the ignorant and the leaders of the black market follow him any longer. I think he is a dead cock in the pit. I hope so."[48]

Apparently in a mood to hold forth on the political scene in general, Sanford spoke more on the Georgia leadership and then ventured to assess national leadership. Georgia Governor Ellis Arnall got good marks. "Ellis Arnall," wrote Sanford, "has made a fine Governor and I hope some way may be found by which he will be eligible to run again. He has given Georgia a good name. He has been my friend and a friend of education." On the national scene Sanford found cautious hope in President Truman. He approved Truman's continuation of Roosevelt men in critical positions, but believed the new president "just a mediocre man compared with the previous 'big three.'"[49] It is not clear if Sanford's "big three" were Roosevelt, Stalin, and Churchill as in wartime events or some Democratic trilogy like Roosevelt, Wilson, and Cleveland, the last three Democratic presidents of Sanford's lifetime, and in fact, the *only* Democratic presidents before Truman during Sanford's almost seventy-five years of life.

The letter closed with a return to family matters. Daughter-in-law Ann Sanford and her sons Charles and Shelton had been visiting in Athens, and it was clear that both grandfather and grandmother Sanford were smitten with the youngsters and relished their visits. "Grace is enjoying Ann and the two children. It is remarkable what affection Charles has for Shelton. He makes an excellent nurse for Shelton. Charles can read the daily paper with more understanding than many of our freshmen." [50]

Later that month Sanford recognized the impact of the recently exploded atomic bombs in Japan. "It looks," he wrote, "as if this global war is nearly at an end, so far as the fighting is concerned. After Japan folds up, then comes the fearful era of reconstruction. I hope we shall have an orgy of spending and above all no such depression as followed World War I." [51]

Steadman Vincent Sanford celebrated his seventy-fourth birthday on August 24, 1945, at the beginning of a new school year for the University System. During the second week of September the Board of Regents met in Atlanta. The news early in the week included the selection of Bess Myerson of New York as Miss America, McArthur's order to arrest Tojo as a war criminal, the promise of a early end to meat rationing, and Kaye Kaiser's retirement as a band leader "to spit and whittle." A small item carried in the Wednesday, September 12, edition of the *Atlanta Constitution* reported that editor and columnist Ralph McGill would be speaking in Athens on Thursday on "Some Social Political Aspects of the Post-war Social Order." Chancellor S. V. Sanford was scheduled to preside at the evening session in the university chapel. [52]

The next day the *Constitution* carried a brief page one notice that Sanford had been stricken with a hemorrhage of the head after complaining of nausea in the midst of a report to the Board of Regents. The minutes of that meeting reveal that Sandy Beaver, vice chairman of the regents, reported that following Sanford's collapse he had spoken with chairman Marion Smith, who was out of town, and that the two recommended the board grant the chancellor an indefinite leave of absence. This was done and Smith was named acting chancellor. A resolution was passed to extend to Sanford the "deepest regret for his sudden illness and its sincerest best wishes for an early and complete recovery." [53]

On September 14, the *Atlanta Constitution's* editorial page carried Ralph McGill's piece about Sanford, "A great fighter is a little tired." McGill had known the chancellor for many years, had traveled thousands of miles with him on trains to and from football games, and was unabashedly one of Sanford's biggest fans. McGill wrote in a tone that suggested that despite the fact that the chancellor had several times been gravely ill, this time the end was near. Reports on his condition from Emory Hospital were not encouraging. Sanford had not regained consciousness since he collapsed following his initial complaints of nausea and then paralysis on one side of his body. McGill, basing his information on someone who was with Sanford when he was stricken, reported that Sanford had, despite the paralysis picked up with his good hand a Coca-Cola that a colleague offered him, lifted it, and drained the bottle's contents. McGill saw in that determined gesture the symbolism of the chancellor's lifelong devotion to the objective at hand. The writer pointed to the concrete evidence of Sanford's accomplishments in the structures on the campuses and the wartime programs he had engineered. "Sanford," he wrote, "stood off the greedy, killing hand of corrupt politicians who wanted to kill off the University." McGill said Sanford "would not have any help on any task and he resented any inference he needed any. The load he carried for almost half a century would have broken three or four other men." It had finally broken Sanford. McGill revealed that the day of his stroke the chancellor was scheduled to leave the regents' meeting in Atlanta, go to Athens to preside at a conference, and then go on to Augusta late in the evening to prepare for a hospital conference there the following morning. "Now he is a little tired." [54]

Chancellor Sanford died early Saturday, September 15, of the cerebral hemorrhage which had stricken him. Funeral services were held in Athens at the fine arts building on the campus of the university, on Monday, September 17. "Next to Sanford Stadium," reported the *Atlanta Constitution*, "Dr. Sanford loved the Fine Arts building best." The occasion of his service brought a large and distinguished gathering of friends, former colleagues and students, and leading political and business leaders from around the state, including Governor Arnall, the presidents of the system colleges, and the members of the Board of Regents of the University System. The Reverend J. C. Wilkinson of the Athens First Baptist Church and the Reverend H. C. Holland of Athens First Methodist Church officiated in Athens; Dr. Louie D. Newton of Atlanta officiated at graveside in Marietta later that day. Sons Charles and Shelton were with their mother; Homer Reynolds was still in China in the service.[55]

Mrs. Sanford and the family received hundreds of messages of sympathy. One of those was from Dr. E. Merton Coulter, professor of history at the University of Georgia and a major figure in the rise of the graduate program which Sanford had encouraged there. Coulter had not been a slavish devotee of Sanford, but rather was considered an objective observer of the comings and goings at the university, with no particular ties to the old establishment. Coulter wrote Mrs. Sanford on September 17: "Dr. Sanford lived a long and satisfactory life, and one useful not only to his own state but to the whole South. And this further, that he worked up to the very end of his life. This is a blessing not given to all." Coulter closed, "Thousands will miss him, his good humor and fine disposition, and his inspiring leadership. You do not mourn alone."[56]

The Board of Regents adopted a resolution recognizing Chancellor Sanford for devoting his life to "building an educational system that will be a model for the entire nation." With Sanford's death, "the cause of education in Georgia and the entire South has lost its most eminent champion. He was undoubtedly one of the outstanding Georgians of all times." The regents hailed Sanford as a "scholar, educator, organizer, and leader of tireless energy, rare culture, and superb personality." The resolution concluded: "He never hesitated to state that no phase of educational work appealed to him like the close personal relation with students in the classroom. Many said of him that he was the best friend the boys and girls of Georgia ever had."[57]

Grace McClatchey Sanford survived her husband seven years. She died in Athens in the spring of 1952. The chancellor's sons, Shelton,

Charles, and Homer Reynolds, all survived their parents. Charles died in the mid-1950s in Savannah leaving two sons to carry the family name. Homer Reynolds died without issue in the early 1960s in Atlanta; the oldest, Shelton, died in the late 1970s in Athens, where he had lived in the Sanford home on Cloverhurst. The house finally passed from the family when Shelton's adopted daughter, Grace, sold the home in the 1980s.[58]

In the days, weeks, and months following Chancellor Sanford's death, there were scores of editorial tributes, resolutions of sympathy for the family, and assorted declarations of praise for his life and work. Some focused on Sanford the athletic champion and stadium builder; others praised his ability to deal with politicians; still others spoke of his popularity as a speaker, his scholarship, his persistence, his humor, his knowledge of literature, his contributions to journalism education in Georgia, his support for all levels of public education, his broad contacts and friendships, his devotion to his family and forebears, his Christian kindness and concern for all. In John Drewry's article on Sanford and Roosevelt in the September 16, 1945, *Athens Banner-Herald,* he touched on all these facets of Sanford and more and deftly refined the many broad areas of accomplishment into the essence of the chancellor's strength and success. Drewry saw in Sanford "a super salesman selling a product in which first of all, he had much faith, and next, which, through his skill of presentation the public had come increasingly to want." The result? "No person in Georgia or the South, living or dead, has contributed more to the educational advancement of Georgia or the South." "Sanford," said Drewry, "was a man of courage and conviction and energy and concern for the public good." Drewry predicted, "He will be remembered as a great teacher, a great administrator, but—greatest of all—a remarkable academic statesman."[59]

Sanford's accomplishments survive him in physical form. The buildings of the University System for which he worked to secure funds have left the imprint of the Sanford name all around Georgia. Most famous as a monument, of course, is the University of Georgia's playing field, Sanford Stadium, now grown to a capacity of scores of thousands, far beyond the professor's dream of the 1920s.

As the years pass, however, fewer and fewer live who recall in much detail the middle or early years of Sanford's life and career. There are a number of former students and relatives who still remember the Sanford of the 1930s and 1940s when he was in his sixties and seventies. For them, the details are beginning to dim, and there is no real recollection of the dynamic years of S. V. Sanford's youth and middle age. While these imperfect memories persist and the physical tributes remain, we are all deprived of the essence of what made Steadman Vincent Sanford the legend that he was at the time of his death. As has been said of other impressive phenomena, "you had to have been there." Those who never came under his spell will not be able to appreciate what must in the end be considered his real strength, the strength of the totality of who he was.

In a 1943 letter to his youngest son, Homer Reynolds, Sanford reported on one of his upcoming trips to Washington on the business of the University System. The chancellor had just returned from a meeting of the Southeastern Conference in Nashville. "We reached Athens late Saturday and Sunday Caldwell and I left for Washington to get many things accomplished—things that only the personal equation can accomplish." [60] In the final analysis, S. V. Sanford's life and career were, in his own words, his exercise of the personal equation.

The S. V. Sanford Line of the Sanford Family, 1816-1997

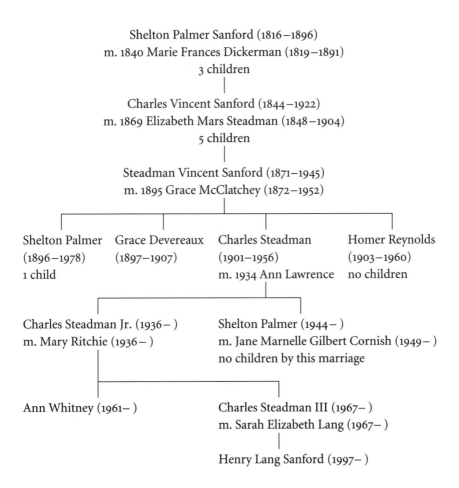

Shelton Palmer Sanford (1816–1896)
m. 1840 Marie Frances Dickerman (1819–1891)
3 children

Charles Vincent Sanford (1844–1922)
m. 1869 Elizabeth Mars Steadman (1848–1904)
5 children

Steadman Vincent Sanford (1871–1945)
m. 1895 Grace McClatchey (1872–1952)

| Shelton Palmer (1896–1978) 1 child | Grace Devereaux (1897–1907) | Charles Steadman (1901–1956) m. 1934 Ann Lawrence | Homer Reynolds (1903–1960) no children |

Charles Steadman Jr. (1936–)
m. Mary Ritchie (1936–)

Shelton Palmer (1944–)
m. Jane Marnelle Gilbert Cornish (1949–)
no children by this marriage

Ann Whitney (1961–)

Charles Steadman III (1967–)
m. Sarah Elizabeth Lang (1967–)

Henry Lang Sanford (1997–)

Notes

ONE. *Beginnings, 1871–1890*

1. Elaine Justesen and Dwight A. Radford, "Sanford Saga" (privately printed, 1992), typescript in the author's possession; Sally Bruce McClatchey, manuscript charts of the Reynolds and Sanford families; Mrs. George O. Marshall Jr., "Sanford Lineage of Chancellor Steadman Vincent Sanford"; editors, "Steadman Vincent Sanford," in *The Dictionary of Georgia Biography,* vol. 2, ed. Kenneth Coleman and Charles Stephen Gurr (Athens: University of Georgia Press, 1983), 867–68.

2. See the appendix.

3. *Mercerian* (Macon: Burke and Company, 1889).

4. Ibid.

5. Thomas Reed, "History of the University of Georgia" (unpublished typescript), vol. 2, 406–12. Special Collection, University of Georgia Library.

6. Ibid.

7. Shelton Palmer Sanford to Steadman Vincent Sanford, October 10, 1890, box 6, Steadman V. Sanford Collection, University of Georgia Library (hereafter cited as Sanford Collection).

8. William Bailey Williford, *The Glory of Covington* (Atlanta: Cherokee Press, 1973), 42; *Covington Enterprise,* September 8, 1871.

9. Obituary for Charles S. Sanford, *Macon Telegraph,* April 3, 1922.

10. Elaine Justesen and Dwight A. Radford, "Sanford Saga: A Genealogy of the Sanford Family" (unpublished, 1992), 36–37, typescript in the author's possession.

11. Dorothy Orr, *A History of Education in Georgia* (Chapel Hill: University of North Carolina Press, 1950), 222–28.

12. Peggie R. Elgin, *Centennial Celebration: Marietta Schools, 1892–1992* (Marietta: Marietta City School System, 1993).

13. Thomas G. Dyer, *Higher Education in Georgia: A Historiographical Prospective* (Athens: Institute of Higher Education, University of Georgia, 1976); E. Merton Coulter, *College Life in the Old South* (Baton Rouge: Louisiana State Univer-

sity Press, 1928); Robert Preston Brooks, *The University of Georgia under Sixteen Administrations, 1785–1955* (Athens: University of Georgia Press, 1956).

14. Dyer, *The University of Georgia: A Bicentennial History, 1785–1985* (Athens: University of Georgia Press, 1985), 119–20.

15. Ibid., 116.

16. Ibid., 142–44.

17. *Covington Enterprise,* 1870–71.

18. *Covington Enterprise,* 1871.

19. *Covington Enterprise,* August 1871.

20. *Conyers Examiner,* 1872.

21. Reed, "University of Georgia," 2772.

22. *Mercerian* (1889), 124–27.

23. Mercer Catalogs, 1889–90.

24. Ibid., 6–7.

25. *Mercerian* (1889), 64.

TWO. *Marietta, 1890–1903*

1. Sarah Blackwell Gober Temple, *The First Hundred Years: A Short History of Cobb County in Georgia,* 6th ed. (Athens: Agee Press, 1989). Temple's book, first published in the 1930s, provides the most comprehensive history of Cobb County and Marietta. This almost 1,000-page tome is not only detailed, but written in a style lively enough to make for pleasant reading. As with many community or local histories there are the usual biographical sketches, statistical tables, church histories, and cemetery records. Temple, however, does an unusually good job of setting the stage with interesting social and cultural details that put all the usual factual material in the context of the community's various periods and historical developments.

2. *Marietta Journal,* November 24, 1892.

3. Notes of Shelton P. Sanford, box 28, Sanford Collection.

4. Ibid.

5. Ibid.

6. Temple, *The First Hundred Years,* 424.

7. *Marietta Journal,* "Marietta Matters," "Local Leaflets," 1890s.

8. Mrs. D. F. McClatchey to Steadman Sanford, August 19, 1893, box 66, Sanford Collection.

9. Ibid.

10. Ibid.

11. Ibid.

12. Steadman Sanford to Grace McClatchey, October 8, 1893, box 66, Sanford Collection.

13. Grace McClatchey to Steadman Sanford, November 5, 1893, box 66, Sanford Collection.

14. Grace McClatchey to Steadman Sanford, February 28, 1894, box 66, Sanford Collection.

15. Grace McClatchey to Steadman Sanford, July 3, 1894, box 66, Sanford Collection.

16. *Marietta Journal,* August 1890.

17. *Marietta Journal,* September 13, 1890; October 2, 1890.

18. *Marietta Journal,* October 23, 1890.

19. *Marietta Journal,* February 26, 1891.

20. *Marietta Journal,* June 4, 1891.

21. *Marietta Journal,* June 4, 1891.

22. Author's interview with Ralph Moor, June 18, 1996. When the author used the term "slick" to describe Sanford's methods, Mr. Moor corrected, "smooth, not slick."

23. *Marietta Journal,* June 25, 1891.

24. *Marietta Journal,* June 25, 1891.

25. *Marietta Journal,* June 25, 1891.

26. *Marietta Journal,* June 28, 1892.

27. Oscar Bane Keeler, clipping from *Atlanta Journal,* 1935, box 53, Sanford Collection.

28. Ibid.

29. Ibid.

30. Marietta Journal, May 24, 1892; James D. Manget to Steadman Sanford, box 6, Sanford Collection.

31. "The First Annual Report of the Public Schools of the City of Marietta, Georgia; with Manual of Instructions and Rules and Regulations, Session 1892–93," 3, box 23, Sanford Collection.

32. Ibid., 5.

33. Ibid., 9.

34. Steadman V. Sanford notes, "Marietta Rifles," 1894, box 20, Sanford Collection.

35. *Marietta Journal,* January 25, 29, February 1, 8, 1894.

36. *Marietta Journal,* March 22, April 12, 26, May 10, 1894.

37. *Marietta Journal,* June 14, 1894.

38. Author's interview with Ralph Moor, May 28, 1996. Moor recalled that when he worked with the chancellor there was occasionally a call or visit from one of his men from the old company. Frequently, it was someone who had seen

better days and was looking for a handout from the "Captain." Sanford remained the beloved leader and was always willing to oblige.

39. *Atlanta Constitution,* June 8, 1945, quoting *Marietta Journal,* June 18, 1895.

40. R. N. Holland to W. A. Little Jr., June 5, 1896, box 6, Sanford Collection.

41. Charles Sanford to S. V. Sanford, August 5, 1896, box 6, Sanford Collection.

42. Charles Sanford to S. V. Sanford, August 5, 1897, box 6, Sanford Collection.

43. John F. Howard to S. V. Sanford, February 1, 1897, box 6, Sanford Collection.

44. R. E. Lawhorn to S. V. Sanford, February 2, 1897, box 6, Sanford Collection.

45. *Marietta Journal,* March 4, May 6, June 10, July 15, 1897.

46. *Marietta Journal,* July 8, July 15, 1897.

47. *Marietta Journal,* July 22, 1897.

48. *Marietta Journal,* June 2, 1898.

49. Temple, *The First Hundred Years,* 556–57.

50. Charles Sanford to S. V. Sanford, July 8, 1898, box 12, Sanford Collection.

51. S. V. Sanford to Adjutant General, U.S. Army, August 27, 1898, box 12, Sanford Collection.

52. S. V. Sanford to Grace Sanford, September 24, 1898, box 12, Sanford Collection.

53. S. V. Sanford to Grace Sanford, September 26, 1898, box 31, Sanford Collection.

54. Special Order no. 231, September 30, 1898, box 36, Sanford Collection.

55. Author's interview with Ralph Moor, May 28, 1996.

56. Grace Sanford to S. V. Sanford, July 5, 1899, box 6, Sanford Collection.

57. Grace Sanford to S. V. Sanford, July 28, 1899, Box 66, Sanford Collection.

58. Laurence R. Veysey, *The Emergence of the American University* (Chicago: University of Chicago Press, 1965), 72, 116.

59. Ibid.

60. Ibid., 367–68.

61. Ibid., 376–77.

62. *Marietta Journal,* February 1, 1900.

63. *Marietta Journal,* February 8, 1900.

64. *Marietta Journal,* June 21, 1900.

65. *Marietta Journal,* May 20, 30, 1901; Dr. Shelton Palmer Sanford notes, box 28, Sanford Collection.

66. Byron Bower to S. V. Sanford, January 6, 1903, box 6, Sanford Collection.

67. W. E. Simmons to S. V. Sanford, February 2, 1903, box 6, Sanford Collection.

68. A. O. Bacon to S. V. Sanford, March 24, 1903, box 6, Sanford Collection.

69. *Marietta Journal,* May 7, 28, October 8, 1903; A. L. Hull to S. V. Sanford, April 13, 1903, box 31, Sanford Collection.

THREE. *Athens, 1903−1917*

1. Dyer, *University of Georgia,* 173.

2. Ibid.

3. *Athens City Directory,* 1904, 1906, 1909.

4. Dr. Shelton Sanford notes, box 28, Sanford Collection.

5. *Athens City Directory,* 1906, f, g.

6. "Souvenir Edition," *Athens Banner,* 1903, 7, 13.

7. Dr. Shelton Sanford notes, box 28, Sanford Collection.

8. Miscellaneous papers, insurance folder, box 2, Sanford Collection; *Atlanta Journal,* September 10, 1903, in scrapbook, box 54, Sanford Collection.

9. Charles Sanford to S. V. Sanford, May 25, 1904, box 6, Sanford Collection.

10. Charles Sanford to S. V. Sanford, August 15, 1906, box 6, Sanford Collection.

11. Alex MacDowell to S. V. Sanford, July 24, 1907, box 6, Sanford Collection.

12. Clippings in possession of Marvin McClatchey family, Atlanta; sympathy notes and letters, box 66, Sanford Collection.

13. W. H. Young to S. V. Sanford, July 1907, box 6, Sanford Collection.

14. Charles Sanford to S. V. Sanford, September 4, 1907, box 6, Sanford Collection.

15. Blanton Winship to S. V. Sanford, October 28, 1905, box 6, Sanford Collection.

16. *Pandora* (1905), "Dedication," no page numbers.

17. Draft agreement, University of Georgia Athletic Department, November 26, 1906, box 6, Sanford Collection.

18. University of Georgia Athletic Association, minute book, April 10, 1907, box 32, Sanford Collection.

19. Ibid., April 10, 1911, December 9, 1913, January 24, 1914.

20. John F. Stegeman and Robert M. Willingham Jr., *Touchdown: A Pictorial History of the Georgia Bulldogs* (Athens: Agee Publishers, 1983), 21.

21. John F. Stegeman, *The Ghosts of Herty Field: Early Days on a Southern Gridiron* (Athens: University of Georgia Press, 1966), 76.

22. Fuzzy Woodruff, *The History of Southern Football, 1890−1928* (Atlanta: Georgia Southern Publishers, 1928), 98.

23. Ibid., 205.

24. Ibid., 208.

25. Stegeman, *The Ghosts of Herty Field,* 69.

26. Ibid., 86–87.

27. Stegeman and Willingham, *Touchdown,* 38–39.

28. Stegeman, *The Ghosts of Herty Field,* 88.

29. Chancellor Barrow to University of Georgia alumni, 1910, box 6, Sanford Collection.

30. Draft of letter, S. V. Sanford to trustees, University of Georgia, June 11, 1908, box 53, Sanford Collection.

31. Clippings and letters, grey ledger, box 53; Col. E. E. Pomeroy to S. V. Sanford, December, 1907, box 53, Sanford Collection.

32. Ibid.

33. Ibid.

34. *Athens Banner,* June 18, 1908.

35. Hughes Spalding to Mrs. S. V. Sanford, July 30, 1912, box 31, Sanford Collection.

36. Governor Joseph M. Brown to S. V. Sanford, August 7, 1912, box 6, Sanford Collection.

37. R. C. Hazlehurst to S. V. Sanford, August 2, 1912, box 6, Sanford Collection; Senator A. O. Bacon, letter of introduction for S. V. Sanford, July 20, 1912, box 6, Sanford Collection; Melville Stone to S. V. Sanford, July 29, 1912, box 53, Sanford Collection.

38. Miscellaneous documents, 1912, box 6, Sanford Collection.

39. Clipping, box 38, Sanford Collection.

40. Dr. Shelton Sanford notes, box 28, Sanford Collection; letters Shelton to family, World War I, box 24, Sanford Collection.

41. Ibid.

42. S. V. Sanford to Marvin McClatchey, November 5, 1912, McClatchey family, Atlanta.

43. Correspondence, 1913, box 6, Sanford Collection.

44. Printed materials; passenger list, receipts, postcards, boxes 53, 62, 65, Sanford Collection.

45. S. V. Sanford to Tom Reed, April 5, 1924, box 8, Sanford Collection.

46. Miscellaneous receipts, box 53, Sanford Collection.

47. Reed, "University of Georgia," 2776.

48. Author interview with Ralph Moor, June 18, 1996.

49. Honorary degree, June 17, 1914, box 58, Sanford Collection.

50. S. V. Sanford to Tom Reed, April 5, 1924, box 8, Sanford Collection.

51. Ibid.

52. Reed, "University of Georgia," 2776–77.

53. George M. Abney Jr., "Forty Years of Communications Education at the Oldest Chartered State University (1915–1955)" (M.A. thesis, University of Georgia, 1959).

54. Trustees' correspondence, 1913, quoted in Abney, 11.

55. Chancellor's report, 1914, box 6, University of Georgia Archives.

56. Trustees' correspondence, 1915, quoted in Abney, 17.

57. Ibid., 18.

58. *Bulletin of the University of Georgia*, 1914–15.

59. Abney, "Forty Years of Communications Education," 20–21.

60. Ibid., 23.

61. Ibid., 26.

62. S. V. Sanford to Tom Reed, April 5, 1924, box 8, Sanford Collection.

63. *Pandora* (1912), pages not numbered.

FOUR. *World War I, 1917–1919*

1. Brooks, *University of Georgia,* 153–57; Benjamin Barrow Tate, "David Crenshaw Barrow, Jr.," in *Dictionary,* vol. 1, ed. Coleman and Gurr, 60–62.

2. Brooks, *University of Georgia,* 139.

3. Scrapbooks, World War I period, box 24, Sanford Collection.

4. S. V. Sanford to Edwin Brown, March 28, 1917, box 6, Sanford Collection.

5. Council on Defense to S. V. Sanford, June 20, 1917, box 6, Sanford Collection.

6. Captain Ralph R. Hess to S. V. Sanford, June 30, 1917, box 6, Sanford Collection.

7. Albert Bushnell Hart to S. V. Sanford, June, 1917, box 6, Sanford Collection.

8. Shelton P. Sanford to S. V. Sanford, July 11, 1917, box 69, Sanford Collection.

9. Shelton P. Sanford to Grace Sanford, August 29, 1917, box 69, Sanford Collection.

10. Shelton P. Sanford to Grace Sanford, September 3, 1917, box 69, Sanford Collection.

11. Shelton P. Sanford to S. V. Sanford, September 18, 1917, box 69, Sanford Collection.

12. Shelton P. Sanford to Grace Sanford, no date, box 70, Sanford Collection.

13. Shelton P. Sanford to Grace Sanford, September 24, 1917, box 69, Sanford Collection.

14. S. V. Sanford to Grace Sanford, October 1, 1917, box 69, Sanford Collection.

15. Copy of S. V. Sanford to Honorable W. J. Harris, October 1, 1917, included in S. V. Sanford to Grace Sanford letter, October 1, 1917, box 69, Sanford Collection.

16. Ibid.

17. S. V. Sanford to Shelton P. Sanford, October 1, 1917, box 69, Sanford Collection.

18. University training course, no date, box 70, Sanford Collection.

19. S. V. Sanford to Capt. Hess, July 7, 1917, box 6, Sanford Collection.

20. S. V. Sanford to Capt. Hess, September 26, 1917, box 6, Sanford Collection.

21. S. V. Sanford to Capt. Hess, October 29, 1917, box 6, Sanford Collection.

22. S. V. Sanford to Shelton P. Sanford, November 4, 1917, box 6, Sanford Collection.

23. Ibid.

24. S. V. Sanford to C. W. Wall, November 25, 1917, box 6, Sanford Collection.

25. Richard N. Schwab to S. V. Sanford, December 11, 1917, box 6, Sanford Collection.

26. Capt. Hess to S. V. Sanford, December 17, 1917, box 6, Sanford Collection.

27. Shelton P. Sanford to Homer Reynolds Sanford, November 5, 1917; Shelton P. Sanford to Charles Sanford, November 7, 1917, box 69, Sanford Collection.

28. Shelton P. Sanford to Grace Sanford, November 9, 1917; Shelton P. Sanford to S. V. Sanford, November (misdated October) 5, 1917, box 69, Sanford Collection.

29. "R.T." (undecipherable) to S. V. Sanford, November 19, 1917, box 69, Sanford Collection.

30. Shelton to S. V. Sanford, December 29, 1917, box 69, Sanford Collection.

31. Shelton to S. V. Sanford, January 4, 1918, box 69, Sanford Collection.

32. Shelton to S. V. Sanford, January 5, 1918, box 69, Sanford Collection.

33. Shelton P. Sanford to S. V. and Grace Sanford, January 6, 1918, box 69, Sanford Collection.

34. S. V. Sanford to Shelton P. Sanford, January 24, 1918, box 69, Sanford Collection.

35. Julius M. Elrod to S. V. Sanford, January 10, 1918, box 7, Sanford Collection.

36. S. V. Sanford to Sgt. L. M. Gardner, January 11, 1918, box 7, Sanford Collection.

37. S. V. Sanford to Shelton P. Sanford, January 13, 1918, box 69, Sanford Collection.

38. Michael Zunch to C. O. Brown, September 26, 1918, box 7, Sanford Collection.

39. Shelton P. Sanford to Charles Sanford, January 23, 1918, box 69, Sanford Collection.

40. Shelton P. Sanford to Grace Sanford, February 1, 1918, box 69, Sanford Collection.

41. Shelton P. Sanford to S. V. Sanford, January 25, 1918, box 69, Sanford Collection.

42. Shelton P. Sanford to S. V. Sanford, February 17, 1918, box 69, Sanford Collection.

43. Ibid.

44. Shelton P. Sanford to Grace Sanford, March 4, 1918, box 69, Sanford Collection.

45. Shelton P. Sanford to S. V. Sanford, March 23, 1918, box 69, Sanford Collection.

46. Shelton P. Sanford to Grace Sanford, November 1, 1918, box 70, Sanford Collection.

47. Shelton P. Sanford to Grace Sanford, November 16, 1918, box 70, Sanford Collection.

48. Shelton P. Sanford to S. V. Sanford, December 10, 1918, box 70, Sanford Collection.

49. Shelton P. Sanford to S. V. Sanford, January 2, 1919, box 70, Sanford Collection.

50. Shelton P. Sanford to S. V. Sanford, March 3, 1919, box 70, Sanford Collection.

51. Shelton P. Sanford to S. V. Sanford, July 10, 1919, box 70, Sanford Collection.

52. Shelton P. Sanford to Grace Sanford, July 28, 1919, box 70, Sanford Collection.

53. Rhodes Scholarship application form, September 26, 1919, box 7, Sanford Collection.

FIVE. *The Decade of Sports, 1920s*

1. Stegeman and Willingham, *Touchdown*, 18.

2. Jesse Outlar, *Between the Hedges: A Story of Georgia Football* (Huntsville, Ala.: Strode Publishers, 1973), appendix.

3. Ledger of the University of Georgia football contracts, 1924–25, box 32, Sanford Collection.

4. Minutes, Georgia Athletic Association, May 20, 1920, box 32, Sanford Collection.

5. Susan Barrow Tate, *Remembering Athens* (Athens: Athens Historical Society, 1996), 176–77.

6. Stegeman and Willingham, *Touchdown,* 26.

7. Ibid., 26.

8. Clark Howell to S. V. Sanford, December 17 and 20, 1920, box 7, Sanford Collection.

9. Marion Smith to S. V. Sanford, November 8, 1921, box 1, Sanford, University of Georgia Archives.

10. S. V. Sanford speech at dedication of Woodruff Hall, Archives of the University of Georgia Athletic Association.

11. Harold Hirsch to S. V. Sanford, October 10, 1921, box 53, Sanford Collection.

12. E. R. King to S. V. Sanford, October 30, 1921, box 7, Sanford Collection.

13. Unsigned to S. V. Sanford, August 8, 1923, box 7, Sanford Collection.

14. George Woodruff to S. V. Sanford, January 17, 1924, box 8, Sanford Collection; John B. Myers, "George Woodruff," in *Dictionary,* vol. 2, ed. Coleman and Gurr, 1085–86.

15. S. V. Sanford to Harold Hirsch, January 30, 1924, box 8, Sanford Collection.

16. Stegeman and Willingham, *Touchdown,* appendix.

17. James F. Ragan to S. V. Sanford, March 5, 1924, box 8, Sanford Collection.

18. Clark Howell to S. V. Sanford, December 12, 1924, box 8, Sanford Collection.

19. Chip Robert to Harold Hirsch, November 30, 1926, Harold Hirsch papers, Athletic Association Archives.

20. Chip Robert to Harold Hirsch, November 30, 1926, Hirsch papers, Athletic Association Archives.

21. Harold Hirsch to S. V. Sanford, December 3, 1926, Hirsch papers, Athletic Association Archives.

22. Stegeman and Willingham, *Touchdown,* appendix.

23. Ibid., 34–38.

24. Robert Sharod, "Sanford the Conference Builder," *Georgia Alumni Record* (November 1927): 35.

25. Ibid.

26. S. V. Sanford, "College Athletics," address to the Southern Association of Colleges and Schools, December 3, 1925, box 62, Sanford Collection.

27. Ibid., 8.

28. Ibid., 12.

29. Ibid., 14–17.

30. Ibid., 17–18.

31. Ibid., 21.

32. Ibid., 22.

33. Ibid., 32.

34. E. K. Hall to S. V. Sanford, December 30, 1927, box 9, Sanford Collection.

35. S. V. Sanford to E. K. Hall, October 2, 1927; Hall to Sanford, December 30, 1928, box 9, Sanford Collection.

36. S. V. Sanford to E. K. Hall, October 2, 1927, box 9, Sanford Collection.

37. Ed Danforth clipping, undated, box 39, Sanford Collection.

38. *Pandora* (1927), 115.

39. Frank Boland to S. V. Sanford, July, 1927, box 9, Sanford Collection.

40. William B. Kent Sr. to S. V. Sanford, November 6, 1928, box 9, Sanford Collection.

41. Ibid.

42. Stegeman and Willingham, *Touchdown,* 38−39.

43. Outlar, *Between the Hedges,* 41−42.

44. *Pandora* (1912), no page numbers.

45. Harold Hirsch to S. V. Sanford, December 12, 1924, box 8, Sanford Collection.

46. Ibid.

47. Sanford, "Address to Southern Association of Colleges and Secondary Schools," 1925, 19, box 62, Sanford Collection.

48. Notes on building of Sanford Stadium, 1990, Athletic Association Archives.

49. Ibid.

50. Minutes of Athletic Association, February 21, 1928; Daniel MacDougald to S. V. Sanford, March 27, 1929, box 9, Sanford Collection.

51. *Georgia Alumni Record* (October 1929): 5, 22; typed list of contributors, Athletic Association Archives.

52. Tate Wright to Charles Snelling, July 4, 1928, box 9, Sanford Collection.

53. Minutes of the Athletic Association, February 23, 1928, Athletic Association Archives.

54. Various letters, January−April 1928, box 9, Sanford Collection.

55. George Nettleton to S. V. Sanford, October 26, 1928, box 9, Sanford Collection.

56. *Georgia Alumni Record* (November 1928).

57. Outlar, *Between the Hedges,* 40.

58. Ibid., 44.

59. Box 24, Archives of the University of Georgia.

60. *Athens Banner-Herald,* October 10, 1929.

61. *Athens Banner-Herald,* October 10, 1929.

62. *Athens Banner-Herald,* October 13, 1929; *Georgia Alumni Record* (October, 1929).

63. *Athens Banner-Herald,* October 13, 1929, 1.

64. *Athens Banner-Herald,* October 13, 1929.

65. *The New Yorker,* October 19, 1929, 55.

66. S. V. Sanford, "An Appreciation," *Pandora* (1929): 303.

SIX. *Beyond Sports, 1920s*

1. Author's interview with Charles S. Sanford Jr., December 2, 1996.

2. Author's interview with Mrs. Marvin McClatchey, August 16, 1996.

3. Author's interview and tour with Charles S. Sanford Jr., May 29, 1996.

4. S. V. Sanford to his sons, box 6, Sanford Collection.

5. Charles Sanford to Grace Sanford, December 15, 1922, box 33, Sanford Collection.

6. D. C. Heath Company to S. V. Sanford, August 21, 1920; November 15, 1921; November 15, 1922, box 7, Sanford Collection.

7. Auto purchase contract, box 5, Sanford Collection.

8. Report of disbursements, estate of Charles V. Sanford, by C. D. Sanford, box 3, Sanford Collection.

9. Details of 359 Cloverhurst from tour of the property by author, May 29, 1996.

10. Guest book, Box 28, Sanford Collection.

11. Clark Howell to S. V. Sanford, February 17, 1922, box 7, Sanford Collection; Oakland contest notes, box 53, Sanford Collection.

12. John G. Harrison to S. V. Sanford, April 24, 1924, box 8, Sanford Collection.

13. Professor S. V. Sanford's class rolls, 1919–1929, box 28, Sanford Collection.

14. R. N. Hardeman to S. V. Sanford, October 11, 1920, box 28, Sanford Collection.

15. Andrew Soule to S. V. Sanford, October 13, 1920, box 7, Sanford Collection.

16. B. P. O'Neal to S. V. Sanford, January 25, 1921, box 7, Sanford Collection.

17. D. C. Heath to S. V. Sanford, September 13, 1921, box 19, Sanford Collection.

18. S. V. Sanford to Thomas Reed, April 5, 1924, box 8, Sanford Collection.

19. Ibid.

20. Ibid.

21. Ibid.

22. Charles E. Martin to S. V. Sanford, May 25, 1924, box 8, Sanford Collection.

23. George Gober to S. V. Sanford, April 15, 1924, box 8, Sanford Collection.

24. Ibid.

25. Ann G. Ragsdale, "The History of Co-Education at the University of Georgia, 1918−1945" (M.A. thesis, University of Georgia, 1948), no page numbers.

26. Dyer, *University of Georgia*, 191.

27. Brooks, *University of Georgia*, 158.

28. Dyer, *University of Georgia*, 175.

29. Brooks, *University of Georgia*, 158−59.

30. George Gober to S. V. Sanford, February 13, 1925, box 8, Sanford Collection.

31. Alexander Cunningham to S. V. Sanford, March 5, 1925, box 8, Sanford Collection.

32. E. T. Holmes to S. V. Sanford, March 26, 1925, box 8, Sanford Collection.

33. H. D. Russell to S. V. Sanford, March 26, 1925, box 8, Sanford Collection.

34. E. T. Holmes to S. V. Sanford, May 12, 1925, box 8, Sanford Collection.

35. E. T. Holmes to S. V. Sanford, 2nd letter, May 12, 1925, box 8, Sanford Collection.

36. A. L. Elrod to Judge Samuel H. Sibley, copy to S. V. Sanford, box 8, Sanford Collection.

37. Various letters, September 1925, box 8, Sanford Collection.

38. Brooks, *University of Georgia*, 158.

39. John Donald Wade to Julia C. Harris, July 3, 1925, quoted in William F. Muggleston, "The Press and Student Activism at the University of Georgia in the 1920's," *Georgia Historical Quarterly* 64 no. 3 (Fall 1980): 241−52.

40. *Athens Banner-Herald,* June 11, 1926.

41. W. C. Kellogg to S. V. Sanford, June 20, 1926, box 8, Sanford Collection.

42. Senator Thomas W. Atkins to S. V. Sanford, July 1, 1926, box 8, Sanford Collection.

43. S. G. Backman to Charles Snelling, September 1, 1926, box 8, Sanford Collection.

44. Harry Hodgson to S. V. Sanford, September 17, 1926, box 8, Sanford Collection.

45. Dyer, *University of Georgia*, 128.

46. *Iconoclast,* quoted in Muggleston, "The Press and Student Activism."

47. S. V. Sanford to Andrew Soule, August 15, 1926, box 8, Sanford Collection.

48. Annual report of the chancellor, June 1919.

49. Annual report of the chancellor, 1922, 8.

50. Annual report of the chancellor, 1925, 20.

51. Annual report of the chancellor, 1926, 154.

52. Dyer, *University of Georgia*, 190−99.

53. Regents of the University System of Georgia, annual report, 1932.

54. S. V. Sanford in annual report of the chancellor, 1926–27.

55. Ibid.

56. Ibid.

57. Ibid., 128.

58. Ibid.

59. Unknown writer to S. V. Sanford, April 8, 1929, box 9, Sanford Collection.

60. Ellis G. Arnall to S. V. Sanford, April 22, 1927; S. V. Sanford to Eugene Talmadge, June 26, 1927, box 9, Sanford Collection.

61. S. V. Sanford to Dean Miller, August 10, 1927, box 9, Sanford Collection.

62. S. V. Sanford in annual report of the chancellor, 1927–28, 28.

63. Ibid.

64. Annual report of the chancellor, 1927–28, 10.

65. Dean's report, 1927–28, 33.

66. Ibid.

67. Veysey, *The Emergence of the American University,* 276.

68. Ibid., 277.

69. Dean's report, 1927–28, 10.

70. George C. Woodruff to S. V. Sanford, March 18, 1929, box 9, Sanford Collection.

71. F. Phinizy Calhoun to S. V. Sanford, March 21, 1929, box 9, Sanford Collection.

SEVEN. *Chancellor-in-Waiting, 1930–1934*

1. Charles Sanford to Grace Sanford, December 15, 1932, box 10, Sanford Collection.

2. Clippings, box 9, Sanford Collection.

3. Hughes Spalding to S. V. Sanford, October 14, 1931, box 1, Archives of the University of Georgia, Sanford (hereafter cited as University of Georgia Archives, Sanford).

4. Brooks, *University of Georgia,* 170–75.

5. Hughes Spalding to S. V. Sanford, January 5, 1932, box 10, Sanford Collection.

6. *Red and Black,* January 22, 1932, 2.

7. George F. Peabody to S. V. Sanford, February 17, 1932, box 10, Sanford Collection.

8. Clippings in scrapbook, no date, box 57, Sanford Collection.

9. Blind copy of Hughes Spalding to W. D. Anderson, January 15, 1932, box 1, University of Georgia Archives, Sanford.

10. S. V. Sanford to Hughes Spalding, January 19, 1932, box 1, University of Georgia Archives, Sanford.

11. S. V. Sanford to Hughes Spalding, April 1, 1932, box 1, University of Georgia Archives, Sanford.

12. Secretary of President Sanford to Lloyd Grady, April 7, 1932, box 1, University of Georgia Archives, Sanford.

13. Hughes Spalding to S. V. Sanford, April, 1932, box 1, University of Georgia Archives, Sanford.

14. Hughes Spalding to S. V. Sanford, April 14, 1932, box 1, University of Georgia Archives, Sanford.

15. Hughes Spalding to S. V. Sanford, April 20, 1932, box 1, University of Georgia Archives, Sanford.

16. Hughes Spalding to J. M. Pound et al., May 11, 1932; Spalding to Sanford et al., May 11, 1932, box 1, University of Georgia Archives, Sanford.

17. Report of the Board of Regents, 1932, box 1, University of Georgia Archives, Sanford.

18. S. V. Sanford to Hughes Spalding, June 20, 1932, box 10, Sanford Collection.

19. Ibid.

20. Hughes Spalding to S. V. Sanford, June 23, 1932, box 10, Sanford Collection.

21. Ibid.

22. S. V. Sanford to Earle Cocke, July 7, 1932, box 1, University of Georgia Archives, Sanford.

23. Hughes Spalding to Andrew Soule, August 30, 1932, box 1, University of Georgia Archives, Sanford.

24. Philip Weltner to S. V. Sanford, September, 1932; Hughes Spalding to S. V. Sanford, September, 1932, box 1, University of Georgia Archives, Sanford.

25. Hughes Spalding to S. V. Sanford, October 4, 5, 6, 1932, box 1, University of Georgia Archives, Sanford.

26. Hughes Spalding to S. V. Sanford, October 20, 30, 1932, box 1, University of Georgia Archives, Sanford.

27. S. V. Sanford to Hughes Spalding, October 30, 1932, box 1, University of Georgia Archives, Sanford.

28. Hughes Spalding to S. V. Sanford, October 28, 1932, box 1, University of Georgia Archives, Sanford.

29. S. V. Sanford to Hughes Spalding, October 31, 1932, box 1, University of Georgia Archives, Sanford.

30. Hughes Spalding to S. V. Sanford, November 1, 1932, box 1, University of Georgia Archives, Sanford.

31. S. V. Sanford to Hughes Spalding, November 2, 1932, box 1, University of Georgia Archives, Sanford.

32. Hughes Spalding to S. V. Sanford, November 7, 1932, box 1, University of Georgia Archives, Sanford.

33. S. V. Sanford to Philip Weltner, December 12, 1932, box 1, University of Georgia Archives, Sanford.

34. Philip Weltner to heads of institutions, December 25, 1932, box 1, University of Georgia Archives, Sanford.

35. Hughes Spalding to Charles Snelling and S. V. Sanford, December 30, 1932, box 1, University of Georgia Archives, Sanford.

36. Harmon Caldwell to S. V. Sanford, December 31, 1932, box 1, University of Georgia Archives, Sanford.

37. Statement of liabilities and unpaid appropriations, December 31, 1932, box 10, Sanford Collection.

38. Files for January and February, 1933, box 1, University of Georgia Archives, Sanford.

39. S. V. Sanford to W. W. Stancil, February 17, 1933, box 1, University of Georgia Archives, Sanford.

40. S. V. Sanford to Hughes Spalding, February 2, 1933, box 1, University of Georgia Archives, Sanford.

41. Hughes Spalding to S. V. Sanford, January 23, 1933, box 1, University of Georgia Archives, Sanford.

42. S. V. Sanford to Hughes Spalding, January 20, 1933, box 1, University of Georgia Archives, Sanford.

43. S. V. Sanford to W. W. Stancil, February 17, 1933, box 1, University of Georgia Archives, Sanford.

44. S. V. Sanford to Senator A. J. Tuten, February 18, 1933, box 1, University of Georgia Archives, Sanford.

45. Robert Hutchins to S. V. Sanford, March 9, 1933, box 10, Sanford Collection.

46. Hughes Spalding to S. V. Sanford, March 14, 1933, box 1, University of Georgia Archives, Sanford.

47. Ibid.

48. Philip Weltner to S. V. Sanford, March 14, 1933, box 1, University of Georgia Archives, Sanford.

49. Notice to faculty from S. V. Sanford, April 3, 1933, box 1, University of Georgia Archives, Sanford.

50. S. V. Sanford to university faculty, March 22, 1933, box 1, University of Georgia Archives, Sanford.

51. Dyer, *University of Georgia*, 216; Brooks, *University of Georgia*, 178.

52. Report of the Board of Regents, 1933, 9.

53. Various letters, May, 1933, box 2, University of Georgia Archives, Sanford.

54. S. V. Sanford to Philip Weltner, May 25, 1933, box 2, University of Georgia Archives, Sanford.

55. S. V. Sanford to Governor Eugene Talmadge, May 25, 1933, box 2, University of Georgia Archives, Sanford.

56. S. V. Sanford to Hughes Spalding, February 23, 1933, box 2, University of Georgia Archives, Sanford.

57. S. V. Sanford to Philip Weltner, June 15, 1933, box 2, University of Georgia Archives, Sanford.

58. Bruce Payne to S. V. Sanford, June 20, 1933, box 2, University of Georgia Archives, Sanford.

59. Hughes Spalding to S. V. Sanford, August 24, 1933, box 2, University of Georgia Archives, Sanford.

60. Ibid.

61. S. V. Sanford to Hughes Spalding, August 24, 1933, box 2, University of Georgia Archives, Sanford.

62. S. V. Sanford in *Athens Banner-Herald,* July 1933 clipping; S. V. Sanford to Hughes Spalding, March 19, 1933, box 2, University of Georgia Archives, Sanford.

63. S. V. Sanford to George H. Denny, October 13, 1933, box 10, Sanford Collection.

64. Brooks, *University of Georgia,* 180–81.

65. S. V. Sanford to President Franklin D. Roosevelt, October 21, 1933, box 10, Sanford Collection.

66. S. Gilbert Price to S. V. Sanford, October 31, 1933, box 2, University of Georgia Archives, Sanford.

67. S. V. Sanford to Hughes Spalding, November 6, 1933; November 28, 1933, box 2, University of Georgia Archives, Sanford.

68. S. V. Sanford to Charles Sanford, November 23, 1933, box 10, Sanford Collection.

69. Hughes Spalding to S. V. Sanford, December 11, 1933; Hughes Spalding to Senator Richard Russell, December 11, 1933, box 10, Sanford Collection.

70. S. V. Sanford to "Dear John," February 3, 1934, box 10, Sanford Collection.

71. Hughes Spalding to S. V. Sanford, February 12, 1934, box 3, University of Georgia Archives, Sanford.

72. S. V. Sanford to Philip Weltner, May 16, 1934, box 3, University of Georgia Archives, Sanford.

73. S. V. Sanford to Hughes Spalding, May 22, 1934, box 3, University of Georgia Archives, Sanford.

74. Dyer, *University of Georgia*, 216–20; Brooks, *University of Georgia*, 179–82.

75. S. V. Sanford to Hughes Spalding, May 22, 1934, box 3, University of Georgia Archives, Sanford.

76. Charles Sanford to S. V. Sanford, October 23, 1934, box 10, Sanford Collection.

EIGHT. *Chancellor Sanford, 1935–1940*

1. S. V. Sanford to Hughes Spalding, September 20, 1934, box 4, University of Georgia Archives, Sanford.

2. Ibid.

3. *Pandora* (1935), no page numbers.

4. Ralph McGill to S. V. Sanford, September 10, 1934, box 31, Sanford Collection.

5. *Atlanta Constitution*, September 11, 1934.

6. *Atlanta Constitution*, September 11, 1934.

7. Author's interview with Herman Talmadge, December 1995; author's interview with Ralph Moor, May 1996.

8. Philip Weltner to institution heads, January 16, 1935, box 4, University of Georgia Archives, Sanford.

9. S. V. Sanford to Eugene Talmadge, March 25, 1935; Governor Talmadge to Sanford, March 26, 1935, box 10, Sanford Collection.

10. S. V. Sanford to Judge Dickerson, April 1, 1935, box 4, University of Georgia Archives, Sanford.

11. Dickerson to Sanford, April 6, 1935, box 4, University of Georgia Archives, Sanford.

12. Various newspaper clippings, scrapbook, box 31, Sanford Collection.

13. Governor Talmadge to Chancellor Sanford, April 1935, box 34, Sanford Collection.

14. Scrapbooks, box 31, Sanford Collection.

15. Undated clipping, *Atlanta Journal*, box 31, Sanford Collection.

16. Files, February 1935, box 10, Sanford Collection.

17. Notes from meetings, May 1935, box 4, University of Georgia Archives, Sanford.

18. *Atlanta Constitution*, September 11, 1934.

19. Clipping, scrapbook, box 31, Sanford Collection.

20. Minutes of the Board of Regents, April 10, 1935, 10, July 15, 1935, 29.

21. S. V. Sanford to S. H. Morgan, June 25, 1935, box 4, University of Georgia Archives, Sanford.

22. Minutes of the Board of Regents, July 15, 1935, 29, May 10, 1935, 101.

23. Author's interview with Charles Gowen, December 1995.

24. J. C. Meadows to S. V. Sanford, January 30, 1936, box 2, Georgia Department of Archives and History, Sanford (hereafter cited as GDAH, Sanford).

25. Minutes of the Board of Regents, April 15, May 15, 1936.

26. S. V. Sanford to Grace Sanford, June 24, 1935, box 10, Sanford Collection.

27. Author interview with Ralph Moor, December 16, 1996.

28. Correspondence, April, 1936, box 2, GDAH, Sanford.

29. S. V. Sanford to W. T. Anderson, October 2, 1936, box 2, GDAH, Sanford.

30. Minutes of the Board of Regents, October 6, 1936.

31. Minutes of the Board of Regents, February 11, 1936.

32. Folder U, box 1, GDAH, Sanford.

33. Speech notes, April 30, 1937, box 1, GDAH, Sanford.

34. Speech notes, July 22, 1937, box 1, GDAH, Sanford.

35. Mrs. Monroe A. Butler to S. V. Sanford, June 21, 1937; Sanford to Butler, July 8, 1937, box 2, GDAH, Sanford.

36. Mary Fletcher to S. V. Sanford, October 12, 1937, box 10, Sanford Collection.

37. S. V. Sanford to Fred Morris, October 2, 1937; Sanford to George Montgomery; Sanford to Oscar Keller, box 2, GDAH, Sanford.

38. Minutes of the Board of Regents, July 1937.

39. Ibid.

40. Minutes of the Board of Regents, December 17, 1937.

41. S. V. Sanford to Board of Regents, November 12, 1937, box 1, GDAH, Sanford.

42. Grace Sanford diary, January 3, 1937, box 27, Sanford Collection.

43. Grace Sanford diary, January 12, 1937; March 27, 1937; July 30, 1937.

44. Grace Sanford diary, January 10, 1937; January 20, 1937; January 17, 1937; January 31, 1937.

45. Grace Sanford diary, February 24, 1937; March 3, 1937; March 22, 1937.

46. Grace Sanford diary, July 30, 1937.

47. Grace Sanford diary, August 24, 1937.

48. *Gainesville Eagle,* May 12, 1938.

49. Author's interview with James Dunlap, February 9, 1996.

50. Minutes of the Board of Regents, July 9 and 10, 1938.

51. Ibid.

52. *Gainesville Eagle,* August 18, 1938.

53. Kelly (no given name) to S. V. Sanford, August 28, 1938, box 2, GDAH, Sanford.

54. Minutes of the Board of Regents, October 7, 1938.

55. Minutes of the Board of Regents, November 26, 1938.

56. Minutes of the Board of Regents, January 13, 1939; March 24, 1939.

57. *Atlanta Constitution,* January 14, 1939.

58. S. V. Sanford to Board of Regents, August 1, 1939.

59. Minutes of the Board of Regents, December 2, 1939.

60. Minutes of the Board of Regents, March 1, 1940.

61. Notes, July 17, 1939, box 1, GDAH, Sanford.

62. Walter B. Hill to S. V. Sanford, July 25, 1939, box 2, GDAH, Sanford.

NINE. *War at Home and Abroad, 1940–1943*

1. Brooks, *University of Georgia,* 185–86.

2. Coleman et al., *History of Georgia,* 318.

3. Minutes of the Board of Regents, April 5, 1940, 9.

4. Minutes of the Board of Regents, April 4, 1940.

5. Ibid.

6. Minutes of the Board of Regents, May 10, 1940; *Atlanta Constitution,* May 10–11, 1940; *Athens Banner-Herald,* May 10, 1940.

7. Letters, May 1940, box 11, Sanford Collection.

8. W. M. Hubbard to Mrs. Sanford, May 22, 1940, box 11, Sanford Collection.

9. John Donald Wade to Mrs. Sanford, May, 1940, box 11, Sanford Collection.

10. Chip Robert to S. V. Sanford, June, 12, 1940, box 11, Sanford Collection.

11. Frank Reade to S. V. Sanford, July 8, 1940, box 11, Sanford Collection.

12. Minutes of the Board of Regents, July 12, 1940.

13. William Anderson, *The Wild Man from Sugar Creek: The Political Career of Eugene Talmadge* (Baton Rouge: Louisiana State University Press, 1975), 185–92.

14. Ibid., 192–93.

15. Clippings, box 39, Sanford Collection.

16. Scrapbook, box 39, Sanford Collection.

17. Anderson, *Wild Man,* 199.

18. James Cook, "Walter D. Cocking," in *Dictionary,* vol. 1, ed. Coleman and Gurr, 208.

19. Anderson, *Wild Man,* 196–97.

20. Ibid., 196; George Rogers and Frank Saunders Jr., "Marvin Pittman," in *Dictionary,* vol. 2, ed. Coleman and Gurr, 799.

21. Minutes of the Board of Regents, May 30, 1941, 2–3.

22. James F. Cook Jr., "Politics and Education in the Talmadge Era: The Controversy over the University System of Georgia, 1941–1942" (Ph.D. diss., University of Georgia, 1972), 59.

23. Dyer, *University of Georgia*, 228–29.

24. Brooks, *University of Georgia*, 188–89.

25. Cook, "Politics and Education," 65.

26. Minutes of the Board of Regents, May 30, 1941.

27. Minutes of the Board of Regents, June 16, 1941.

28. *Atlanta Constitution*, June 17, 1941.

29. *Atlanta Constitution*, June 21, 1941.

30. *Atlanta Constitution*, June 2, July 14, 1941.

31. *Atlanta Constitution*, July 15, 1941.

32. Minutes of the Board of Regents, August, 1941; Cook, "Politics and Education," 210–16; Dyer, *University of Georgia*, 234.

33. Cook, "Politics and Education," 156.

34. Ibid., 157.

35. John Curtis Dixon, "Facts Relating to the Appointment and Discharge of J. C. Dixon," September 26, 1941, typescript, University of Georgia Special Collections.

36. Ibid., 78.

37. Ibid., 80.

38. Ibid., 81.

39. Ibid., 81–82.

40. Cook, "Politics and Education," 303–4.

41. Testimony before the November 1941 Southern Association of Colleges and Schools Committee, "Dixon Statement," 82–83, typescript, University of Georgia Special Collections.

42. Ralph Moor to Steve Gurr, May 12, 1997, author's files.

43. Author's phone interview with Benjamin Moore, August 10, 1996.

44. Testimony before SACS, November 1941, "Sanford Statement," 84.

45. Cook, "Politics and Education," 302.

46. Ibid., 303.

47. Scrapbook labeled "Talmadge," July 1941, box 46, Sanford Collection.

48. *Atlanta Journal*, July 21, 1941.

49. *Atlanta Constitution*, July 12, 1941.

50. Minutes of the Board of Regents, October 11, 1941.

51. *Red and Black*, October 17, 1941; *Life*, October 27, 1941, 43–46.

52. Anderson, *Wild Man*, 201.

53. Ibid.; minutes of the Board of Regents, November 1, 1941.

54. Testimony before SACS, November 1941, "Sanford Statement," Special Collections, University of Georgia Library.

55. Ibid., g.

56. Anderson, *Wild Man*, 205.

57. Mrs. Marvin Branscomb to S. V. Sanford, November 22, 1941, box 2, GDAH, Sanford.

58. Minutes of the Board of Regents, June 1942.

59. *Atlanta Constitution,* August 30, 1941.

60. *Statistical Register,* 1941, 42; Anderson, *Wild Man,* 210–11.

61. *Georgia Laws,* 1943.

62. Minutes of the Board of Regents, January 1943.

TEN. *The Last Years, 1943–1945*

1. Notes for S. V. Sanford, Spanish-American War Veterans Speech, Augusta, 1943, box 1, GDAH, Sanford.

2. Minutes of the Board of Regents, January 26, 1943; March 25, 1943.

3. Governor Arnall to S. V. Sanford, January 16, 1943, box 11, Sanford Collection.

4. Minutes of the Board of Regents, March 25, 1943.

5. Minutes of the Board of Regents, April 23, 1943.

6. Ibid., 5.

7. Minutes of the Board of Regents, July 8, 1943.

8. Dyer, *University of Georgia,* 251; chancellor's report, 1943, 44.

9. Minutes of the Board of Regents, August 11, 1943.

10. Minutes of the Board of Regents, April 23, 1943.

11. Ibid.

12. B. Carlyle Ramsey, "The University System Controversy Reexamined: The Talmadge-Holley Connection," *Georgia Historical Quarterly* 64 (Summer 1980): 199.

13. Minutes of the Board of Regents, April 23, 1943.

14. S. V. Sanford to Sam Seibert, October 24, 1943, box 52, GDAH, Sanford.

15. Minutes of the Board of Regents, October 13, 1943.

16. Sandy Beaver to S. V. Sanford, December 12, 1943, box 52, GDAH, Sanford.

17. Sanford personal files, box 52, GDAH, Sanford.

18. S. V. Sanford to Albert Davidson, January 1943, box 52, GDAH, Sanford.

19. Box 52, GDAH, Sanford.

20. S. V. Sanford to Guy Jackson, September 25, 1943, box 52, GDAH, Sanford.

21. S. V. Sanford to McGregor Company, December 31, 1943, box 52, GDAH, Sanford.

22. Author interview with Charles S. Sanford Jr., June 4, 1996.

23. S. V. Sanford to Athens Rationing Board, December 31, 1943, box 11, Sanford Collection.

24. S. V. Sanford to Mrs. Mike Fleming, December 1, 1943, box 52, GDAH, Sanford.

25. Minutes of Board of Regents, January 12, 1944.

26. Ibid.

27. Author's interview with Benjamin Moore, July 25, 1996.

28. S. V. Sanford to Marvin McClatchey, January 17, 1944, box 52, GDAH, Sanford.

29. S. V. Sanford to Shelton Sanford, November 16, 1944, box 11, Sanford Collection.

30. *Savannah Morning News,* clippings, October, 1944, box 54, Sanford Collection.

31. S. V. Sanford, speech notes for October 9, 1944, box 1, GDAH, Sanford.

32. S. V. Sanford to General P. B. Fleming, September 12, 1944, Sanford personal papers, box 52, GDAH, Sanford.

33. Clippings, box 54, Sanford Collection.

34. Minutes of the Board of Regents, January 17, 1945.

35. Ibid.

36. Minutes of the Board of Regents, February 14, 1945.

37. Minutes of the Board of Regents, April 19, 1945.

38. Box 52, GDAH, Sanford.

39. *Columbus Ledger,* April 27, 1945.

40. *Athens Banner-Herald,* September 16, 1945.

41. S. V. Sanford to Shelton Sanford, May 27, 1945, box 11, Sanford Collection.

42. Grace Sanford diary, box 27, Sanford Collection.

43. S. V. Sanford to Colonel Alton Hosch, June 6, 1945, box 52, GDAH, Sanford.

44. S. V. Sanford to Clarke County draft board, June 4, 1945, box 52, GDAH, Sanford.

45. *Athens Banner-Herald,* June 17, 1945.

46. *Athens Banner-Herald,* June 17, 1945.

47. S. V. Sanford to Shelton Sanford, June 29, 1945, box 11, Sanford Collection.

48. S. V. Sanford to Shelton Sanford, August 9, 1945, box 11, Sanford Collection.

49. Ibid.

50. Ibid.

51. S. V. Sanford to Shelton Sanford, August 13, 1945, box 11, Sanford Collection.

52. *Atlanta Constitution,* September 12, 1945.

53. Minutes of the Board of Regents, September 17, 1945; *Atlanta Constitution,* September 13, 1945.

54. Ralph McGill, editorial, *Atlanta Constitution,* September 14, 1945.

55. *Atlanta Constitution,* September 18, 1945.

56. E. Merton Coulter to Grace Sanford, September 17, 1945, box 22, E. M. Coulter Collection, University of Georgia.

57. Resolution of the Board of Regents, no date, box 52, Sanford personal papers, GDAH, Sanford.

58. Family records in possession of Sally Bruce McClatchey; Sanford notes from Mrs. George Marshall.

59. *Athens Banner-Herald,* September 16, 1945.

60. S. V. Sanford to Homer Reynolds Sanford, December 20, 1943, box 52, GDAH, Sanford.

Bibliographic Essay

The history of the University of Georgia has been examined most completely in Thomas Dyer, *The University of Georgia: A Bicentennial History, 1785–1985* (Athens: University of Georgia Press, 1985). Robert Preston Brooks, *The University of Georgia under Sixteen Administrations, 1785–1955* (Athens: University of Georgia Press, 1956) is a valuable and less formal treatment of the university to mid-twentieth century. E. Merton Coulter, *College Life in the Old South* (Baton Rouge: Louisiana State University Press, 1928) is a delightful view of students and faculty as well as administrative matters in the antebellum period. Thomas Reed, long-time university staffer and observer, left a multivolume typescript informal history of the school to the eve of World War II. A bound copy is available in the reference section of the Georgia Room, Hargrett Library, in the University of Georgia main library.

The Hargrett Library and the Archives of the university, also housed in the main library of the university, are chief depositories of the records and manuscript collections pertaining to the history of the university: minutes of the trustees, administrative reports, university publications, minutes of the Board of Regents of the University System, as well as the papers of the leading administrative officers and many important faculty members. The Georgia collections also contain guides to the theses and dissertations related to Georgia topics.

The Steadman Vincent Sanford Collection in the Hargrett (MS 1578) includes seventy-one boxes of letters, scrapbooks, speeches, personal and official documents, and notes. A most helpful guide to the collection is available, and the materials are organized topically and chronologically. A much smaller collection of materials related to Sanford's chancellorship is housed in the collections of the Georgia Department of Archives and History, a unit of the Office of the Secretary of State of Georgia in Atlanta.

The office of the Board of Regents houses copies of the minutes of the Board of Regents with index. Except for the index, these are duplicated in the university library in Athens. The Archives of the Athletic Association of the University of Georgia are housed in Butts-Myer Hall and Stegeman Colosseum. Vertical files there include helpful information on various sports programs and the building of Sanford Stadium. There are a few early documents duplicated in the University Archives and the Sanford Collection.

A number of published histories of football at the university are available and were valuable in considering Sanford's role in that part of the sports program. John F. Stegeman, *The Ghosts of Herty Field: Early Days on a Southern Gridiron* (Athens: University of Georgia Press, 1966) is the best single source for the first few decades (1891–1916).

One of the most valuable sources for this study was the interviews with people who had known S. V. Sanford or who had special knowledge that helped better understand him. The following people were consulted as part of my research during the period 1995–97. While not all of them were formally interviewed, some provided information via phone conversations, brief visits, notes, and E-mail messages; all were helpful. The hours spent with these people were some of the most personally enjoyable parts of the project.

Interviews

Abney, George, interview, May 24, 1995
Baxter, Harry, interview, January 31, 1996
Bell, Griffin, telephone interview, March 10, 1996
Butler, Tyus, interview, September 26, 1996
Cabaniss, Ann, interview, April 3, 1996
Caldwell, Gwendolyn, interview, March 27, 1996
Cheatham, Mike, interview, March 20, 1996
Dodd, Lamar, interview, April 3, 1996
Dunlap, James, interview, February 9, 1996
Embry, Charters, interview, January 5, 1996
Esley, Albert, interview, June 19, 1996
Gatchell, Roy, interview, February 6, 1996
Gowen, Charles, interview, December 8, 1995
Hartman, Bill, interview, March 1, 1996
Hudson, Billy, interview, December 22, 1995
Kenyon, Richard, interview, February 8, 1996
McClatchey, Marvin and Sally Bruce, interview, December 11, 1995
Moor, Ralph, interviews, May 28, June 18, 1996; E-mail, May 12, 19, 20, 1997
Moore, Benjamin, interview, July 25, 1996; telephone interview, August 10, 1996
Paris, Tom, interview, February 20, 1996
Pennell, Tim, interview, February 6, 1996
Powell, Elizabeth, interview, June 19, 1995

Reynolds, Allie, interview, February 1, 1997

Sanford, Charles S. Jr., interviews, E-mail, telephone interviews, December, 1995–June, 1997

Smith, J. Aubry, interview, February 19, 1996

Spalding, Jack, interview, December 8, 1995

Stanford, Henry King, telephone interview, December 21, 1995

Stegeman, John F., telephone interview, December 18, 1995

Stephens, Robert, interview, February 5, 1997

Talmadge, Herman, interview, December 19, 1995

Tate, Susan Barrow, interview, June 28, 1994

Upson, Stephen Lumpkin, telephone interview, April 13, 1995

Waldrip, Klon M. and Patricia, interview, April 9, 1996

Walter, Nelly Rucker Lamar, telephone interview, February 27, 1995

Ward, Judson, interview, March 13, 1996

Yeomans, Jasper, interview, March 27, 1996

Index